i-Ready Classroom
Mathematics

Grade 3 • Volume 1

Curriculum Associates

NOT FOR RESALE

978-1-4957-8036-3
©2020–Curriculum Associates, LLC
North Billerica, MA 01862
No part of this book may be reproduced
by any means without written permission
from the publisher.
All Rights Reserved. Printed in USA.
11 12 13 14 15   21

Contents

Contents (continued)

UNIT 2

Multiplication and Division
Concepts, Relationships, and Patterns

UNIT

3

Multiplication
Finding Area, Solving Word Problems, and Using Scaled Graphs

UNIT 4

Fractions
Equivalence and Comparison, Measurement, and Data

$\frac{1}{8}$ mile

UNIT 5

Measurement
Time, Liquid Volume, and Mass

Contents (continued)

UNIT 6

Shapes
Attributes and Categories, Perimeter and Area, and Partitioning

☑ SELF CHECK

Before starting this unit, check off the skills you know below. As you complete each lesson, see how many more skills you can check off!

I can . . .	Before	After
Use place value to round numbers to the nearest ten and to the nearest hundred, for example: • 315 rounded to the nearest ten is 320. • 826 rounded to the nearest hundred is 800.	☐	☐
Use place value to add and subtract, for example: $329 + 148 = (300 + 100) + (20 + 40) + (9 + 8)$ $\qquad\quad = 400 + 60 + 17$ $\qquad\quad = 477$	☐	☐
Solve word problems by adding and subtracting using place value.	☐	☐

Build Your Vocabulary

Math Vocabulary

Define the review words. Work with your partner to clarify.

Review Word	Current Thinking	Revise Your Thinking
place value		
regroup		
difference		
number line		

Academic Vocabulary

Put a check next to the academic words you know. Then use the words to complete the sentences.

☐ arrange   ☐ estimate   ☐ critical   ☐ discuss

1 I can .... the length of my foot without actually measuring it.

2 Regrouping is a .... skill for adding numbers.

3 We will work together and .... our roles and responsibilities for the class project.

4 You can .... the numbers on the place-value chart by putting them in their proper columns.

Use Place Value to Round Numbers

Dear Family,

This week your child is learning to use place value to round numbers.

Rounding is useful to give you an idea of the size of a number when you do not have to be exact. For example, when you buy several items you might round each price to the nearest dollar before adding them all in your head.

These blocks show the number 217. How do you round 217 to the nearest hundred?

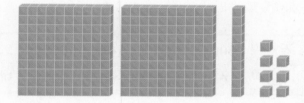

217 is 2 hundreds + 1 ten + 7 ones.

To round 217 to the nearest hundred, decide whether 217 is *more than* or *less than halfway* between 200 and 300. To do this, look at the tens.

5 tens is exactly half of 100. So, if there are fewer than 5 tens in 217, it is closer to 200. If there are 5 or more tens, 217 is closer to 300.

Because 217 has only 1 ten, 217 rounded to the *nearest hundred* is 200. So, it *rounds down* to 200.

To round 217 to the *nearest ten*, look at the ones. 217 is between 210 and 220. If there are fewer than 5 ones, it is closer to 210. If there are 5 or more ones, it is closer to 220.

Because 217 has 7 ones, 217 *rounds up* to 220.

Invite your child to share what he or she knows about using place value to round numbers by doing the following activity together.

ACTIVITY ROUNDING NUMBERS

Do this activity with your child to use place value to round numbers.

Materials 0–8 digit cards, bag, game board, and recording table below

Play this game with your child to practice rounding.

• Cut out digit cards and place them in a bag.

• Choose 3 digit cards from the bag and record them in any order.
  Then replace the cards. *Example: 2, 7, 4*

• Write a 3-digit number using the numbers drawn. *Example: 472*

• Round the number to the nearest hundred. *Example: 500*

• Shade in the hundred number on your game board.

• The first player with five numbers shaded wins.

Player 1	100	200	300	400	500	600	700	800	900
Player 2	100	200	300	400	500	600	700	800	900

Player 1:

Digits	3-digit number	Rounded to nearest hundred

Player 2:

Digits	3-digit number	Rounded to nearest hundred

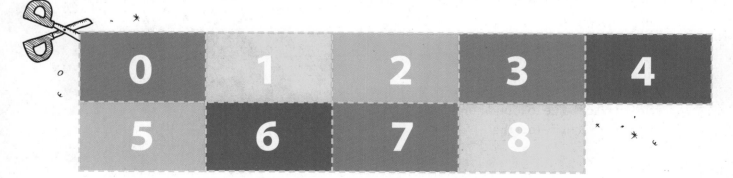

Explore Using Place Value to Round Numbers

You know that three-digit numbers are formed by groups of hundreds, tens, and ones. Use what you know to try to solve the problem below.

> **Look at the number 384 in the place-value chart. Between which two tens does it fall? Between which two hundreds does it fall?**

Hundreds	Tens	Ones
3	8	4

TRY IT

Math Toolkit
- base-ten blocks
- hundreds place-value charts
- number lines

DISCUSS IT

Ask your partner: How did you get started?

Tell your partner: A model I used was . . . It helped me . . .

CONNECT IT

1 LOOK BACK

a. Between which two tens is 384?   **b.** Between which two hundreds is 384?

2 LOOK AHEAD

Locating a number between two tens or two hundreds can help you **round** up or down to the nearest ten or hundred number. When a number is halfway between two tens or two hundreds, the rule is to round up.

Rounding to the Nearest Ten

Look at **8**, **14**, and **5** on the number line. Fill in the blanks to tell how to round these numbers to the **nearest ten**.

a. 8 rounds *up* to ....   **b. 14** rounds *down* to ....

c. 5 rounds *up* to ....

Rounding to the Nearest Hundred

Find **25**, **175**, and **50** on the number line to round them to the **nearest hundred**.

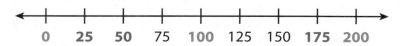

d. 25 rounds to ....   **e. 175** rounds to ....

f. 50 rounds to ....

3 REFLECT

Explain your answer to problem 2f.

....

....

Prepare for Using Place Value to Round Numbers

1 Think about what you know about rounding. Fill in each box. Use words, numbers, and pictures. Show as many ideas as you can.

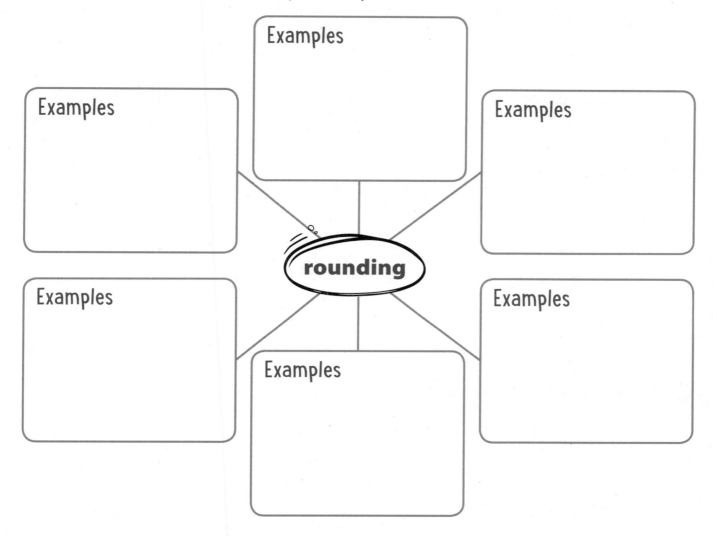

2 Round 451 to the nearest hundred. Explain your answer.

3 Solve the problem. Show your work.

Look at the number 253 in the place-value chart. Between which two tens does it fall? Between which two hundreds does it fall?

Hundreds	Tens	Ones
2	5	3

Solution ....

4 Check your answer. Show your work.

Develop Rounding to the Nearest Ten

Read and try to solve the problem below.

> **Ally records the time she spends doing homework. She rounds each time to the nearest ten minutes. If Ally spends 37 minutes on her homework, how does she record this time?**

TRY IT

 **Math Toolkit**
- base-ten blocks
- hundred charts
- hundreds place-value charts
- number lines

DISCUSS IT

Ask your partner: Why did you choose that strategy?

Tell your partner: I knew . . . So, I . . .

Lesson 1 Use Place Value to Round Numbers   **9**

Explore different ways to understand rounding to the nearest ten.

> Ally records the time she spends doing homework. She rounds each time to the nearest ten minutes. If Ally spends 37 minutes on her homework, how does she record this time?

PICTURE IT

You can use a hundred chart to help round to the nearest ten.

37 is between the tens **30** and **40**.

1	2	3	4	5	6	7	8	9	10
11	12	13	14	15	16	17	18	19	20
21	22	23	24	25	26	27	28	29	30
31	32	33	34	35	36	37	38	39	40
41	42	43	44	45	46	47	48	49	50
51	52	53	54	55	56	57	58	59	60
61	62	63	64	65	66	67	68	69	70
71	72	73	74	75	76	77	78	79	80
81	82	83	84	85	86	87	88	89	90
91	92	93	94	95	96	97	98	99	100

SOLVE IT

Use what you know about rounding to solve the problem.

The **halfway** number between **30** and **40** is **35**.

37 is greater than **35**, so round **37** up to **40**.

Ally records the time as 40 minutes.

CONNECT IT

Now you will use the problem from the previous page to help you understand how to solve a new problem involving rounding to the nearest ten.

Round 943 to the nearest ten.

1 The number 943 is between which two tens? ....

2 What number is halfway between these two tens? ....

3 Is 943 *less than* or *greater than* the halfway number? ....

4 Do you round 943 up or down? ....

5 What is 943 rounded to the nearest ten? ....

6 Explain how to round a number to the nearest ten.

7 REFLECT

Look back at your **Try It**, strategies by classmates, and **Picture It** and **Solve It**. Which models or strategies do you like best for rounding to the nearest ten? Explain.

....

....

....

....

....

APPLY IT

Use what you just learned to solve these problems.

8 What is 106 rounded to the nearest ten? Show your work.

Solution ....

9 Round to the nearest ten.

a. What is a number less than 180 that rounds to 180?
Show your work.

Solution ....

b. What is a number greater than 180 that rounds to 180?
Show your work.

Solution ....

10 Which numbers round to 640 when rounded to the nearest ten?

Ⓐ 644

Ⓑ 634

Ⓒ 645

Ⓓ 635

Ⓔ 600

Ⓕ 649

Practice Rounding to the Nearest Ten

**Study the Example showing rounding to the nearest ten.
Then solve problems 1–8.**

EXAMPLE

Robert always tells his friend how many points he earns on his video game. He rounds the number to the nearest ten. On Saturday, Robert earned 63 points. How many points did he tell his friend that he earned?

51	52	53	54	55	56	57	58	59	**60**
61	62	**63**	64	65	66	67	68	69	**70**

63 is between the tens **60** and **70**. Because 63 is closer to 60, Robert tells his friend that he earned 60 points.

1 Later that afternoon, Robert spent more time playing the video game. He earned 88 points. How many points did he tell his friend that

he earned? ....

2 The number 157 is between which two tens? Circle the two tens on the number line.

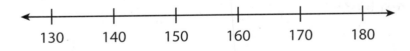

130   140   150   160   170   180

3 What is 157 rounded to the nearest ten? ....

> ### Vocabulary
>
> **round** to find a number that is close in value to the given number by finding the nearest ten, hundred, or other place value.

4   To earn money, you brush dogs. You are so busy that you hire your friends to help. You pay your friends $1 for each dog that they brush. You only have $10 bills to pay them with. You must round each payment to the nearest ten. Complete the table to show how much each friend gets paid.

Friend	Number of Dogs Brushed	Payment to the Nearest $10
Jessica	12	$
Sophie	18	$
Mia	22	$

5   **a.** The number 767 is between which two tens?

.... and ....

b. What number is halfway between these two tens? ....

c. Is 767 less than or greater than the halfway number?

....

d. Will it round up or down? ....

e. What is 767 rounded to the nearest ten? ....

6   **a.** The number 342 is between which two tens?

.... and ....

b. Will it round up or down? ....

c. What is 342 rounded to the nearest ten? ....

7   What is a number less than 930 that rounds to 930?

8   What is a number greater than 930 that rounds to 930?

Develop Rounding to the Nearest Hundred

Read and try to solve the problem below.

> There are 236 third graders at Huron
> Elementary School. What is 236 rounded
> to the nearest hundred?

TRY IT

 Math Toolkit
- base-ten blocks
- hundreds place-value charts
- number lines

DISCUSS IT

Ask your partner: Do you agree with me? Why or why not?

Tell your partner: The strategy I used to find the answer was . . .

Explore different ways to understand rounding to the nearest hundred.

> **There are 236 third graders at Huron Elementary School. What is 236 rounded to the nearest hundred?**

PICTURE IT

Use base-ten blocks to show the number you are rounding.

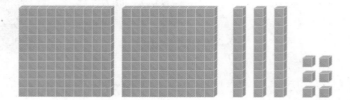

236 has 2 hundreds, so it is between 200 and 300.

The drawing shows that 236 is 2 hundreds + 3 tens + 6 ones.

SOLVE IT

Use what you know about rounding to solve the problem.

There are 10 tens in each hundred. **Halfway** between 0 tens and 10 tens is **5 tens**.

236 has 2 hundreds, **3 tens**, and 6 ones. Because 3 tens is less than 5 tens, round down.

236 rounded to the nearest hundred is 200.

CONNECT IT

Now you will use the problem from the previous page to help you understand how to solve a new problem involving rounding to the nearest hundred.

Round 358 to the nearest hundred.

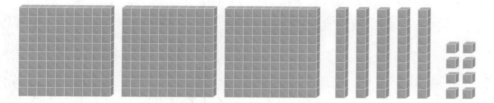

1 The number 358 is between which two hundreds? ....

2 What digit is in the tens place? ....

3 What number of tens is halfway between hundreds? ....

4 What is 358 rounded to the nearest hundred? ....

5 Did you round up or round down? Explain how you knew which hundred to round to.

6 REFLECT

Look back at your **Try It**, strategies by classmates, and **Picture It** and **Solve It**. Which models or strategies do you like best for rounding to the nearest hundred? Explain.

....

....

....

....

APPLY IT

Use what you just learned to solve these problems.

7 What is 476 rounded to the nearest hundred? Show your work.

Solution ....

8 You are rounding to the nearest hundred. What numbers less than 100 would round to 100? Show your work.

Solution ....

9 Which numbers will round to 300 when rounded to the nearest hundred?

Ⓐ 248

Ⓑ 348

Ⓒ 250

Ⓓ 350

Ⓔ 308

Practice Rounding to the Nearest Hundred

Study the Example showing rounding to the nearest hundred. Then solve problems 1–10.

EXAMPLE

There are 127 crayons in a bin. What is 127 rounded to the nearest hundred?

In the drawing, you can see that 127 is 1 hundred + 2 tens + 7 ones.

The number 127 is between 100 and 200. The halfway number between 100 and 200 is 150. The number 127 is less than the halfway number.

So, 127 is nearer to 100 than to 200. 127 rounded to the nearest hundred is 100.

1 The number 684 is between which two hundreds? Circle the two hundreds on the number line.

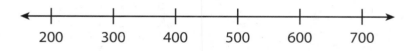

200   300   400   500   600   700

2 What is the halfway number between the two hundreds you circled? ....

3 What is 684 rounded to the nearest hundred? ....

4 What is 694 rounded to the nearest hundred? ....

5 What is 674 rounded to the nearest hundred? ....

6 What is 624 rounded to the nearest hundred? ....

7 Answer the questions below to round 377 to the nearest hundred.

   a. The number 377 is between which two hundreds?

   .... and ....

   b. What number is halfway between these two hundreds? ....

   c. Is 377 *less than* or *greater than* the halfway number? ....

   d. Will you round up or down? ....

   e. What is 377 rounded to the nearest hundred? ....

8 The table below shows the miles between U.S. cities. Round each distance to the nearest hundred miles.

Cities	Distance in Miles	Distance to the Nearest Hundred Miles
Phoenix and Las Vegas	292	
Los Angeles and San Francisco	386	

9 Which of these numbers could it be? Here are the clues.

   • The number is between the two hundreds, 500 and 600.

   • The number is greater than the halfway number.

   • You will round up to round this number to the nearest hundred.

   What is the number? Circle the correct answer.

   525   575   501   650

10 What is 999 rounded to the nearest hundred? ....

Refine Using Place Value to Round Numbers

Complete the Example below. Then solve problems 1–9.

EXAMPLE

What is 362 rounded to the nearest ten?

Look at how you could show your work using base-ten blocks.

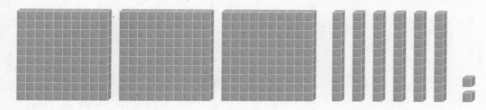

The halfway number between the nearest tens is 5 ones.
Because 2 ones is less than 5 ones, round down.

Solution ....

The blocks show the number of hundreds, tens, and ones in 362.

PAIR/SHARE
If you add 3 ones to the model, will you still round to the same ten? Explain.

APPLY IT

1 What is 879 rounded to the nearest hundred? Show your work.

Read the problem carefully. Are you rounding to the nearest ten or to the nearest hundred?

PAIR/SHARE
Which digit in the number helps you decide whether to round up or down?

Solution ....

2 Mr. Edwards picked out a TV for $479 and a DVD player for $129. He rounded each price to the nearest $10 to estimate the total cost. What is each price rounded to the nearest $10? Show your work.

Between which two tens is 479?

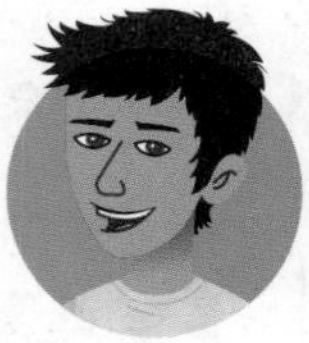

PAIR/SHARE
Why do you think Mr. Edwards rounded the prices to the nearest $10 and not to the nearest $100?

Solution ....

3 There are 416 third grade students at Lincoln School. What is the number of third grade students rounded to the nearest hundred?

Ⓐ 400

Ⓑ 410

Ⓒ 420

Ⓓ 500

How many hundreds and tens are in the number?

Lien chose Ⓒ as the correct answer. How did he get that answer?

PAIR/SHARE
What kinds of mistakes could Lien have made?

4 Jolon scored 194 points during the basketball season. What is 194 rounded to the nearest hundred?

Ⓐ 100

Ⓑ 180

Ⓒ 190

Ⓓ 200

5 Round to the nearest ten. Which number will NOT round to 590?

Ⓐ 596

Ⓑ 594

Ⓒ 588

Ⓓ 585

6 Tell whether each sentence is *True* or *False*.

	True	False
496 rounded to the nearest hundred is 500.	Ⓐ	Ⓑ
496 rounded to the nearest ten is 500.	Ⓒ	Ⓓ
205 rounded to the nearest ten is 200.	Ⓔ	Ⓕ
745 rounded to the nearest hundred is 800.	Ⓖ	Ⓗ

7 Which numbers will round to 250 when rounded to the nearest ten?

Ⓐ

200   250

Ⓑ

Hundreds	Tens	Ones
2	5	0

Ⓒ

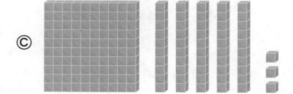

Ⓓ 259

Ⓔ 245

8 A total of 778 tickets are sold to a charity event. Round the number of tickets to the nearest ten and to the nearest hundred. Fill in the blanks to show about how many tickets are sold.

Rounded to the nearest ten, ... tickets are sold.

Rounded to the nearest hundred, ... tickets are sold.

9 MATH JOURNAL

Round 465 to the nearest hundred. Explain your thinking.

☑ SELF CHECK Go back to the Unit 1 Opener and see what you can check off.

Add Three-Digit Numbers

Dear Family,

This week your child is using different strategies to add three-digit numbers.

For example, one way to use **place value** to find the sum of 153 + 260 is shown below.

You can add the ones first, then add the tens, and then add the hundreds, writing each sum on a line by itself. Then you add the three **partial sums** to get the total.

```
  153
+ 260
———
    3  ⟶ 3 ones + 0 ones = 3 ones, or 3
  110  ⟶ 5 tens + 6 tens = 11 tens, or 1 hundred + 1 ten, or 110
  300  ⟶ 1 hundred + 2 hundreds = 3 hundreds, or 300
———
  413
```

Another way to solve this problem using place value is to use the standard addition **algorithm**. This involves **regrouping** when the digits in one of the place-value columns add up to 10 or more. Here is how the same addition problem would look when solved using the algorithm.

The small 1 represents the regrouped 100.

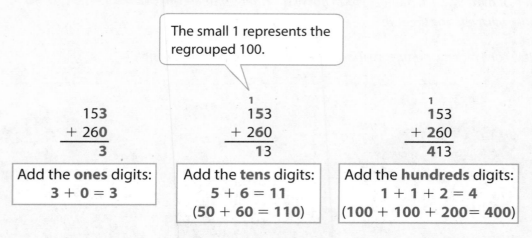

```
    153            ¹             ¹
  + 260           153           153
  ————          + 260         + 260
    3             ————          ————
                   13            413
```

Add the **ones** digits:	Add the **tens** digits:	Add the **hundreds** digits:
3 + 0 = 3	**5 + 6 = 11**	**1 + 1 + 2 = 4**
	(50 + 60 = 110)	**(100 + 100 + 200 = 400)**

Invite your child to share what he or she knows about adding three-digit numbers by doing the following activity together.

ACTIVITY ADD THREE-DIGIT NUMBERS

Do this activity with your child to add three-digit numbers.

Materials 3 number cubes, pencil and paper

Play this adding game with your child to practice adding three-digit numbers. The goal of this game is to get a sum greater than 500 by adding a three-digit number to 250.

- Have your child roll three number cubes.

- Ask your child to form a three-digit number from the number cubes. (If the rolls are 2, 6, and 1, the possible numbers are 126, 162, 216, 261, 612, and 621.) Write down the chosen number.

- Your child adds 250 to the number, using any addition strategy.

- If the sum is greater than 500, then he or she wins the round. If not, you win the round.

- Switch roles. Play five rounds for best out of five.

- Ask your child questions during the game, such as:

  - *Does it matter which number I form out of the three number cubes? How will it change the sum?*

  - *How can I pick my number to make sure my sum is as great as possible?*

Explore Adding Three-Digit Numbers

In this lesson you will learn strategies for adding numbers. Use what you know to try to solve the problem below.

> Rodney has 147 songs on his MP3 player. Elaine has 212 songs on her MP3 player. How many songs do Rodney and Elaine have in all?

TRY IT

 Math Toolkit
• base-ten blocks
• hundreds place-value charts
• number lines

DISCUSS IT

Ask your partner: How did you get started?

Tell your partner: I knew . . . so I . . .

CONNECT IT

1 LOOK BACK

Explain how to find the number of songs Rodney and Elaine have in all.

2 LOOK AHEAD

You can solve addition problems in different ways. Breaking apart numbers is one way to make a problem easier.

Suppose you had the addition problem $374 + 122$.

a. Break apart 374 into ones, tens, and hundreds.

b. Break apart 122 into ones, tens, and hundreds.

c. Add ones and ones, tens and tens, and hundreds and hundreds to find $374 + 122$.

d. Check your answer by estimating. Round 374 and 122 to the nearest ten and add. Does your answer make sense? Explain.

3 REFLECT

What is another way you could find $374 + 122$?

....

....

....

Prepare for Adding Three-Digit Numbers

1 Think about what you know about breaking apart numbers. Fill in each box. Use words, numbers, and pictures. Show as many ideas as you can.

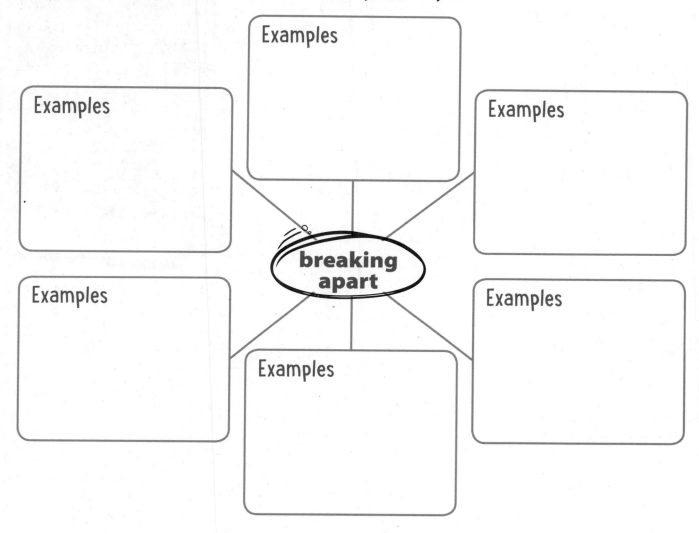

Examples

Examples

Examples

breaking apart

Examples

Examples

Examples

2 List two different ways to break apart 247.

3 Solve the problem. Show your work.

Benoit has 215 photos on his phone. Sara has 173 photos on her phone. How many photos do Benoit and Sara have in all?

Solution ....

4 Check your answer. Show your work.

Develop Using Place-Value Strategies to Add

Read and try to solve the problem below.

> **Garcia has 130 trading cards.**
> **Mark has 280 trading cards.**
> **How many trading cards do**
> **Garcia and Mark have together?**

TRADING CARD

TRY IT

 **Math Toolkit**
- base-ten blocks
- hundreds place-value charts
- number lines

DISCUSS IT

Ask your partner: Why did you choose this strategy?

Tell your partner: A model I used was . . . It helped me . . .

Explore different ways to understand how to add three-digit numbers.

> Garcia has 130 trading cards. Mark has 280 trading cards. How many trading cards do Garcia and Mark have together?

PICTURE IT

You can use base-ten blocks to help add three-digit numbers.

This model shows the 130 trading cards Garcia has.

This model shows the 280 trading cards Mark has.

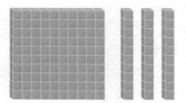

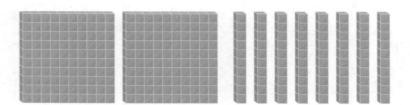

The model below shows the total number of trading cards Garcia and Mark have.

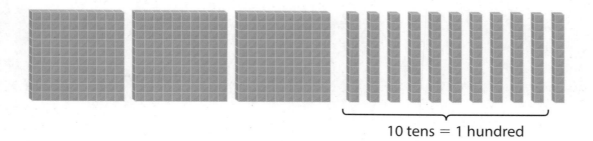

10 tens = 1 hundred

MODEL IT

You can also use place value and partial sums to help add three-digit numbers.

$$
\begin{array}{r}
130 \\
+\ 280 \\
\hline
\end{array}
$$

0 ⟶ There are **0 ones** in both numbers.

110 ⟶ 3 tens + 8 tens = **11 tens**, or 1 hundred + 1 ten, or **110**

300 ⟶ 1 hundred + 2 hundreds = **3 hundreds**, or **300**

CONNECT IT

Now you will use the problem from the previous page to help you understand how to use different strategies to add.

1 Look at **Picture It**. Each number is broken apart into hundreds and tens. What is the total number of hundreds and tens?

.... hundreds and .... tens

2 There are enough tens to make another hundred. Regroup the tens.

11 tens is the same as .... hundred and .... ten.

3 Now what is the total number of hundreds and tens?

.... hundreds and .... ten

4 How many trading cards do Garcia and Mark have together?

.... + 10 = ...

5 Look at **Model It**. How do the sums in this model match the blocks in **Picture It**?

6 Explain how to use place value and regrouping to add three-digit numbers.

7 REFLECT

Look back at your **Try It**, strategies by classmates, and **Picture It** and **Model It**. Which models or strategies do you like best for adding three-digit numbers? Explain.

APPLY IT

Use what you just learned to solve these problems.

8 Fill in the sums of the ones, the tens, and the hundreds. Then add to find the sum.

```
   275
 + 216
```

.... ⟶ 5 ones + 6 ones

.... ⟶ 7 tens + 1 ten

.... ⟶ 2 hundreds + 2 hundreds

.... ⟶ sum

9 A farm's new milk tank holds 185 more gallons than the old tank. The old tank holds 275 gallons. How many gallons does the new tank hold? Show your work.

Solution ....

10 What is 649 + 184? Show your work.

Solution ....

Practice Using Place-Value Strategies to Add

Study the Example showing how to add three-digit numbers. Solve problems 1–6.

EXAMPLE

This week, 248 people came to watch the school play on Tuesday night. 175 people came on Thursday night. How many people came to see the play on these two nights?

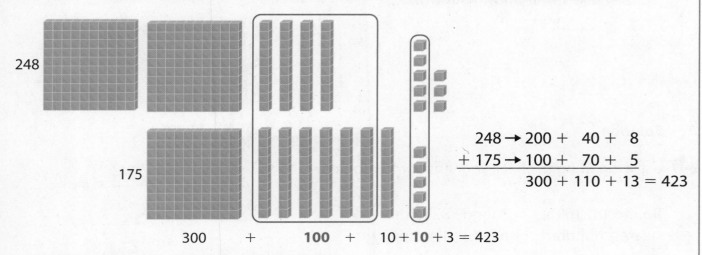

$$248 \rightarrow 200 + 40 + 8$$
$$+ 175 \rightarrow 100 + 70 + 5$$
$$300 + 110 + 13 = 423$$

248

175

$$300 \quad + \quad 100 \quad + \quad 10 + 10 + 3 = 423$$

423 people came to the play on these nights.

Solve. Fill in the blanks to add.

1   631 $\longrightarrow$ 600   + ...   +   1

   + 368 $\longrightarrow$ ....   +   60   +   8

   900   +   90   + ... = ...

2   167
   + 208

   .... $\longrightarrow$ 7 ones + 8 ones = ... ones, or .... ten + ... ones

   60 $\longrightarrow$ 6 tens + 0 tens = ... tens

   .... $\longrightarrow$ 1 hundred + 2 hundreds = ... hundreds

   ....

3) Find 157 + 291. Show your work.

Solution ....

4) Felice takes 142 photos on vacation. Her mother takes 382. How many photos did they take in all? Show your work.

Solution ....

5) Use estimating to check your answer to problem 4.

Round 142 to the   Round 382 to the
nearest hundred.   nearest hundred.

.... + ... = ...

Is your answer to problem 4 reasonable? Explain.

6) Use two of the numbers in the box to make the greatest possible sum. Then use two of the numbers to make the least possible sum. Explain how you got your answers.

348   256   289   361

Develop Connecting Place-Value Strategies to an Algorithm

Read and try to solve the problem below.

> **What is the sum?**
> **Use place value to help you add.**
>
> 225
> $+\ 229$

TRY IT

 **Math Toolkit**
- base-ten blocks
- hundreds place-value charts

DISCUSS IT

Ask your partner: Do you agree with me? Why or why not?

Tell your partner: I am not sure how to find the answer because . . .

Explore another way to understand how to add using place value.

> **What is the sum?**   225
> **Use place value to help you add.**   + 229

MODEL IT

You can use place value and partial sums to add. Add ones to ones, tens to tens, and hundreds to hundreds.

```
    225
  + 229
  ─────
     14 ⟶ 5 ones + 9 ones = 14 ones, or 1 ten + 4 ones
     40 ⟶ 2 tens + 2 tens = 4 tens
  + 400 ⟶ 2 hundreds + 2 hundreds = 4 hundreds
```

MODEL IT

You can record your work in a shorter way.

Add ones to ones, tens to tens, and hundreds to hundreds. Record your work by showing regrouping above the problem and writing the sum in one row. A grid can help you keep track of the place value of the digits.

Step 1: Add ones.
$5 + 9 = 14$
1 ten and 4 ones

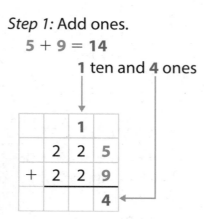

Step 2: Add tens.
$1 + 2 + 2$

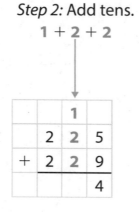

Step 3: Add hundreds.
$2 + 2$

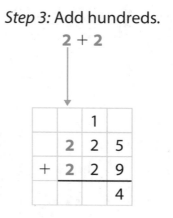

CONNECT IT

Now you will use the problem from the previous page to help you understand how to add using place value.

1 Look at the first **Model It**. What place-value sum must be regrouped? Explain.

2 Look at the second **Model It**. The sum of the ones is 14. Where do you see the 14 ones in the **Model It**?

3 What is the sum? Did you need to regroup again? Explain.

4 How are the two ways of adding in each **Model It** alike and different?

5 Use the grid to find 158 + 363. Add by place value and show the sum in one row. Explain your work.

		1	5	8
+		3	6	3

6 **REFLECT**

Look back at your **Try It**, strategies by classmates, and **Model Its**. Which models or strategies do you like best for adding? Explain.

....

....

....

APPLY IT

Use what you just learned to solve these problems.

7 Find the sum.

	2	4	5
	1	1	4
+	3	2	8

8 The third grade students collect 507 cans of food for Lake Park Elementary School's food drive. The fourth grade students collect 435 cans. How many cans did the students collect in all? Check your answer by estimating. Show your work.

Round to the nearest ten to check:

Solution ....

9 Find the sum.

```
  284
+ 258
```

Practice Connecting Place-Value Strategies to an Algorithm

Study the Example showing how using an algorithm can help you add three-digit numbers. Then solve problems 1–7.

EXAMPLE

On the weekend, 172 adults and 253 children went to the fair. How many people went to the fair on the weekend?

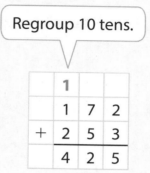

Regroup 10 tens.

	1		
	1	7	2
+	2	5	3
	4	2	5

$$
\begin{array}{r}
172 \\
+\ 253 \\
\hline
5 \\
120 \\
300 \\
\hline
425
\end{array}
$$

5 ⟶ 2 ones + 3 ones
120 ⟶ 7 tens + 5 tens
300 ⟶ 1 hundred + 2 hundreds

So, 425 people went to the fair on the weekend.

Fill in the blanks to add.

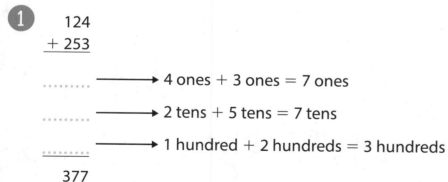

1

$$
\begin{array}{r}
124 \\
+\ 253 \\
\end{array}
$$

.... ⟶ 4 ones + 3 ones = 7 ones

.... ⟶ 2 tens + 5 tens = 7 tens

.... ⟶ 1 hundred + 2 hundreds = 3 hundreds

377

2

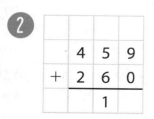

	4	5	9
+	2	6	0
			1

Fill in the blanks to add.

3

```
    2  2  8
+   1  3  6
```

4

```
    2  5  1
+   2  5  4
          5
    1  0  0
    4  0  0
```

5

```
  151
+ 154
```

6

```
  368
+ 245
```

300   + ...   +   8

....   +   40   +   5

500   +   100   + ... = ...

7

```
    4  1  8
    2  5  4
+   3  2  8
```

Refine Adding Three-Digit Numbers

Complete the Example below. Then solve problems 1–9 using any strategy you choose.

EXAMPLE

On Monday, a flower store sold 617 roses. On Tuesday, the store sold 279 roses. How many roses were sold in all on Monday and Tuesday?

Look at how you could show your work by breaking apart 617 and 279.

$$617 + 279 = (600 + 200) + (10 + 70) + (7 + 9)$$
$$= 800 + 80 + 16$$
$$= 896$$

Solution ....

The student broke apart 617 and 279 into hundreds, tens, and ones. That makes it easy to add the two numbers.

PAIR/SHARE
How else could you solve this problem?

APPLY IT

1 Diana has 109 magnets. Roger has 56 more magnets than Diana. How many magnets do Diana and Roger have in all? Show your work.

How many magnets does Roger have?

PAIR/SHARE
How did you know what to do first?

Solution ....

2 Find the sum of 345 and 626.

What place value do you need to regroup?

Solution ....

PAIR/SHARE
How can you estimate to see if your answer makes sense?

3 What is 149 + 293?

Ⓐ 442

Ⓑ 432

Ⓒ 342

Ⓓ 440

Finn chose Ⓑ as the correct answer. How did he get that answer?

Where do you write a regrouped ten? Where do you write a regrouped hundred?

PAIR/SHARE
Does Finn's answer make sense?

4 Mr. Coleman drives 129 miles on Monday. He drives 78 more miles on Tuesday than on Monday. How many miles does Mr. Coleman drive altogether on Monday and Tuesday?

Ⓐ 51

Ⓑ 207

Ⓒ 285

Ⓓ 336

5 Find the sum of 258 and 436. Estimate to check if your answer makes sense. Show your work.

Solution ....

6 The sum of the equation below can be written using tens and ones.

$68 + 16 =$ ......?...... tens and ......?...... ones.

Select one number from each column to make the equation true.

Tens	Ones
○ 2	○ 4
○ 7	○ 9
○ 8	○ 12
○ 9	○ 14

7 Find 147 + 123. Show your work.

8 Fill in the table to show how many hundreds, tens, and ones are in the number 746.

Number	Hundreds	Tens	Ones
746			

Write a number that meets the following conditions:

• The number must be a one-digit number.

• When the number is added to 746, the digit in the ones place of the sum is less than the ones digit in 746.

Solution ....

9 MATH JOURNAL

What strategy would you use to find 379 + 284? Explain and then find the sum.

☑ SELF CHECK Go back to the Unit 1 Opener and see what you can check off.

Subtract Three-Digit Numbers

Dear Family,

This week your child is using different strategies to subtract three-digit numbers.

For example, one way to find the difference $260 - 153$ is to use a number line to show the related addition equation, $153 + ? = 260$.

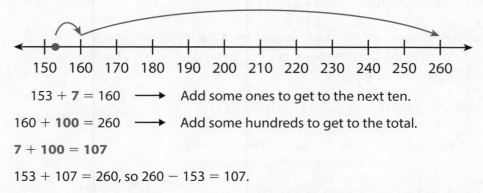

150 160 170 180 190 200 210 220 230 240 250 260

$153 + 7 = 160$ $\longrightarrow$ Add some ones to get to the next ten.

$160 + 100 = 260$ $\longrightarrow$ Add some hundreds to get to the total.

$7 + 100 = 107$

$153 + 107 = 260$, so $260 - 153 = 107$.

Another way to solve this problem is to use place value and the standard subtraction algorithm. This involves regrouping when you cannot subtract the digits in one of the place-value columns because the digit being subtracted is greater than the digit it is being subtracted from. Here is how the same subtraction problem would look when solved using the algorithm.

6 tens become 5 tens and 10 ones.

$$\begin{array}{r} {\scriptstyle 5\,10} \\ 2\cancel{6}\cancel{0} \\ -\ 153 \\ \hline 7 \end{array}$$

$$\begin{array}{r} {\scriptstyle 5\,10} \\ 2\cancel{6}\cancel{0} \\ -\ 153 \\ \hline 07 \end{array}$$

$$\begin{array}{r} {\scriptstyle 5\,10} \\ 2\cancel{6}\cancel{0} \\ -\ 153 \\ \hline 107 \end{array}$$

Subtract the **ones** digits: **3 cannot be subtracted from 0; regroup a 10** $10 - 3 = 7$	Subtract the **tens** digits: $5 - 5 = 0$ $(50 - 50 = 0)$	Subtract the **hundreds** digits: $2 - 1 = 1$ $(200 - 100 = 100)$

Invite your child to share what he or she knows about subtracting three-digit numbers by doing the following activity together.

ACTIVITY SUBTRACT THREE-DIGIT NUMBERS

Do this activity with your child to subtract three-digit numbers.

Materials 3 number cubes, pencil and paper

Play this subtraction game with your child to practice subtracting three-digit numbers. The goal of this game is to get the least possible difference when subtracting a three-digit number from 880.

• Each player rolls three number cubes.

• Have each player form a three-digit number from the number cubes. (If the rolls are 2, 6, and 1, the possible numbers are 126, 162, 216, 261, 612, and 621.) Write down the chosen number.

• Each player subtracts their number from 880, using any subtraction strategy.

• Whoever has the least difference wins the round.

• Play five rounds for best out of five.

• Ask your child questions during the game, such as:

  • *Does it matter which number I form out of the three number cubes? How will it change the difference?*

  • *How can I pick my number to make sure I have the least possible difference?*

Explore Subtracting Three-Digit Numbers

In this lesson you will learn strategies for subtracting numbers. Use what you know to try to solve the problem below.

> Eva bought a bag of 475 glass beads. She used 134 beads to make a necklace. How many beads are left in the bag?

Learning Target

- Fluently add and subtract within 1000 using strategies and algorithms based on place value, properties of operations, and/or the relationship between addition and subtraction.

SMP 1, 2, 3, 4, 5, 6, 7, 8

TRY IT

Math Toolkit

- base-ten blocks
- hundreds place-value charts
- number lines

DISCUSS IT

Ask your partner: How did you get started?

Tell your partner: I am not sure how to find the answer because . . .

CONNECT IT

1 **LOOK BACK**

Explain how to find how many beads Eva has left.

2 **LOOK AHEAD**

You can solve subtraction problems in different ways. Breaking apart numbers is one way to make a problem easier.

Suppose you had the subtraction problem $525 - 213$.

a. Break apart 525 into hundreds, tens, and ones.

b. Break apart 213 into hundreds, tens, and ones.

c. Subtract ones from ones, tens from tens, and hundreds from hundreds to find $525 - 213$.

d. Check your answer by estimating. Round 525 and 213 to the nearest ten or hundred and subtract. Does your answer make sense? Explain.

3 **REFLECT**

What is another way you could find $525 - 213$?

....

....

....

Prepare for Subtracting Three-Digit Numbers

1 Think about what you know about regrouping. Fill in each box. Use words, numbers, and pictures. Show as many ideas as you can.

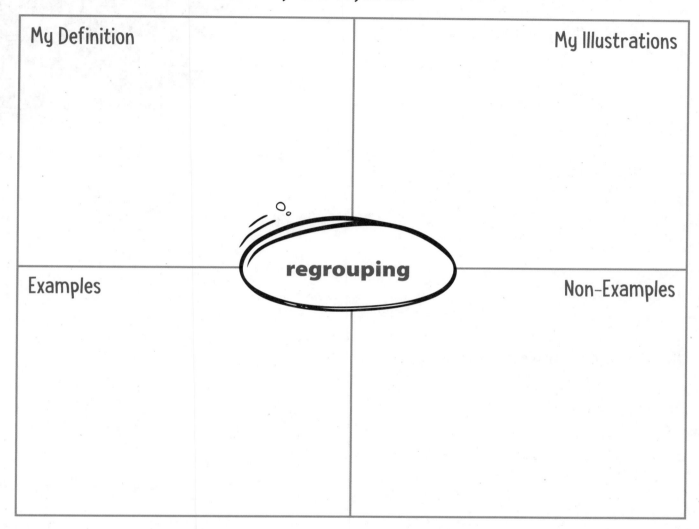

My Definition	My Illustrations

Examples	Non-Examples

regrouping

2 Explain how you would regroup to find 194 − 187.

3 Solve the problem. Show your work.

Alexi needs to plant 355 flowers in a garden. He plants 223 flowers before taking a break. How many flowers does he still need to plant?

Solution ....

4 Check your answer. Show your work.

Develop Using Place-Value Strategies to Subtract

Read and try to solve the problem below.

> Catalina records the weather for 365 days. It is sunny
> 186 days. How many days are not sunny?

TRY IT

Math Toolkit
- base-ten blocks
- hundreds place-value charts
- number lines

DISCUSS IT

Ask your partner: Can you explain that again?

Tell your partner: I do not understand how . . .

Explore different ways to understand subtracting three-digit numbers.

> **Catalina records the weather for 365 days. It is sunny 186 days. How many days are not sunny?**

PICTURE IT
You can use base-ten blocks to subtract three-digit numbers.

This model shows 365 − 186. All the blocks show 365. One ten and one hundred are regrouped. The blocks crossed out show 186.

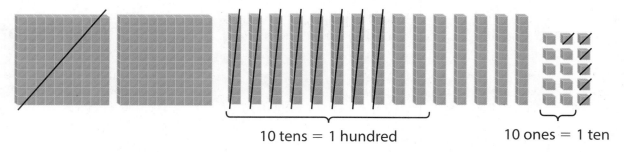

10 tens = 1 hundred   10 ones = 1 ten

Blocks that are left: 1 hundred + 7 tens + 9 ones

MODEL IT
You can also break apart by place value to subtract three-digit numbers.

365 = 3 hundreds + 6 tens + 5 ones
= 3 hundreds + 5 tens + 15 ones
= **2 hundreds + 15 tens + 15 ones**

186 = 1 hundred + 8 tens + 6 ones

Subtract ones, tens, and hundreds.
15 ones − 6 ones = 9 ones
15 tens − 8 tens = 7 tens
2 hundreds − 1 hundred = 1 hundred

Combine these differences.
1 hundred + 7 tens + 9 ones

CONNECT IT

Now you will use the problem from the previous page to help you understand how to use different strategies to subtract.

$365 - 186 = \square$

Step 1:	$365 = 300 + 60 + 5$	$186 = 100 + 80 + 6$
Step 2:	$= 300 + 50 + 15$	$= 100 + 80 + 6$
Step 3:	$= 200 + 150 + 15$	$= 100 + 80 + 6$

1 Look at 365 in Step 1. Can you subtract ones from ones, tens from tens, and hundreds from hundreds?

2 Explain the regrouping used to go from Step 1 to Step 2.

Explain the regrouping used to go from Step 2 to Step 3.

3 Subtract each place:

$200 - 100 =$ .... $150 - 80 =$ .... $15 - 6 =$ ....

Now find what is left by adding the three differences. ....

How many days are not sunny? ....

4 Explain how to subtract three-digit numbers when you need to regroup twice.

5 REFLECT

Look back at your **Try It**, strategies by classmates, and **Picture It** and **Model It**. Which models or strategies do you like best for subtracting three-digit numbers? Explain.

....
....
....

APPLY IT

Use what you just learned to solve these problems.

6 Find 362 − 125. Show your work.

Solution ....

7 Ellie is reading a book with 853 pages. Over the weekend, she reads 146 pages. How many more pages does she need to read to finish the book?

Ⓐ 670 pages

Ⓑ 703 pages

Ⓒ 707 pages

Ⓓ 713 pages

8 Find 425 − 289. Show your work.

Solution ....

Practice Using Place-Value Strategies to Subtract

Study the Example showing how place value can help you subtract three-digit numbers. Then solve problems 1–5.

EXAMPLE

The balloon artist at the fair sold 253 balloons. Of those, 129 were monster heads. How many balloons were not monster heads?

Find 253 − 129.

$$253 = 2 \text{ hundreds} + \textbf{5 tens} + \textbf{3 ones}$$
$$\textbf{or } 2 \text{ hundreds} + \textbf{4 tens} + \textbf{13 ones}$$
$$129 = 1 \text{ hundred} + 2 \text{ tens} + 9 \text{ ones}$$
$$253 - 129 = 1 \text{ hundred} + 2 \text{ tens} + 4 \text{ ones}$$

124 balloons were not monster heads.

1 Fill in the blanks to find 352 − 147.

352 = ... hundreds + ... tens + 2 ones

or .... **hundreds** + **4 tens** + ... **ones**

147 = ... **hundred** + **4 tens** + ... **ones**

Subtract: .... hundreds + 0 tens + ... ones

352 − 147 = ...

2 Fill in the blanks to find 459 − 260.

459 = ... hundreds + ... tens + 9 ones

or **3 hundreds** + **15 tens** + ... **ones**

260 = ... **hundreds** + ... **tens** + ... **ones**

Subtract: .... hundreds + ... tens + ... ones

459 − 260 = ...

3 Fill in the blanks to find 905 − 425.

905 = ... +   0   + 5

   or .... +   100   + 5

425 = ... + ... + 5

Subtract hundreds: ....

Subtract tens: ....

Subtract ones: ....

905 − 425 = ...

Subtract. Regroup if needed.

4 Find 252 − 136. Show your work.

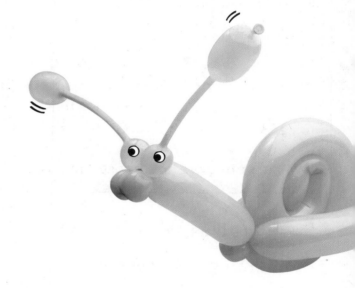

Solution ....

5 Find 636 − 158. Show your work.

Solution ....

Develop Adding On to Subtract

Read and try to solve the problem below.

> **Perez has 205 seeds.**
> **He plants 137 seeds.**
> **How many seeds does**
> **Perez have left?**

TRY IT

🧰 **Math Toolkit**
- base-ten blocks 🖱
- hundreds place-value charts
- number lines

DISCUSS IT

Ask your partner: Do you agree with me? Why or why not?

Tell your partner: I knew . . . so I . . .

Explore another way to understand subtracting three-digit numbers.

> **Perez has 205 seeds. He plants 137 seeds. How many seeds does Perez have left?**

MODEL IT

You can use a number line to add on to find a difference.

To solve the problem, you can use the subtraction equation $205 - 137 = \square$.
You can also solve the problem with the addition equation $137 + \square = 205$.
Use a number line to add on to 137 to get to 205.

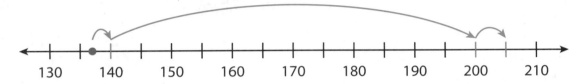

Find the numbers that you add to get to the next number:

$137 + 3 = 140$ ⟵ Add on ones to get to the next ten.

$140 + 60 = 200$ ⟵ Add on tens to get to the next hundred.

$200 + 5 = 205$ ⟵ Add on ones to get to the total, 205.

You added $3 + 60 + 5$ to get from 137 to 205.

CONNECT IT

Now you will use the problem from the previous page and a place-value chart to help you understand how to add on to subtract.

1 Start at 137. What is the next ten? ....
How many ones do you add to get to the

next ten? ....

This first number is written in the chart
for you.

	Hundreds	Tens	Ones	
137 +			3	= 140
140 +				= 200
200 +				= 205

2 How many tens do you add to get from 140 to the hundred you need?
Write your answer in the chart.

3 Now what do you add to get from 200 to 205? Write your answer in the chart.

4 Write an addition equation to show what you added.

How many seeds does Perez have left? .... seeds

5 Explain how you would add on to find this difference: 202 − 195.

6 REFLECT

Look back at your **Try It**, strategies by classmates, and **Model It**. Which models
or strategies do you like best for subtracting three-digit numbers? Explain.

....

....

....

APPLY IT

Use what you just learned to solve these problems.

7 Edith has $600. She spends $84. How much does Edith have left? Show your work.

Solution ....

8 Find the difference between 430 and 182.

Ⓐ 148

Ⓑ 240

Ⓒ 248

Ⓓ 310

9 Juan sent and received 800 text messages. He sent 379 text messages. How many text messages did Juan receive? Show your work.

Solution ....

Practice Adding On to Subtract

**Study the Example showing how to subtract by adding on.
Then solve problems 1–8.**

EXAMPLE

310 students went to the art museum. 195 students left at 9 AM. The others left at
9:30 AM. How many students left for the museum at 9:30 AM?

$310 - 195 = \boxed{}$, or $195 + \boxed{} = 310$

Add on to 195 to get to 310.

Add 5: $195 + \ \mathbf{5} = 200$
Add 100: $200 + \mathbf{100} = 300$
Add 10: $300 + \ \mathbf{10} = 310$

$\mathbf{5 + 100 + 10} = 115$
$195 + 115 = 310$ $310 - 195 = 115$

So, 115 students left at 9:30.

Fill in the blanks to show adding on to subtract.

1 $75 + 5 + \text{.............} = 100$, so $100 - 75 = \text{.............}$.

2 $114 + 6 + \text{.............} + \text{.............} = 132$, so $132 - 114 = \text{.............}$.

3 $162 + 8 + \text{.............} + 1 = 201$, so $201 - 162 = \text{.............}$.

Solve.

4 $501 - 470 = \text{.............}$

Explain how you can start with 470 and add on to solve.

Solve.

5 100 − 78 = ...

Explain how you can start with 78 and add on to solve.

6 200 − 96 = ...

Explain how you can start with 96 and add on to solve.

7 305 − 212 = ...

Explain how you can start with 212 and add on to solve.

8 303 − 196 = ...

Explain how you can start with 196 and add on to solve.

Develop Connecting Place-Value Strategies to an Algorithm

Read and try to solve the problem below.

What is the difference?
Use place value to help you subtract.

385
− 158

TRY IT

 **Math Toolkit**
- base-ten blocks
- hundreds place-value charts
- number lines

DISCUSS IT

Ask your partner: Why did you choose this strategy?

Tell your partner: The model I used was . . .
It helped me . . .

Explore another way to understand how to subtract using place value.

> **What is the difference?**
> **Use place value to help you subtract.**

$$385 - 158$$

MODEL IT

You can regroup when needed so you can subtract.

You cannot subtract 8 from 5. You need to regroup. Write 385 in a place-value chart.

Regroup a ten into the ones place.

Hundreds	Tens	Ones
3	(8)	5

Hundreds	Tens	Ones
3	7	10 + 5 = 15

8 tens = 7 tens + 10 ones

Now you have enough ones to subtract.

	Hundreds	Tens	Ones
	3	7	15
−	1	5	8

MODEL IT

You can record your work in a shorter way.

Subtract ones from ones, tens from tens, and hundreds from hundreds. Record your work by showing regrouping above the problem and writing the difference in one row. A grid can help you keep track of the place value of the digits.

Regroup **8 tens** to **7 tens** and **10 ones**.

```
      7  15
   3  8̷  5̷
-  1  5  8
         7
```

Step 1: Subtract ones.
Regroup? Yes.
$15 - 8 = 7$

```
      7  15
   3  8̷  5̷
-  1  5  8
         7
```

Step 2: Subtract tens.
Regroup? No.
$7 - 5$

```
      7  15
   3  8̷  5̷
-  1  5  8
         7
```

Step 3: Subtract hundreds.
Regroup? No.
$3 - 1$

66 **Lesson 3** Subtract Three-Digit Numbers

CONNECT IT

Now you will use the problem from the previous page to help you understand how to subtract using place value.

1 Look at the first **Model It**. Does the way one of the tens was regrouped into ones make sense? Explain.

2 Look at the second **Model It**. Why are the **8** in the tens place and the **5** in the ones place crossed out? Why are **7** tens and **15** ones then shown?

3 How would you complete the problem to find the difference?

4 When you need to regroup a ten and the tens digit is 0, you will need to regroup from the hundreds place. Use the grid and the steps from the second **Model It** to find 500 − 219. Explain your work.

		5	0	0
−		2	1	9

5 REFLECT

Look back at your **Try It**, strategies by classmates, and **Model Its**. Which models or strategies do you like best for subtracting? Explain.

....

....

....

APPLY IT

Use what you just learned to solve these problems.

6 Solve each subtraction problem. Show your work.

a.

	8	7	2
−	7	4	1

b.

	4	0	9
−	2	4	3

7 In one year, there are 180 days of school. If there are 365 days in a year, on how many days is there no school? Check your answer by rounding. Show your work.

Round to the nearest hundred to check:

Solution ....

8 Find the difference. Show your work.

345
− 187

Solution ....

Practice Connecting Place-Value Strategies to an Algorithm

Study the Example showing how using an algorithm can help you subtract three-digit numbers. Then solve problems 1–9.

EXAMPLE

Ayla has a container with 562 grams of orange juice. She pours 381 grams of juice into a glass. How many grams of juice are left in the container?

$$
\begin{array}{rcl}
 & & \textbf{4 hundreds} \quad\quad \textbf{16 tens} \\
\overset{\text{4 16}}{\cancel{562}} & = & 5\text{ hundreds} \ + \ 6\text{ tens} \ + \ 2\text{ ones} \\
-\ 381 & = & 3\text{ hundreds} \ + \ 8\text{ tens} \ + \ 1\text{ one} \\
\hline
181 & = & 1\text{ hundred} \ + \ 8\text{ tens} \ + \ 1\text{ one}
\end{array}
$$

There are 181 grams of juice left in the container.

Fill in the blanks to subtract.

1 Subtract 849 from 960.

$$
\begin{array}{rcl}
 & & \text{............ tens} \quad\quad \text{............ ones} \\
960 & = & \text{............ hundreds} \ + \ \cancel{6}\text{ tens} \ + \ \cancel{0}\text{ ones} \\
-\ 849 & = & \text{............ hundreds} \ + \ 4\text{ tens} \ + \ 9\text{ ones} \\
\hline
\text{............} & = & \text{............ hundred} \ + \ \text{............ ten} \ + \ \text{............ one}
\end{array}
$$

2

$$
\begin{array}{r}
6\ 4\ 9 \\
-\ 3\ 6\ 6 \\
\hline
\end{array}
$$

Subtract.

3

```
    2  8  6
 -  1  9  9
```

4

```
    8  0  0
 -  5  1  2
```

5
```
   998
 - 657
```

6
```
   865
 - 328
```

7
```
   382
 - 195
```

8
```
   280
 - 153
```

9
```
  1,000
 -  595
```

Refine Subtracting Three-Digit Numbers

Complete the Example below. Then solve problems 1–8 using any strategy you choose.

EXAMPLE

Find the difference of 805 and 279.

Look at how you could show your work by using the algorithm.

Regroup twice:

$$800 + 0 + 5 = 700 + 100 + 5$$
$$= 700 + 90 + 15$$

```
        9
      7 10 15
       8̶0̶5̶
     − 279
     ─────
       526
```

Solution ....

The student regrouped 1 hundred to the tens first. This made it possible to regroup 1 ten to the ones to make 15.

PAIR/SHARE
How else can you solve this probem?

APPLY IT

1 Find 450 − 131. Show your work.

How can you use place value to help you regroup?

PAIR/SHARE
How did you know you need to regroup?

Solution ....

2 Corey works 144 hours a month. He has worked 72 hours so far this month. How many more hours does Corey have to work this month? Show your work.

Solution ....

3 Chad practiced batting for 205 minutes this week. Doug practiced batting for 110 minutes. How many more minutes did Chad practice than Doug?

Ⓐ 90 minutes

Ⓑ 95 minutes

Ⓒ 195 minutes

Ⓓ 315 minutes

Sam chose Ⓓ as the correct answer. How did he get that answer?

4 Gail drove to a family reunion 900 miles from home. At one point during her drive back home, she saw that she still had 455 miles to go before she reached home. How many miles had she already driven toward home?

Ⓐ 545

Ⓑ 455

Ⓒ 555

Ⓓ 445

5 Which diagrams or solutions represent the difference 354 − 298?

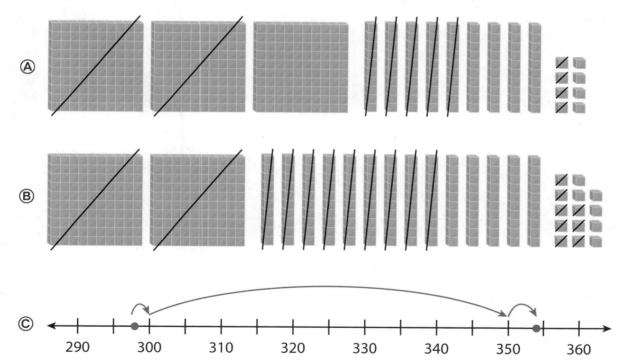

Ⓓ 2 hundreds − 2 hundreds = 0 hundreds
15 tens − 9 tens = 6 tens
14 ones − 8 ones = 6 ones

Ⓔ
```
    14
  2 ⁴14
  3̶5̶4̶
− 298
─────
   56
```

6 Find 907 − 199. Show your work.

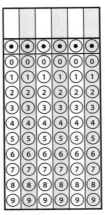

7 Neke has 308 craft sticks. She buys a package of 625 craft sticks. She uses 245 craft sticks for a project. How many craft sticks does Neke have left? Show your work.

Neke has .... craft sticks left.

8 MATH JOURNAL

What strategy would you use to find 379 − 284? Explain and then find the difference.

☑ SELF CHECK Go back to the Unit 1 Opener and see what you can check off.

In this unit you learned to . . .

Skill	Lesson
Use place value to round numbers to the nearest ten and to the nearest hundred, for example: • 315 rounded to the nearest ten is 320. • 826 rounded to the nearest hundred is 800.	1
Use place value to add and subtract, for example: $329 + 148 = (300 + 100) + (20 + 40) + (9 + 8)$ $\qquad\qquad = 400 + 60 + 17$ $\qquad\qquad = 477$	2, 3
Solve word problems by adding and subtracting using place value.	2, 3

Think about what you learned.

Use words, numbers, and drawings.

1 Two important things I learned are . . .

2 Something I know well is . . .

3 One thing I could do better is . . .

Use Rounding and Operations

Study an Example Problem and Solution

SMP 1 Make sense of problems and persevere in solving them.

Read this problem that uses rounding with addition. Then look at Alex's solution to this problem.

Adopt an Animal

The Wildlife Protectors save endangered animals. Alex helps them raise money. Her goal is to raise at least $750. Alex asks her neighbors to buy adoption kits. Here are her notes.

ADOPT-AN-ANIMAL KITS

Tiger	
$59 kit	
$95 kit	
$199 kit	

Snowy Owl	
$29 kit	
$55 kit	
$99 kit	

My Notes

- Two people will spend up to $200.
- Two people will spend about $100.
- Others will spend less than $75.

Use the information in the notes. Show what kits and how many of each Alex can sell to reach her goal. Explain your choices.

Read the sample solution on the next page. Then look at the checklist below. Find and mark parts of the solution that match the checklist.

☑ PROBLEM-SOLVING CHECKLIST

- ☐ Tell what is known.
- ☐ Tell what the problem is asking.
- ☐ Show all your work.
- ☐ Show that the solution works.

a. **Circle** something that is known.

b. **Underline** something that you need to find.

c. **Draw a box around** what you do to solve the problem.

d. **Put a checkmark** next to the part that shows the solution works.

ALEX'S SOLUTION

- **I can round the prices. Then I can estimate how many kits to sell.**

  $59 → $60 $95 → $100 $199 → $200

  $29 → $30 $55 → $60 $99 → $100

- **The two people who will spend up to $200 can buy the $199 kits.**

  $200 + $200 = $400

- **The two people who will spend about $100 can buy the $99 kits. That's about $200 more.**

  Now I have $400 + $200, or $600.

- **$59 < $75. If two people buy $59 kits, I'll have about $120 more.**

  Now I have about $600 + $120, or $720.

- **$29 < $75. If two people buy $29 kits, I'll have about $60 more.**

  Now I have about $720 + $60, or $780. This is at least $750.

- **Now I can find the actual prices.**

  Two kits for $199: $199 + $199 = $398

  Two kits for $99: $99 + $99 = $198

  Two kits for $59: $59 + $59 = $118

  Two kits for $29: $29 + $29 = $58

$$\begin{array}{r} \overset{2\ 3}{\$398} \\ \$198 \\ \$118 \\ +\$\ \ 58 \\ \hline \$772 \end{array}$$

$772 > $750, so the plan works.

Hi, I'm Alex. Here's how I solved the problem.

I can use rounded numbers first. I can get an idea of what numbers will work before doing all the adding.

Each addend is 1 less than the rounded numbers. That means that each actual sum is 2 less than the estimated sum.

Try Another Approach

There are many ways to solve problems. Think about how you might solve the Adopt an Animal problem in a different way.

Adopt an Animal

The Wildlife Protectors save endangered animals. Alex helps them raise money. Her goal is to raise at least $750. Alex asks her neighbors to buy adoption kits. Here are her notes.

My Notes

- Two people will spend up to $200.
- Two people will spend about $100.
- Others will spend less than $75.

ADOPT-AN-ANIMAL KITS

Tiger	
$59 kit	
$95 kit	
$199 kit	
Snowy Owl	
$29 kit	
$55 kit	
$99 kit	

Use the information in the notes. Show what kits and how many of each Alex can sell to reach her goal. Explain your choices.

PLAN IT

Answer these questions to help you start thinking about a plan.

A. What kit that costs about $100 was not used in Alex's solution?

B. What kit that costs about $60 was not used in Alex's solution?

SOLVE IT

**Find a different solution for the Adopt an Animal problem.
Show all your work on a separate sheet of paper.**

You may want to use the Problem-Solving Tips to get started.

PROBLEM-SOLVING TIPS

- **Tools** You may want to use . . .
  - mental math.
  - paper and pencil.

- **Word Bank**

round	sum	about
add	estimate	greater than

- **Sentence Starters**

- I'll round _____

- _____ is greater than _____

☑ PROBLEM-SOLVING CHECKLIST

Make sure that you . . .
- ☐ tell what you know.
- ☐ tell what you need to do.
- ☐ show all your work.
- ☐ show that the solution works.

REFLECT

Use Mathematical Practices As you work through the problem, discuss these questions with a partner.

- **Be Precise** Why do you have to find actual sums to solve this problem?

- **Reason Mathematically** What addition strategies can you use to solve this problem?

Discuss Models and Strategies

Read the problem. Write a solution on a separate sheet of paper. Remember, there can be lots of ways to solve a problem!

Better Farms

One way to help endangered animals is to make better farms. When land is cleared for farming, it is taken away from wild animals. Alex wants to help farms grow more food so new farms are not needed.

The Wildlife Protectors raise money to buy farming supplies.

- Compost: $10 each bag
- Wooden Planters: $5 each box
- Garden Washing Station: $40
- Wooden Raised Bed: $109

Alex wants to know what the money from a $199 animal adoption kit can buy. The kit costs $8 to make. The rest of the money can buy farming supplies. Show Alex what the money from a $199 kit can buy.

PLAN IT AND SOLVE IT

Find a solution for the Better Farms problem.

- Find how much money the sale of one kit makes.

- Find at least two different items that this money can buy.

- Tell how much money is left, if there is any.

You may want to use the Problem-Solving Tips to get started.

PROBLEM-SOLVING TIPS

- **Questions**

  - How do you find the amount left after paying for making the kit?

  - What items do you think farms need the most?

- **Sentence Starters**

- There is _____ left after _____

- The sale of a $199 kit can buy _____

✓ PROBLEM-SOLVING CHECKLIST

Make sure that you . . .
- ☐ tell what you know.
- ☐ tell what you need to do.
- ☐ show all your work.
- ☐ show that the solution works.

REFLECT

Use Mathematical Practices As you work through the problem, discuss these questions with a partner.

- **Make Sense of Problems** What will you do first? Why?

- **Persevere** What are some different ways that you might solve this problem?

Persevere On Your Own

Read the problems. Write a solution on a separate sheet of paper.

Ticket Sales

Alex works at a zoo. The zoo donates money to the Wildlife Protectors for every ticket sold on Saturday morning. They donate $1 for each child ticket and $2 for each adult ticket.

Alex looks at ticket records for the past 5 weeks.

Saturday Morning Ticket Sales					
	Week 1	**Week 2**	**Week 3**	**Week 4**	**Week 5**
Adult Tickets Sold	74	68	76	78	72
Child Tickets Sold	93	96	99	103	106

Estimate how much money the zoo will donate to the Wildlife Protectors for Week 6.

SOLVE IT

Help Alex estimate the donation amount.

• Find the usual number of adult and child tickets that are sold on Saturday mornings. Use rounding.

• Then use the ticket numbers to estimate the amount of money that the zoo will donate.

REFLECT

Use Mathematical Practices After you complete the task, choose one of these questions to discuss with a partner.

• **Make an Argument** Why do the numbers you used make sense with the problem?

• **Be Precise** Can you find an exact answer for this problem? Why or why not?

Zoo Decorations

Alex wants to make a new ticket booth for the zoo. She will decorate it with silver stars. Alex estimates that she will need about 800 stars.

The stars come in boxes. Here are the boxes she can choose from:

Box A: 96 stars $2

Box B: 204 stars $3

Box C: 300 stars $4

Box D: 348 stars $5

What boxes should Alex buy? How much will the boxes cost?

SOLVE IT

Find a way to buy about 800 stars.

- Tell which boxes and how many of each box Alex should buy.

- Explain how you know Alex will get about 800 stars.

- Find the total cost.

REFLECT

Use Mathematical Practices   After you complete the task, choose one of these questions to discuss with a partner.

- **Reason with Numbers**   How could estimation help you begin this problem?

- **Use Models**   How did you use equations to help you solve the problem?

    Unit 1 Math in Action   Use Rounding and Operations

1 What is 388 rounded to the nearest hundred?

    Ⓐ 300

    Ⓑ 380

    Ⓒ 390

    Ⓓ 400

2 Find $436 + 542$. Record your answer on the grid. Then fill in the bubbles.

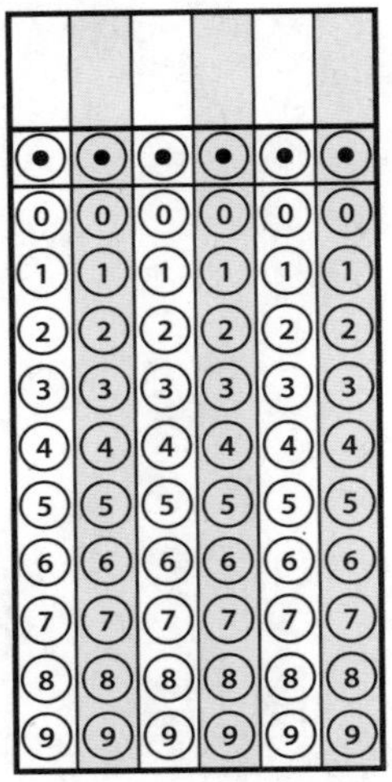

3 What is the difference between 723 and 285? Show your work.

Solution ....

4 Add on to subtract. Write your answer in the blanks.

$326 + 4 + $ .... $ + 2 = 392$ so $392 - 326 = $ ....

5 Dakota takes 426 photos of plants. He rounds to tell people how many photos he takes.

Write your answers in the blanks.

Rounded to the nearest ten, Dakota takes .... photos of plants.

Rounded to the nearest hundred, Dakota takes .... photos of plants.

6 Which of these diagrams or solutions represents $176 + 139$? Choose all the correct answers.

Ⓐ
$$
\begin{array}{r}
100 + 70 + 6 \\
100 + 30 + 9 \\
\hline
200 + 100 + 15
\end{array}
$$

Ⓑ
$$
\begin{array}{r}
176 \\
+ 139 \\
\hline
5 \\
10 \\
200
\end{array}
$$

Ⓒ 1 hundred + 1 hundred = 2 hundreds
70 tens + 30 tens = 100 tens
6 ones + 9 ones = 15 ones

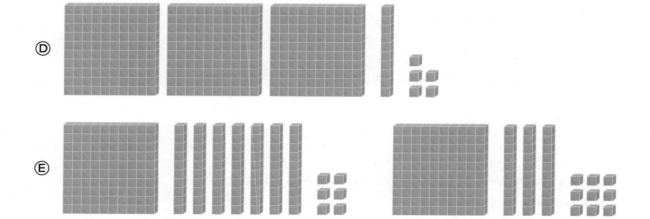

Ⓓ

Ⓔ

Performance Task

Answer the questions and show all your work on separate paper.

Mr. Gemelli runs the school cafeteria. He needs your help ordering compostable lunch trays and bananas for the students' lunches. He needs to order lunch trays and bananas for lunch next week. Here are Mr. Gemelli's instructions:

"I need 1 tray and 1 banana for each lunch ordered. I usually round the number of lunches for each day to the nearest ten when I order bananas. I think this will give me some extra bananas in case students want more than one. I round the number of lunches for each day to the nearest hundred when I order lunch trays because they are sold in packages of 100."

The table below shows the number of lunches ordered for each day next week.

	Monday	Tuesday	Wednesday	Thursday	Friday
Number of lunches	159	245	113	104	162

Use Mr. Gemelli's guidelines to find the total number of trays and bananas he should order for student lunches for next week. Write a letter to Mr. Gemelli telling him how many of each item he should order and explain how you know.

REFLECT

Use Mathematical Practices After you complete the task, choose one of the following questions to answer.

- **Be Precise** How did you decide how to round the numbers in Mr. Gemelli's table?

- **Reason Mathematically** What strategies did you use to add the numbers in this problem?

> ### Checklist
> Did you . . .
> - ☐ organize your information?
> - ☐ check your calculations?
> - ☐ write a letter with a complete explanation?

Vocabulary

Draw or write to show examples for each term. Then draw or write to show other math words in the unit.

algorithm   a set of routine steps used to solve problems.

My Example

partial sums   the sums you get in each step of the partial-sums strategy. You use place value to find partial sums. For example, the partial sums for 124 + 234 are 100 + 200 or 300, 20 + 30 or 50, and 4 + 4 or 8.

My Example

round   to find a number that is close in value to a given number by finding the nearest ten, hundred, or other place value.

My Example

My Word: _____

_____

_____

My Example

My Word: _____

_____

_____

My Example

My Word: _____

_____

_____

My Example

My Word: _____

_____

_____

My Example

My Word: _____

_____

_____

My Example

My Word: _____

_____

_____

My Example

My Word: _____

_____

_____

My Example

My Word: _____

_____

_____

My Example

My Word: _____

_____

_____

My Example

☑ SELF CHECK

Before starting this unit, check off the skills you know below. As you complete each lesson, see how many more skills you can check off!

I can . . .	Before	After
Explain multiplication using equal groups and arrays.	☐	☐
Break apart numbers to make multiplying easier, for example: 3×8 is equal to $(3 \times 4) + (3 \times 4)$.	☐	☐
Use order and grouping to make multiplying easier, for example: $2 \times 6 \times 5$ is equal to $6 \times (2 \times 5)$.	☐	☐
Use place value to multiply, for example: 3×40 is equal to $3 \times 4 \times 10$.	☐	☐
Explain division using equal groups and arrays.	☐	☐
Understand division as a multiplication problem, for example: $10 \div 2 = ?$ can be shown as $2 \times ? = 10$.	☐	☐
Use multiplication and division facts up through the facts for 10.	☐	☐
Find the rule for a pattern and explain it.	☐	☐

Build Your Vocabulary

Math Vocabulary

Play "Math Tac Toe" with a partner. Select a space and tell your partner the meaning of the word, numbers, or picture before you place your X or O marker.

array	⬤⬤⬤ ⬤⬤⬤⬤	$4 + 6 = 10$
even number	2, 4, 6, 8, 10	odd number
sum	1, 3, 5, 7, 9	⬤⬤⬤⬤ ⬤⬤⬤⬤

Academic Vocabulary

Put a check next to the academic words you know. Then use the words to complete the sentences.

☐ prepare   ☐ review   ☐ organize   ☐ process

1 The .... of how a caterpillar turns into a butterfly is called a life cycle.

2 It is helpful to go back and .... my work to make sure I got the right answer.

3 When I build arrays, I .... my tiles into rows and columns.

4 Before we begin to cook our favorite meal, we .... all our ingredients.

Understand the Meaning of Multiplication

Dear Family,

This week your child is exploring the meaning of multiplication.

Multiplication can involve working with equal groups of objects. For example:

3 groups of 5 flowers is 15 flowers in all.

Multiply: $3 \times 5 = 15$

The **product** tells how many in all.

The first **factor** tells how many groups.

The second **factor** tells how many in each group.

Your child is also using arrays to show multiplication. An array is a set of objects arranged in equal rows and equal columns.

4 rows of 6 apples is 24 apples in all. Use the **multiplication equation** $4 \times 6 = 24$.

Invite your child to share what he or she knows about the meaning of multiplication by doing the following activity together.

ACTIVITY MULTIPLICATION

Do this activity with your child to explore the meaning of multiplication.

Materials 30 pennies or other small items, 4 to 6 small cups

- Ask your child to show 4 × 5 by putting pennies in cups.

- Using the pennies in the cups, complete this sentence:

  .... groups of .... pennies equals .... pennies in all.

- Next, ask your child to remove the pennies from the first cup and arrange them in a row to begin an array.

- Have your child create the second, third, and fourth rows of the array with the pennies from the other three cups, as shown.

- Using the array, ask your child to multiply to find the total.

$$\underset{\text{how many rows}}{.......} \times \underset{\text{how many in each row}}{.......} = \underset{\text{total}}{.......}$$

- Repeat this activity for equal groups of other sizes, such as 5 × 3, 2 × 4, or 3 × 6.

As your child becomes more familiar with the idea of multiplication, point out examples of multiplication in real life; for example, 3 groups of 2 socks shows 3 × 2 = 6.

Answers:

4 groups of 5 pennies equals 20 pennies in all.

Array:

4 × 5 = 20

Explore the Meaning of Multiplication

What is going on when you multiply numbers?

MODEL IT

Complete the problems below.

1 You can add to find the total number of objects in different groups. When the groups are equal, you can also **multiply** to find the total.

Draw a picture of 3 equal groups of 2 balloons.

2 Write an addition equation to represent the total your picture shows.

3 Complete the sentence to describe the equal groups in your picture. Then use the same numbers to complete the **multiplication** equation.

.... groups of .... is .... in all.

↓   ↓   ↓   ↓   ↓

.... × .... = ...

DISCUSS IT

• How is your addition equation like your partner's addition equation?

• I think the × in problem 3 means . . .

MODEL IT

Complete the problems below.

4 You can model multiplication with equal groups. Circle the tennis balls to show 3 equal groups of 4 tennis balls.

5 Use the picture of equal groups above to show what the **multiplication equation** means. Fill in the blanks.

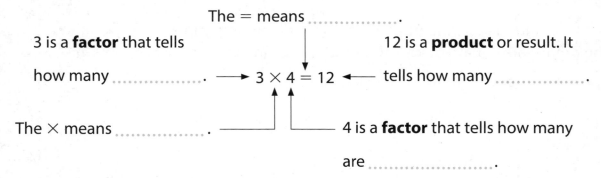

The = means ....

3 is a **factor** that tells

how many .... ⟶ 3 × 4 = 12 ⟵ tells how many ....

12 is a **product** or result. It

The × means .... ⟶ 4 is a **factor** that tells how many

are ....

When you see 3 × 4 = 12, you say: *Three times four equals 12.*

6 You can also model multiplication with an array. Fill in the blanks.

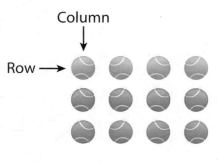

Column

Row ⟶

.... rows with .... columns is .... in all.

.... × .... = ...

7 REFLECT

Look at the way the chairs in your classroom are set up. Could they show a multiplication problem or not? Explain.

....

....

Prepare for Multiplication

1 Think about what you know about multiplication. Fill in each box.
Use words, numbers, and pictures. Show as many ideas as you can.

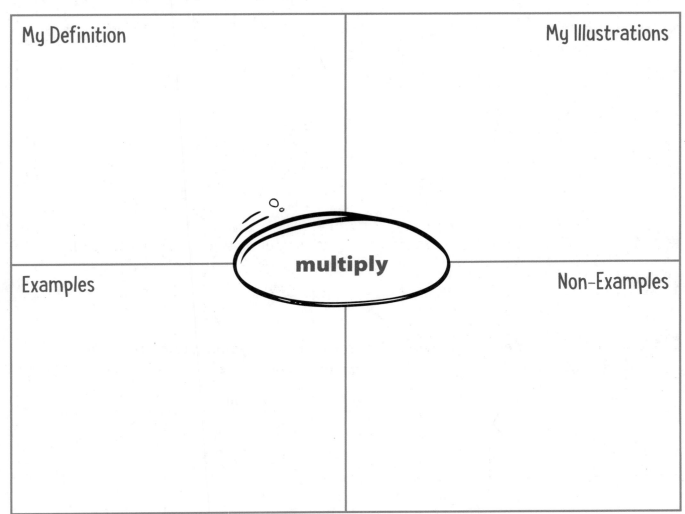

My Definition

My Illustrations

Examples

multiply

Non-Examples

2 Explain how you can write a multiplication equation for the picture.

Solve.

③ Draw a picture of 4 equal groups of 3 buttons.

④ Write an addition equation to represent the total your picture shows.

⑤ Complete the sentence to describe the equal groups in your picture. Then use the same numbers to complete the multiplication equation.

.... groups of .... is .... in all.

.... × .... = ...

Develop Understanding of Multiplication Models

MODEL IT: EQUAL GROUPS AND ARRAYS

Try these two problems.

1 Show what the **expression** 4 × 5 means by using equal groups.

a. Draw equal groups.

b. Use words to describe your drawing of 4 × 5.

c. Write the product. 4 × 5 = ...

2 Show what the expression 4 × 5 means by using an array.

a. Draw an array.

b. Use words to describe your drawing of 4 × 5.

c. Write the product. 4 × 5 = ...

DISCUSS IT

- How did you and your partner know how many equal groups to draw in problem 1?

- I think equal groups and arrays both show multiplication because . . .

MODEL IT: SQUARE TILES

Use square tiles to model multiplication.

3 You can push the tiles in an array together to make a rectangle. Write the multiplication equation the rectangle below shows.

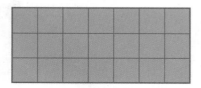

....

4 Draw a rectangle made up of square tiles that shows $5 \times 3 = 15$.

DISCUSS IT

• How can you use words instead of a drawing to describe 5×3?

• I think rectangles with square tiles show multiplication because . . .

CONNECT IT

Complete the problems below.

5 How can words and drawings of equal groups, arrays, or square tiles all be used to describe what a multiplication problem means?

6 Use any model to show and find 4×7. Write a complete multiplication equation and explain what each number in the equation tells you.

Practice Using Multiplication Models

Study how the Example represents a multiplication equation with equal groups. Then solve problems 1–9.

EXAMPLE

Draw a picture and use words for the multiplication equation 2 × 6 = 12.

There are 2 groups of 6 ladybugs, or 12 ladybugs in all.

Use the picture below to answer problems 1–4.

1 How many equal groups are there? ....

2 How many ladybugs are in each group? ....

3 How many ladybugs are there altogether? ....

4 Write a multiplication equation that matches the picture.

.... × .... = ...

Use the picture at the right to solve problems 5–7.

5 The basketball cart has 3 shelves. There is already 1 basketball on each shelf. Draw the rest of the basketballs to create an array to show the expression 3 × 5.

6 Look at your picture of the basketballs on the cart. Think about the basketballs as an array.

How many rows are in the array? ....

How many basketballs are in each row? ....

How many basketballs are on the cart? ....

7 Fill in the blanks to represent the array of basketballs with a multiplication equation.

.... × .... = ...

8 Which of the following shows 3 × 6?

Ⓐ 3 + 3 + 3 + 3 + 3

Ⓑ 3 groups of 6

Ⓒ

Ⓓ

Ⓔ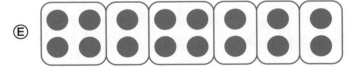

9 John says his drawing shows 4 × 6. Is John correct? Explain.

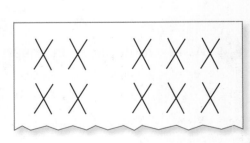

Refine Ideas About the Meaning of Multiplication

APPLY IT

Complete these problems on your own.

① EXPLAIN

Travis drew the picture below to show 4 × 6.

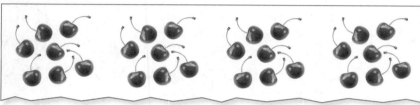

What did he do wrong?

② CREATE

Write a story problem that could be solved using the
multiplication equation 9 × 4 = 36.

③ ANALYZE

Amelia draws the array at the right to show
3 × 2 = 6.

How will Amelia's array change if she wants to
show 4 × 2 = 8?

If Amelia draws one more triangle on each row of the original
array, what multiplication equation would this show?

PAIR/SHARE
Discuss your solutions for
these three problems with
a partner.

Lesson 4 Understand the Meaning of Multiplication   **101**

Use what you have learned to complete problem 4.

4 Tucker wants to use pennies to show 5 × 8. Show what Tucker can do.

Part A Draw a model to show the 5 × 8 pennies. Explain what each number means.

Part B Write a story problem about Tucker's pennies that can be solved using the model you drew in Part A. Tell how many pennies Tucker has in all.

5 MATH JOURNAL

Write a story problem for 3 × 4 and solve it. Then write the complete multiplication equation and explain what each number means.

Dear Family,

This week your child is learning multiplication facts for 0, 1, 2, 5, and 10.

You can use what you know about multiplication and skip-counting to build fluency with the multiplication facts for 0, 1, 2, 5, and 10.

Look at the two models below.

Both models show $3 \times 2 = 6$.
You can also skip-count by twos in each model.

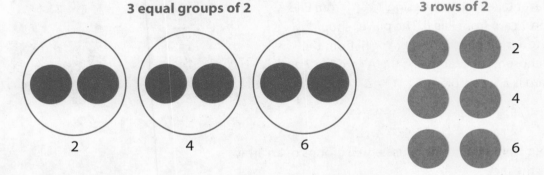

3 equal groups of 2

2   4   6

3 rows of 2

2
4
6

Your child will also explore what it means to multiply with 0 and 1.

Your child will build understanding of facts by thinking about what facts mean and not by just trying to memorize facts.

$3 \times 5 = ?$ →

3 groups of 5 is 15!

Invite your child to explore multiplication facts and share what he or she knows about skip-counting by doing the following activity together.

ACTIVITY MULTIPLICATION FACTS FOR 0, 1, 2, 5, AND 10

Do this activity with your child to multiply with 0, 1, 2, 5, and 10.

Materials 20 index cards or slips of paper in 2 colors (10 of each color), paper, pencil

Play this game with your child to practice multiplication facts for 0, 1, 2, 5, and 10. The winner of the game will have collected the most cards at the end.

- Create 2 groups of 10 colored cards. Write the numbers 1, 2, 3, 4, 5, 6, 7, 8, 9, and 10 on one color of cards (Pile A) and the numbers 0, 0, 1, 1, 2, 2, 5, 5, 10, and 10 on the other color (Pile B).

- Shuffle each pile and place each pile of cards facedown.

- Each player takes turns choosing 1 card from Pile A and then 1 card from Pile B. The player should complete a multiplication fact (A × B) from the factors chosen. For example, if the A card is a 7 and the B card is a 1, complete 7 × 1 = ?.

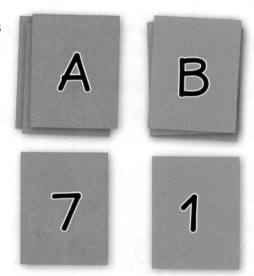

$$7 \times 1 = ?$$

- Help your child skip-count or use equal groups or an array to show the fact.

- If the product is correct, the player keeps the cards. If the product is incorrect, the cards are placed on the bottom of each pile and play moves to the next player.

- Continue taking turns until the cards are gone. The player with the most cards wins.

- Shuffle each pile of cards and play again.

Look for other opportunities to practice multiplication facts with your child.

Explore Multiplying with 0, 1, 2, 5, and 10

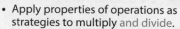
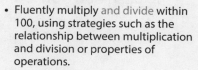

Previously, you learned about the meaning of multiplication. This lesson will take a closer look at certain multiplication facts. Use what you know to try to solve the problem below.

> Jenny draws 6 cartoon bugs. Each bug has 10 legs. How many legs did she draw?

TRY IT

Math Toolkit
- base-ten blocks
- counters
- hundred charts
- multiplication models

DISCUSS IT

Ask your partner: How did you get started?

Tell your partner: A model I used was . . . It helped me . . .

CONNECT IT

1 LOOK BACK

Explain how you found the number of legs Jenny drew for the 6 cartoon bugs.

2 LOOK AHEAD

You can show and solve multiplication problems in different ways, such as using arrays or equal groups.

One way to find products when multiplying with 2, 5, or 10 is to use skip-counting.

Suppose Jenny draws 8 cartoon bugs with 10 legs each.

a. Show how you could use skip-counting to find the number of legs Jenny drew.

10, 20, ...

b. Write a multiplication fact to find the number of legs.

number of bugs ✕ legs on each bug = total number of legs

.... ✕ .... = ...

3 REFLECT

Suppose you have 8 bugs with 8 legs each. What other method besides skip-counting can you use to find the total number of legs?

....

....

Prepare for Multiplying with 0, 1, 2, 5, and 10

1 Think about what you know about multiplication. Fill in each box. Use words, numbers, and pictures. Show as many ideas as you can.

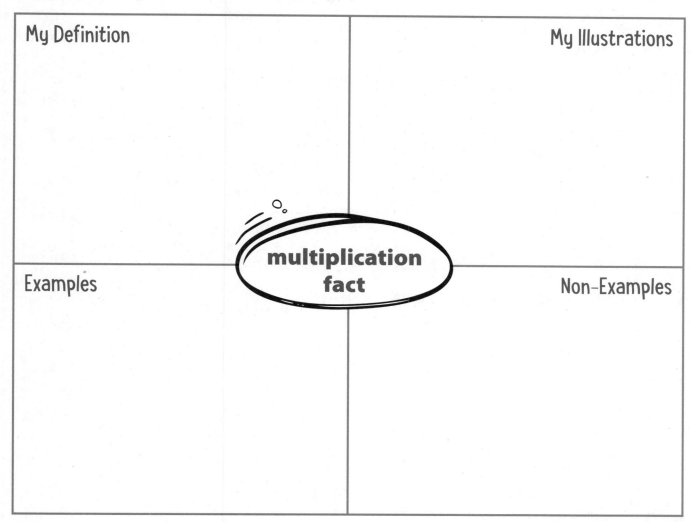

My Definition

My Illustrations

multiplication fact

Examples

Non-Examples

2 What multiplication fact is shown by the model?

3 Solve the problem. Show your work.

Julio makes 7 cookies. Each cookie has 5 chocolate chips. How many chocolate chips did he use?

Solution ....

4 Check your answer. Show your work.

Develop Multiplying with 2, 5, and 10

Read and try to solve the problem below.

> A company makes a toy robot that has 2 antennas and
> 5 buttons. How many antennas and buttons are needed
> for 6 robots?

TRY IT

 Math Toolkit
- counters
- cups
- 1-centimeter grid paper
- multiplication models

DISCUSS IT

Ask your partner: Why did you choose this strategy?

Tell your partner: I started by . . .

Explore different ways to understand multiplying with 2, 5, and 10.

> A company makes a toy robot that has **2** antennas and **5** buttons.
> How many antennas and buttons are needed for **6** robots?

MODEL IT

You can use equal groups and skip-count.

The drawings show the antennas and buttons of **6** robots.

You can skip-count by **twos** to find the number of antennas.

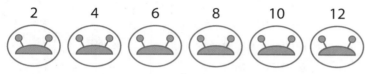

6 groups of **2** antennas

You can skip-count by **fives** to find the number of buttons.

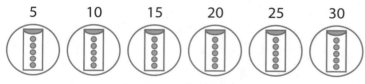

6 groups of **5** buttons

MODEL IT

You can use arrays and skip-count.

The left array shows the number of antennas. You can skip-count by **twos**.
The right array shows the number of buttons. You can skip-count by **fives**.

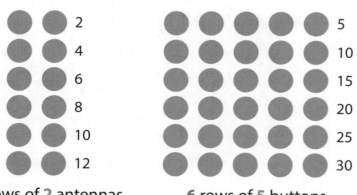

6 rows of **2** antennas   6 rows of **5** buttons

CONNECT IT

Now you will use the problem from the previous page to help you understand how to multiply with 2, 5, and 10.

1 Look at both **Model Its**. What multiplication equations can you write for the number of antennas and number of buttons?

2 How do both models use skip-counting?

3 If you take the antenna array in the second **Model It** and turn it, what would the equation be for each array?

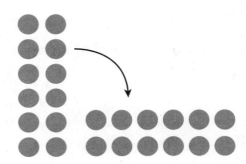

4 Did the order of the factors in problem 3 change the product? Explain why or why not.

5 What addition doubles fact can you write for the turned array in problem 3? Why can you use a doubles fact when you multiply with 2?

6 REFLECT

Look back at your **Try It**, strategies by classmates, and **Model Its**. Which models or strategies do you like best for multiplying with 2 and 5? Explain.

....

....

....

APPLY IT

Use what you just learned to solve these problems.

7 How much is 5 groups of 10? Write a multiplication equation. Show your work.

Solution ....

8 How much is 10 groups of 5? Write a multiplication equation. Show your work.

Solution ....

9 Each cabin at camp has 5 beds. There are 4 cabins. How many beds are there at camp? Show your work.

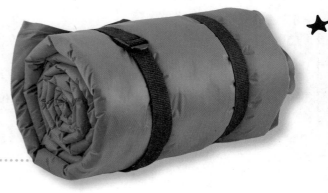

Solution ....

Practice Multiplying with 2, 5, and 10

Study the Example showing how to multiply with 5. Then solve problems 1–5.

EXAMPLE

Wes has 3 rows of tomato plants. There are 5 plants in each row. How many tomato plants does Wes have in all?

$3 \times 5 = 15$. Wes has 15 tomato plants.

1. Circle equal groups of 2. Then fill in the blanks to show the multiplication fact.

.... groups of .... is .... , so .... × .... = ...

2. Each box of pencils has 10 pencils. Write a multiplication fact for 8, 9, and 10 boxes of pencils.

   a. 8 boxes: .... × 10 = ... pencils

   b. 9 boxes: .... × .... = ... pencils

   c. 10 boxes: .... × .... = ... pencils

3 Cole arranges his blueberries into different arrays before he eats them. Write a multiplication fact for each array.

a.

b.

....

4 Fill in the blanks to complete the multiplication facts for 2.

$0 \times 2 =$ .... $6 \times 2 =$ ....

$1 \times 2 =$ .... $7 \times 2 =$ ....

$2 \times 2 =$ .... $8 \times 2 =$ ....

$3 \times 2 =$ .... $9 \times 2 =$ ....

$4 \times 2 =$ .... $10 \times 2 =$ ....

$5 \times 2 =$ ....

5 Fill in the blanks to complete the multiplication facts for 5.

$0 \times 5 =$ .... $6 \times 5 =$ ....

$1 \times 5 =$ .... $7 \times 5 =$ ....

$2 \times 5 =$ .... $8 \times 5 =$ ....

$3 \times 5 =$ .... $9 \times 5 =$ ....

$4 \times 5 =$ .... $10 \times 5 =$ ....

$5 \times 5 =$ ....

Develop Multiplying with 0 and 1

Read and try to solve the problem below.

> Jon says 6 × 1 = 6. Jeff says 6 × 0 = 6. Who is right?
> Explain how you know.

TRY IT

 **Math Toolkit**
- counters
- cups
- number lines
- 1-centimeter grid paper

DISCUSS IT

Ask your partner: Can you explain that again?

Tell your partner: I do not understand how . . .

Explore different ways to understand multiplying with 0 and 1.

> Jon says 6 × 1 = 6. Jeff says 6 × 0 = 6. Who is right?
> Explain how you know.

MODEL IT

You can use equal groups to understand multiplying with 1.

6 × 1 means there are 6 groups with 1 in each group.

MODEL IT

You can use equal groups to understand multiplying with 0.

6 × 0 means there are 6 groups with 0 in each group. A group of 0 is empty.

CONNECT IT

Now you will use the problem from the previous page to help you understand how to multiply with 1 and 0.

1 Look at the first **Model It** for 6 × 1. There are .... groups

of .... , so 6 × 1 = ... Is Jon right? ....

2 Draw the first **Model It** and add another group of 1.

Now there are .... groups of 1, so .... × 1 = ...

3 What do you notice about the number of groups and the product when you multiply 6 × 1? 7 × 1?

4 Look at the second **Model It** for 6 × 0. There are .... groups

of .... , so 6 × 0 = ... Is Jeff right? ....

5 Explain what would happen if more groups of 0 were added.

6 What do you think is true about the product of any number multiplied by 1? Multiplied by 0?

7 REFLECT

Look back at your **Try It**, strategies by classmates, and **Model Its**. Which models or strategies do you like best for multiplying by 1 and 0? Explain.

....

....

....

....

APPLY IT

Use what you just learned to solve these problems.

8 Fill in the missing numbers to complete each fact.

    a. $5 \times 0 =$ ....

    b. .... $\times 1 = 5$

    c. $3 \times$ .... $= 0$

    d. $3 \times 1 =$ ....

9 Which of the following facts have a product of 0?

    Ⓐ $1 \times 0 = ?$

    Ⓑ $0 \times 1 = ?$

    Ⓒ $10 \times 1 = ?$

    Ⓓ $5 \times 1 = ?$

    Ⓔ $5 \times 0 = ?$

10 Draw a model to show 4×0. Then find the product.

    $4 \times 0 =$ ....

Practice Multiplying with 0 and 1

Study the Example showing how to multiply with 1. Then solve problems 1–4.

EXAMPLE

Steve uses a model to create a list of multiplication facts for 1. He starts with 0 equal groups of 1 and then keeps adding a group of 1 for each fact as shown. Describe a pattern he can use to find the 1s facts for 6, 7, 8, 9, and 10.

$0 \times 1 = 0$	
$1 \times 1 = 1$	★
$2 \times 1 = 2$	★ ★
$3 \times 1 = 3$	★ ★ ★
$4 \times 1 = 4$	★ ★ ★ ★
$5 \times 1 = 5$	★ ★ ★ ★ ★

Steve can see that any number times 1 equals that number.

$6 \times 1 = 6$
$7 \times 1 = 7$
$8 \times 1 = 8$
$9 \times 1 = 9$
$10 \times 1 = 10$

The number of groups of 1 is the same as the product.

1. Create a model of 7×1 and 1×7. How are they different? How are they the same?

Solution ....

....

2 Jenna makes a table to show the school supplies she has. Write a multiplication fact to show how many of each school item Jenna has.

Materials	Number of Boxes	Multiplication Fact
Box of 8 crayons	0	
Box of 10 pencils	1	
Box of 5 erasers	1	
Box of 6 markers	0	

3 Is each multiplication fact correct?

	Yes	No
$1 \times 0 = 1$	Ⓐ	Ⓑ
$9 \times 1 = 0$	Ⓒ	Ⓓ
$0 \times 5 = 0$	Ⓔ	Ⓕ
$6 \times 0 = 6$	Ⓖ	Ⓗ

4 Xavier starts to create a list of multiplication facts for 1. Explain the mistake he is making. What will make his facts correct?

$1 \times 1 = 2$

$2 \times 1 = 3$

$3 \times 1 = 4$

Refine Multiplying with 0, 1, 2, 5, and 10

Complete the Example below. Then solve problems 1–9.

EXAMPLE

Liam says 2 × 5 has the same product as 5 × 2. Do you agree?

Look at how you could show your work using an array.

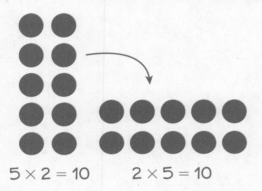

$5 \times 2 = 10$ $2 \times 5 = 10$

Solution ....

> Liam created 5 rows of 2 and 2 rows of 5.

PAIR/SHARE
How can you find the total once you create an array?

APPLY IT

1 Find 7 × 2. Then find 8 × 2 and 9 × 2 using the same model. Explain the pattern you see in the products. Show your work.

> How many are in each group?

Solution ....

....

PAIR/SHARE
How did finding all three facts with the same model help you see the pattern?

2 Rami has 1 bag with 7 apples, 8 bags with 0 oranges, and 3 bags with 10 peaches. How many apples, oranges, and peaches does Rami have? Show your work.

Think about what you know about multiplying with 0 and 1.

PAIR/SHARE
How are your models the same as your partner's models? How are they different?

Solution ....

3 Which of the following equals 10?

Ⓐ 2 × 5

Ⓑ 5 × 5

Ⓒ 10 × 0

Ⓓ 1 × 9

Rey chose Ⓒ as the correct answer. How did he get that answer?

Find the product of each choice first.

PAIR/SHARE
What strategy for multiplying do you like best?

4 Which factor will correctly complete all of the following facts:

$1 \times$ _____ $= 1$ $2 \times$ _____ $= 2$ $3 \times$ _____ $= 3$ $4 \times$ _____ $= 4$

Ⓐ 0

Ⓑ 1

Ⓒ 2

Ⓓ 10

5 Fill in the blanks to complete the multiplication facts for 10.

$0 \times 10 =$ .... $6 \times 10 =$ ....

$1 \times 10 =$ .... $7 \times 10 =$ ....

$2 \times 10 =$ .... $8 \times 10 =$ ....

$3 \times 10 =$ .... $9 \times 10 =$ ....

$4 \times 10 =$ .... $10 \times 10 =$ ....

$5 \times 10 =$ ....

6 Is each multiplication fact *True* or *False*?

	True	False
$7 \times 2 = 14$	Ⓐ	Ⓑ
$10 \times 0 = 10$	Ⓒ	Ⓓ
$1 \times 10 = 10$	Ⓔ	Ⓕ
$5 \times 0 = 5$	Ⓖ	Ⓗ
$2 \times 1 = 2$	Ⓘ	Ⓙ
$3 \times 10 = 30$	Ⓚ	Ⓛ

Lesson 5 Multiply with 0, 1, 2, 5, and 10   **123**

7 Emile has 4 packs of shirts. Each pack has 2 shirts. He also has 2 packs of shorts. Each pack has 3 shorts. Does he have more shirts or shorts? Show your work.

Solution ....

8 Principal Green talks to 5 different students every school day. How many students does she talk to in 10 school days?

Noa says this is a 10 groups of 5 problem and can be solved by multiplying 10 × 5 or skip-counting by fives 10 times. Sara says this problem can be solved by skip-counting by tens 5 times or finding 5 × 10. Who is correct? Explain and provide the answer.

9 MATH JOURNAL

Explain how you would solve the problem below. What multiplication fact could you use?

Lauren paints 8 paintings. She puts 2 trees in each painting. How many trees does Lauren paint?

☑ SELF CHECK Go back to the Unit 2 Opener and see what you can check off.

Multiply with 3, 4, and 6

Dear Family,
This week your child is learning multiplication facts for 3, 4, and 6.

Your child can use known multiplication facts for 1, 2, and 5 to learn multiplication facts for 3, 4, and 6. To solve a harder multiplication equation, you can break apart one factor into lesser numbers to make two easier multiplication equations.

Consider the following multiplication situation.

> Pete plants 6 rows of carrots in his garden. Each row has 4 carrots. How many carrots did Pete plant?

Maybe you do not know 6×4, but you do know 6×2.

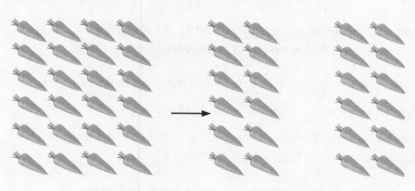

6 rows of 4 carrots is the same as 6 rows of 2 carrots and 6 rows of 2 carrots.

$$6 \times 4 = (6 \times 2) + (6 \times 2) = 12 + 12 = 24$$

So, Pete plants 24 carrots.

Invite your child to share what he or she knows about breaking apart numbers to multiply by doing the following activity together.

ACTIVITY SPLITTING NUMBERS

Do this activity with your child to multiply with 3, 4, and 6.

Materials 36 pennies or other small objects, a paper clip, a pencil, a spinner showing 2–6

Do this activity with your child to practice breaking apart numbers to learn multiplication facts.

- Start by making a spinner. You can do this by putting the tip of a pencil through a paper clip at the center of a paper plate divided into five equal parts and labeled 2–6 as shown at the right.

- Have your child spin the spinner twice to determine the number of rows and columns in an array.

- Work together to build the array using the pennies.

- Have your child write the multiplication expression shown by the array. For example, if the array has 6 rows and 4 columns, your child would write 6 × 4.

- Ask your child to choose where to separate two columns in the array to show breaking apart a factor.

- Have your child write the two multiplication expressions he or she has made by breaking apart the columns in the array. For example: (6 × 2) + (6 × 2).

- Ask your child to find the two products and then add the products to find the answer to the original problem. For example: 12 + 12 = 24.

- Together, count the objects in the array to check the answer and then write the multiplication fact. For example: 6 × 4 = 24.

- Repeat several times.

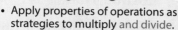

Explore Multiplying with 3, 4, and 6

In previous lessons, you learned multiplication facts for several numbers. This lesson will show you a strategy where you can use the facts you know to learn the facts for 3, 4, and 6. Use what you know to try to solve the problem below.

> **Ty has 6 bunches of carrots. There are 3 carrots in each bunch. How many carrots does Ty have?**

TRY IT

 Math Toolkit

- counters and cups
- 1-centimeter grid paper
- multiplication models
- number lines

DISCUSS IT

Ask your partner: How did you get started?

Ask your partner: A model I used was . . . It helped me . . .

CONNECT IT

1 LOOK BACK

Explain how you found how many carrots Ty has in all.

2 LOOK AHEAD

The array shows the multiplication problem from the previous page, 6 × 3.

To solve a multiplication problem you do not know, you can break apart the problem into simpler facts you might know.

a. Look at the way the array has been broken apart. Write the multiplication fact for each smaller array.

Left array: ....

Right array: ....

Add the products to find the total. ....

b. Compare your answer to Part a with the answer you wrote in problem 1. What do you notice?

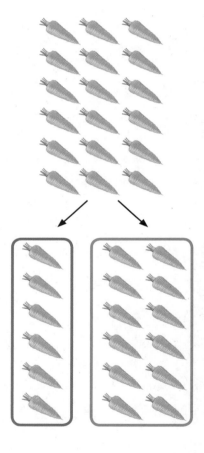

3 REFLECT

Why does the number of items in an array not change when you break it apart into two smaller arrays?

....

....

Prepare for Multiplying with 3, 4, and 6

1. Think about what you know about multiplication. Fill in each box. Use words, numbers, and pictures. Show as many ideas as you can.

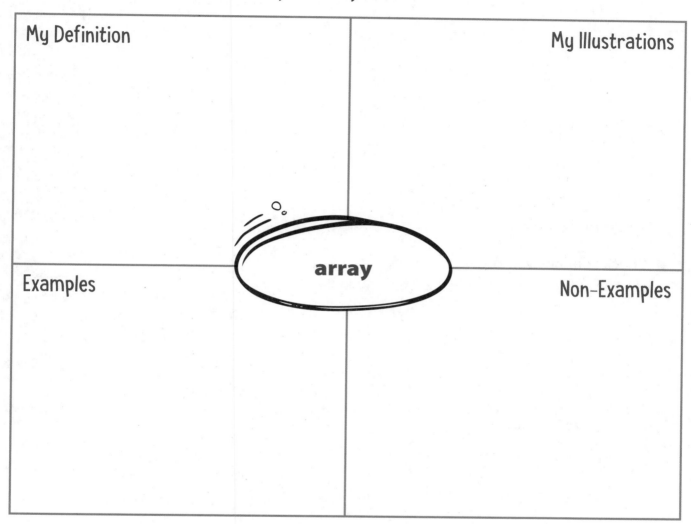

My Definition	My Illustrations

array

Examples	Non-Examples

2. Ramona makes an array to find 3×4. She decides to break apart the array as shown. Explain how her diagram can help her find 3×4.

③ Solve the problem. Show your work.

René has 4 packages of markers. There are 6 markers in each package. How many markers does René have?

Solution ....

④ Check your answer. Show your work.

Develop Multiplying with 3

Read and try to solve the problem below.

Nadia hangs her photos on the wall. She makes
4 rows of photos with 3 photos in each row.
How many photos did Nadia hang on the wall?

TRY IT

 Math Toolkit
- counters
- cups
- 1-centimeter grid paper
- multiplication models
- number lines

DISCUSS IT

Ask your partner: Why did you choose this strategy?

Tell your partner: I started by . . .

Explore different ways to understand multiplying with 3.

> Nadia hangs her photos on the wall. She makes 4 rows of photos with 3 photos in each row. How many photos did Nadia hang on the wall?

PICTURE IT

You can use a picture to understand the problem.

MODEL IT

You can use an array to understand the problem.

Break the array into two smaller arrays to solve the problem.

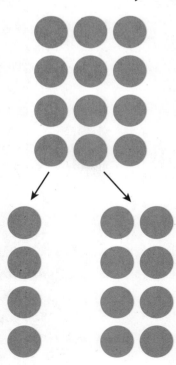

CONNECT IT

Now you will use the problem from the previous page to help you understand how to multiply with 3.

1 Look at **Picture It**. How could you multiply to find the number of photos in the diagram? How could you find the product?

2 Look at **Model It**. What two numbers was 3 broken into to help solve the problem?

3 What two multiplication equations could you use then for the two smaller arrays?

4 How could you use the two smaller arrays to find the number of photos Nadia hung?

5 Fill in the blanks to show two different expressions that each represents the total number of photos.

one large array: $4 \times$ ....

two small arrays: $(4 \times$ ....$) + (4 \times$ ....$)$

6 REFLECT

Look back at your **Try It**, strategies by classmates, and **Picture It** and **Model It**. Which models or strategies do you like best for multiplying with 3? Explain.

....

....

....

APPLY IT

Use what you just learned to solve these problems.

7 Find 5 × 3. Draw a picture and show a way to break apart the problem to find the product. Show your work.

5 × 3 = ...

8 Cassie set up 9 tables with 3 chairs at each table for a party. How many chairs did she use? Show your work.

Solution ....

9 Which expressions can be used to find 8 × 3?

Ⓐ (8 + 2) × (8 + 1)

Ⓑ (8 × 2) + (8 × 1)

Ⓒ (8 × 1) + (8 × 2)

Ⓓ (8 × 1) × (8 × 2)

Ⓔ 3 + 3 + 3 + 3 + 3 + 3 + 3 + 3

Practice Multiplying with 3

Study the Example showing how to break apart the factor 3 to multiply. Then solve problems 1–6.

EXAMPLE

Lacey walks 3 miles every day. How many miles does she walk in 7 days?

$7 \times 3 = ?$

You may be more familiar with multiplying with 1 and 2. So, you can break apart the 3 columns into 1 column and 2 columns and then multiply.

$7 \times 1 = 7$ and $7 \times 2 = 14$

Then add the two products.

$7 + 14 = 21$

So, $7 \times 3 = 21$. Lacey walks 21 miles.

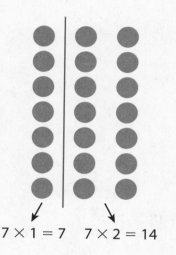

$7 \times 1 = 7$ $7 \times 2 = 14$

Use the array at the right to solve problems 1–4.

1. How many rows and columns are in the array?

.... rows and .... columns

2. Circle the columns to break apart the array into 2 parts.

3. Write multiplication facts to show the total for each part of the array.

.... × .... = ...

.... × .... = ...

4. How can you use the facts from problem 3 to find 5×3? Explain.

5 Draw a line to the pair of multiplication equations that can be used to solve each multiplication problem. Write the missing product for each equation.

$7 \times 2 =$ ....

$5 \times 3 =$ ....

$7 \times 1 =$ ....

$5 \times 2 =$ ....

$(6 \times 1) + (6 \times 2) =$ ....

$5 \times 1 =$ ....

$8 \times 2 =$ ....

$7 \times 3 =$ ....

$8 \times 1 =$ ....

$9 \times 1 =$ ....

$(8 \times 2) + (8 \times 1) =$ ....

$9 \times 2 =$ ....

$6 \times 1 =$ ....

$9 \times 3 =$ ....

$6 \times 2 =$ ....

6 Auggie has 4 trees in his backyard. He hangs 3 bird feeders in each tree. How many bird feeders does Auggie hang in all? Show your work.

Solution ....

Develop Multiplying with 4

Read and try to solve the problem below.

> Jenna is making a quilt. She cuts fabric squares and decides to make the quilt with 5 rows of squares. Each row will have 4 squares. How many fabric squares will she need to make the quilt?

TRY IT

🧰 **Math Toolkit**
- counters
- cups
- 1-centimeter grid paper
- multiplication models
- number lines

DISCUSS IT

Ask your partner: Can you explain that again?

Tell your partner: I do not understand how . . .

Explore different ways to understand multiplying with 4.

> **Jenna is making a quilt. She cuts fabric squares and decides to make the quilt with 5 rows of squares. Each row will have 4 squares. How many fabric squares will she need to make the quilt?**

MODEL IT
You can make an array to understand the problem.

You can break apart the array to show simpler facts. The red line shows one way to split the array.

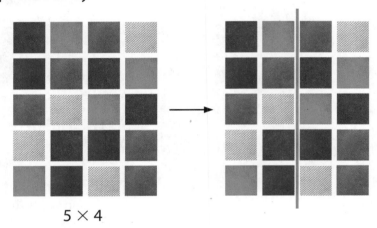

5×4

MODEL IT
You can turn the array to show another fact.

You have already multiplied problems such as 1×5, 2×5, 3×5, and 4×5. So, 4×5 shows a fact you might know.

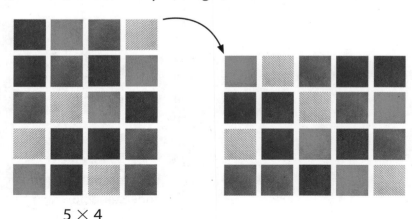

5×4

CONNECT IT

Now you will use the problem from the previous page to help you understand how to multiply with 4.

1 Look at the two smaller arrays in the first **Model It**. What two facts are shown by these smaller arrays?

2 Fill in the blanks to show how the smaller arrays can be used to find 5 × 4.

$5 \times 4 = (5 \times \underline{\hspace{1.5cm}}) + (5 \times \underline{\hspace{1.5cm}})$

$= \underline{\hspace{1cm}} + \underline{\hspace{1cm}} = \underline{\hspace{1cm}}$

3 Look at the second **Model It**. What new multiplication expression is created by turning the array? How are the factors alike and different from 5 × 4?

4 You multiplied with 5 in a previous lesson. What is the product of the multiplication fact for the turned array? Would the product be the same for 5 × 4? Explain.

5 How do both **Model Its** try to make the problem 5 × 4 simpler?

6 REFLECT

Look back at your **Try It**, strategies by classmates, and **Model Its**. Which models or strategies do you like best for multiplying with 4? Explain.

APPLY IT

Use what you just learned to solve these problems.

7 Show how to find the product of 3 × 4 by breaking apart the problem and also by changing the order of the factors. Show your work.

3 × 4 = ...

8 Break apart the array to find 9 × 4.
Fill in the blanks to show your work.

9 × 4 = (9 × ....) + (9 × ....)

= .... + ... = ...

9 × 4 = ...

9 Which expressions can be used to find 8 × 4?

Ⓐ 4 + 4 + 4 + 4 + 4 + 4 + 4 + 4

Ⓑ (8 × 2) + (8 × 2)

Ⓒ (8 + 2) + (8 + 2)

Ⓓ (8 × 1) + (8 × 3)

Ⓔ (8 + 8 + 8 + 8) × 4

Practice Multiplying with 4

Study the Example showing how to break apart the factor 4 to multiply. Then solve problems 1–6.

EXAMPLE

Two friends play tennis together. Each friend brings 4 tennis balls. How many tennis balls do they have in all?

$2 \times 4 = ?$

You might break apart 4 into 2 and 2.

Each part is $2 \times 2 = 4$.

Double the product: $4 + 4 = 8$.

You could also change the order of factors to a fact you know.

$4 \times 2 = 8$

So, $2 \times 4 = 8$. They have 8 tennis balls.

Solve problems 1 and 2 to find how many are in 3 groups of 4.

1 Find 3×4 by breaking apart the array or by changing the order of factors.

$3 \times 4 =$ ....

2 Explain why you broke apart the array or changed the order of factors.

3 Complete these 4s facts using any strategy you choose.

    a. $1 \times 4 =$ ....

    b. $7 \times 4 =$ ....

    c. $6 \times 4 =$ ....

    d. $10 \times 4 =$ ....

    e. $8 \times 4 =$ ....

    f. $5 \times 4 =$ ....

Use the array at the right to solve problems 4–6.

4 Bronson drew the array to solve a problem. What multiplication problem is he trying to solve?

    .... $\times$ .... $= ?$

5 Circle columns to break the array into two parts. Then fill in the blanks to show how you can use the parts to solve the problem.

    (............... $\times$ ....) + (............... $\times$ ....) $= ?$

    So, ... $+$ .... $=$ ....

    So, ... $\times$ .... $=$ ....

6 Describe another way you can break apart the same array to solve the problem.

Develop Multiplying with 6

Read and try to solve the problem below.

> Mario has 4 vases of flowers. There are 6 flowers in each vase. How many flowers does Mario have in all?

TRY IT

 **Math Toolkit**
- counters
- cups
- 1-centimeter grid paper
- multiplication models
- number lines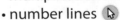

DISCUSS IT

Ask your partner: Do you agree with me? Why or why not?

Tell your partner: At first, I thought . . .

Explore different ways to understand multiplying with 6.

> **Mario has 4 vases of flowers. There are 6 flowers in each vase. How many flowers does Mario have in all?**

MODEL IT

You can use an array to understand the problem.

Make an array and then break it apart into two smaller arrays.

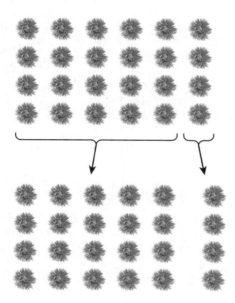

PICTURE IT

You can also use equal groups to understand the problem.

Break apart the number of groups to find the answer.

CONNECT IT

Now you will use the problem from the previous page to help you understand how to multiply with 6.

1 What multiplication equation can you write for the problem?

$\underset{\text{vases}}{\rule{3cm}{0.4pt}} \times \underset{\text{flowers}}{\rule{3cm}{0.4pt}} = ?$

2 Look at **Model It**.

a. Fill in the blanks to show how the array is broken apart.

$4 \times 6 = (4 \times \rule{2cm}{0.4pt}) + (4 \times \rule{2cm}{0.4pt})$

b. Use the equation you wrote in Part a to find 4×6. Remember that

parentheses show you what operations to do first. ....

3 Look at **Picture It**.

a. Fill in the blanks to show how to break apart the number of vases.

$4 \times 6 = (\rule{2cm}{0.4pt} \times 6) + (\rule{2cm}{0.4pt} \times 6)$

b. Use the equation you wrote in Part a to find 4×6. ....

4 Why do you get the same answer with the equation for the array and the equation for the vases?

5 REFLECT

Look back at your **Try It**, strategies by classmates, and **Model It** and **Picture It**. Which models or strategies do you like best for multiplying with 6? Explain.

....

....

....

....

APPLY IT

Use what you just learned to solve these problems.

6 Show two different ways to break apart 3 × 6. Draw models and write the equations for each model. Show your work.

3 × 6 = ...

7 Find 5 × 6 by breaking apart 6. Show how you broke apart 6 on the array.

(5 × ....) + (5 × ....) = ... + ...

= ....

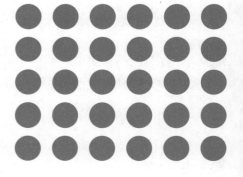

8 Which expression would NOT help you find 8 × 6?

Ⓐ (5 × 6) + (3 × 6)

Ⓑ (8 + 3) × (8 + 3)

Ⓒ (8 × 5) + (8 × 1)

Ⓓ (6 + 6 + 6 + 6 + 6) + (6 + 6 + 6)

Practice Multiplying with 6

Study the Example showing how to break apart the factor 6 to multiply. Then solve problems 1–5.

EXAMPLE

Gabriella has 2 tanks of fish. Each tank has 6 fish. How many fish does Gabriella have in all?

You can use an array to show 2×6. You can break apart the array.

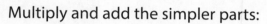

Multiply and add the simpler parts:

$(2 \times 3) + (2 \times 3) = ?$

Then add the products:

$6 + 6 = 12$

So, $2 \times 6 = 12$. Gabriella has 12 fish.

Solve problems 1–3 to find 4×6.

1 Create an array to show 4×6. Draw a line to break apart the array into two smaller arrays.

2 Write an equation for each of your smaller arrays.

3 Add the two products. What is 4×6?

4   Draw a line to the pair of multiplication equations that can be used to solve each multiplication problem. Write the missing product for each equation.

$5 \times 6 =$ ....

$5 \times 3 =$ ....
$5 \times 3 =$ ....

$(9 \times 5) + (9 \times 1) =$ ....

$7 \times 2 =$ ....
$7 \times 4 =$ ....

$7 \times 6 =$ ....

$9 \times 5 =$ ....
$9 \times 1 =$ ....

$(6 \times 4) + (6 \times 2) =$ ....

$4 \times 6 =$ ....
$4 \times 6 =$ ....

$8 \times 6 =$ ....

$6 \times 4 =$ ....
$6 \times 2 =$ ....

5   Tyquan draws 3 ants. Each ant has 6 legs. How many ant legs did Tyquan draw? Show your work.

Tyquan drew .... ant legs.

Refine Multiplying with 3, 4, and 6

Complete the Example below. Then solve problems 1–8.

EXAMPLE

Stacy is making 7 bracelets. Each bracelet uses 4 green beads. How many green beads does Stacy need? Show how to break apart 4 to make the problem easier to solve.

Look at how you could show your work using an array.

$14 + 14 = ?$

$7 \times 2 = 14$ $7 \times 2 = 14$

Solution ....

> The student broke apart the 4 into $2 + 2$ and then added the two products together.

PAIR/SHARE
How else could you have broken apart 4 to solve this problem?

APPLY IT

1 There are 6 bowls of apples. There are 6 apples in each bowl. Show how to break apart the number 6 to make the problem easier to solve.

> What ways do you know to break apart the number 6? Which way do you think is easiest?

PAIR/SHARE
What is another model you could have used to show how to break apart the number?

2 Mrs. Harris has 3 tables in her art class. She seats 6 students at each table. How many students does Mrs. Harris have in her art class? Show how you can break apart one factor to make the problem easier to solve. Show your work.

Can you use facts you know to help solve the problem?

Solution ....

3 Julio finds 8 × 6 by breaking apart the 6 into 4 + 2. Which expression correctly shows the next step in finding the product?

Ⓐ (6 × 4) + (6 × 2)

Ⓑ (8 × 6) + (8 × 2)

Ⓒ (8 + 4) × (8 + 2)

Ⓓ (8 × 4) + (8 × 2)

Don chose Ⓐ as the correct answer. How did he get that answer?

PAIR/SHARE
What factor did you break apart?

Julio broke apart the 6 in 8 × 6. What will he do next?

PAIR/SHARE
Does Don's answer make sense?

4 Rebeccah finds 8 × 4 by breaking it apart as shown below.

$$(8 \times 2) + (8 \times \underline{\quad})$$

What number belongs in the blank?

Ⓐ 1

Ⓑ 2

Ⓒ 3

Ⓓ 4

5 Decide if each equation is true. Choose *Yes* or *No* for each equation.

	Yes	No
8 × 3 = 22	Ⓐ	Ⓑ
4 × 3 = 12	Ⓒ	Ⓓ
2 × 6 = 12	Ⓔ	Ⓕ
6 × 2 = 13	Ⓖ	Ⓗ
4 × 4 = 16	Ⓘ	Ⓙ

6 Which expressions can be used to find 7 × 4?

Ⓐ (7 × 2) + (7 × 2)

Ⓑ (7 + 2) + (7 + 2)

Ⓒ (7 × 3) × (7 × 1)

Ⓓ (5 × 4) + (2 × 4)

Ⓔ 4 + 4 + 4 + 4 + 4 + 4 + 4

7 Owen is at the beach for 5 days. He collects 6 seashells each day. Show two different ways to find the number of seashells Owen collects.

Way 1

Owen collects .... seashells.

Way 2

Owen collects .... seashells.

8 MATH JOURNAL

Describe one way you could find 9×6 by breaking apart the problem into simpler problems.

 SELF CHECK Go back to the Unit 2 Opener and see what you can check off.

Multiply with 7, 8, and 9

Dear Family,

This week your child is learning multiplication facts for 7, 8, and 9.

Your child can use known multiplication facts for 1, 2, 3, 4, 5, 6, and 10 to learn the multiplication facts for 7, 8, and 9. To help learn facts for these greater numbers, you can break apart the number into two lesser numbers to make the problem easier.

Take a look at this problem.

A tree farm plants 3 rows of trees. Each row has 8 trees. How many trees are planted?

If you do not know 3 × 8, you can break apart the problem into simpler problems you do know. You can do this in different ways.

$(3 \times 4) + (3 \times 4)$
12 + 12 = 24
So, 3 × 8 = 24.

$(3 \times 5) + (3 \times 3)$
15 + 9 = 24
So, 3 × 8 = 24.

Invite your child to share what he or she knows about multiplying with 7, 8, and 9 by doing the following activity together.

ACTIVITY TILE CAPTURE GAME

Do this activity with your child to multiply with 7, 8, and 9.

Materials grid paper, colored pencils or markers, index cards numbered 1–10 (at least 2 cards per number), paper to keep score

Play this game with your child to practice multiplication facts for 1–10. The object of the game is to fill in the greatest number of squares on the grid paper.

- Each player chooses a colored pencil or marker that will be his or her color for the whole game.

- Shuffle the index cards and place them in one pile, facedown. On each turn, a player will draw two cards from the pile. The numbers are the factors in a multiplication problem, in order as drawn (for example, drawing 4 and then 9 makes 4 × 9).

- Have your child state the multiplication fact for these numbers and then "capture" and color a rectangle of tiles on the grid paper that represents the multiplication fact.

- After a player colors in his or her rectangle, record the product of the multiplication fact as points. Add on to each player's points as you go.

- As players take turns and the grid paper fills up, there will be times when a rectangle for a multiplication fact will not exactly fit on the paper. In this case, play passes to the next player. When the cards run out, the game is finished. The player who captured the most tiles—and has the most points—wins.

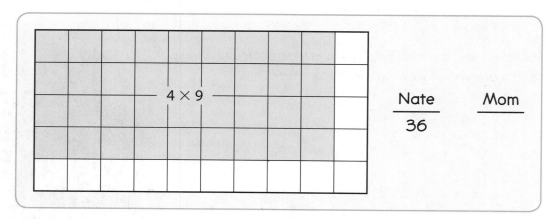

Be sure to have your child state the full multiplication fact that each rectangle represents. Encourage your child to try different strategies as he or she approaches a multiplication fact that is unfamiliar, such as skip-counting or breaking apart a factor.

Prepare for Multiplying 7, 8, and 9

1 Think about what you know about multiplication. Fill in each box.
Use words, numbers, and pictures. Show as many ideas as you can.

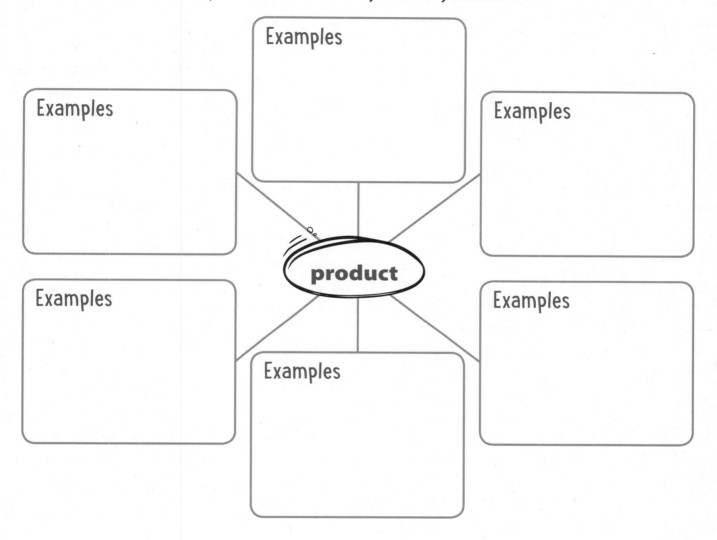

Examples

Examples

Examples

Examples

product

Examples

Examples

2 Explain how you can use the facts $8 \times 5 = 40$ and
$8 \times 2 = 16$ to find 8×7.

3 Solve the problem. Show your work.

Hana and Mario are both finding 6 × 9. They each break apart the problem in a different way. Show two different ways to break apart 6 × 9 and find the product.

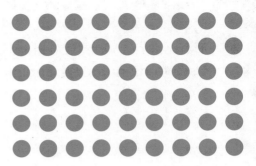

4 Check your answer. Show your work.

Develop Multiplying with 7

Read and try to solve the problem below.

> Matt gives crackers to 8 friends. Each friend gets 7 crackers. How many crackers does Matt give away?

TRY IT

 Math Toolkit
- counters
- cups
- 1-centimeter grid paper
- multiplication models
- number lines

DISCUSS IT

Ask your partner: Why did you choose this strategy?

Tell your partner: I started by . . .

Explore different ways to understand multiplying with 7.

> **Matt gives crackers to 8 friends. Each friend gets 7 crackers. How many crackers does Matt give away?**

MODEL IT
You can use an array to help understand the problem.

Matt broke apart the columns (the number of crackers).

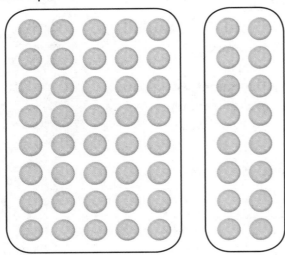

MODEL IT
You can also use words and multiplication expressions to help understand the problem.

Giving **8 friends 7 crackers** each is the same as giving 8 friends **5 crackers** each and then giving each of them **2 more crackers**. You can write the multiplication three ways:

$$8 \times 7 \quad \text{or} \quad 8 \times (5 + 2) \quad \text{or} \quad (8 \times 5) + (8 \times 2)$$

CONNECT IT

Now you will use the problem from the previous page to help you understand how to multiply with 7.

1 What multiplication problem is Matt trying to solve?

2 Write an addition expression to show how Matt broke apart 7.

3 Rewrite the multiplication expression from problem 1 by replacing 7 with the addition expression you wrote in problem 2.

8 × .... = 8 × (................. + ...)

4 Complete the equation to show the products being added to find the total number of crackers.

(8 × ....) + (8 × ....) =

.... + ... = ...

5 Explain why someone might want to break apart one of the factors in a multiplication problem.

6 REFLECT

Look back at your **Try It**, strategies by classmates, and **Model Its**. Which models or strategies do you like best for multiplying with 7? Explain.

....

....

....

....

APPLY IT

Use what you just learned to solve these problems.

7 Use a model and equations to show how knowing the answer to 2 × 7 can help you find 4 × 7.

4 × 7 = ...

8 Show two ways you can break apart a factor to find 3 × 7. Write an equation for each way.

3 × 7 = ...

9 Which expressions can be used to find 5 × 7?

Ⓐ 7 × 5

Ⓑ 5 × (2 + 5)

Ⓒ (5 × 2) + 5

Ⓓ (2 × 7) + (3 × 7)

Ⓔ (3 × 5) + (2 × 2)

Practice Multiplying with 7

Study the Example showing how to break apart the factor 7 to multiply. Then solve problems 1–6.

EXAMPLE

Chef Mel can feed 7 people with 1 pot of soup. How many people can she feed with 3 pots of soup?

$3 \times 7 = ?$

$3 \times 2 = 6$

$3 \times 5 = 15$

You may know how to multiply with 2 and 5, so break apart the 7 into 2 and 5.

Then add the two products. $6 + 15 = 21$

So, $7 \times 3 = 21$. She can feed 21 people.

Use the array at the right to answer problems 1–4.

1 How many rows and columns are in the array? Fill in the blanks.

.... rows and .... columns

2 Circle columns to break apart the array into two parts.

3 Write multiplication facts to show the total for each part of the array.

.... × .... = ... × .... = ...

4 How can you use your answer to problem 3 to find the product of 6×7? Explain.

5 Draw a line to the pair of multiplication equations that can be used to solve each multiplication problem. Write the missing product for each equation.

$4 \times 7 =$ ....

$6 \times 5 =$ ....

$6 \times 2 =$ ....

$5 \times (1 + 6) =$ ....

$4 \times 6 =$ ....

$4 \times 1 =$ ....

$6 \times 7 =$ ....

$7 \times 3 =$ ....

$7 \times 4 =$ ....

$7 \times 7 =$ ....

$8 \times 2 =$ ....

$8 \times 5 =$ ....

$8 \times (2 + 5) =$ ....

$5 \times 1 =$ ....

$5 \times 6 =$ ....

6 The art teacher has 9 crates of art supplies for the class. Each crate has 7 paintbrushes. How many paintbrushes does she have altogether? Show your work.

Solution

Develop Multiplying with 8

Read and try to solve the problem below.

> Stella plants 6 rows of pumpkins with 8 pumpkins in each row.
> How many pumpkins does she plant in all?

TRY IT

 **Math Toolkit**
- counters
- cups
- 1-centimeter grid paper
- multiplication models
- number lines

DISCUSS IT

Ask your partner: Can you explain that again?

Tell your partner: I do not understand how . . .

Explore different ways to understand multiplying with 8.

> **Stella plants 6 rows of pumpkins with 8 pumpkins in each row.**
> **How many pumpkins does she plant in all?**

MODEL IT

You can break the columns of the array into equal groups of facts you know.

You know the multiplication facts for 4.

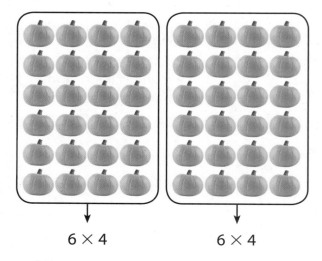

       6 × 4   6 × 4

MODEL IT

You can further break the columns of the array into equal groups of facts you know.

You know the multiplication facts for 2.

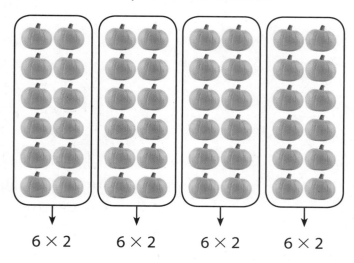

  6 × 2   6 × 2   6 × 2   6 × 2

CONNECT IT

Now you will use the problem from the previous page to help you understand how to multiply with 8.

1 Look at the first **Model It**. Fill in the blanks to show how the factor 8 is broken apart.

6 × (.............. + ...)

2 Fill in the blanks to show how you can use the two simpler problems to find the product.

(6 × ....) + (6 × ....) =

.... + ... = ...

3 Look at the second **Model It**. Fill in the blanks to show how the factor 8 is broken apart.

6 × (.............. + ... + ... + ...)

4 Fill in the blanks to show how you can use the four simpler problems to find the product.

(6 × ....) + (6 × ....) + (6 × ....) + (6 × ....) =

.... + ... + ... + ... = ...

5 When breaking apart the factor 8, what is the benefit of breaking it apart into two 4s or four 2s?

6 **REFLECT**

Look back at your **Try It**, strategies by classmates, and **Model Its**. Which models or strategies do you like best for multiplying with 8? Explain.

....

....

....

APPLY IT

Use what you just learned to solve these problems.

7 Use the model for 7×8 to show how you can break apart 8 to find this product. Show your work.

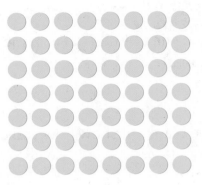

$7 \times 8 =$ ....

8 Use what you know about 5×2 to find 5×8. Show your work.

$5 \times 8 =$ ....

9 Find 8×8. Show your work.

$8 \times 8 =$ ....

Practice Multiplying with 8

Study the Example showing how to break apart the factor 8 to multiply. Then solve problems 1–7.

EXAMPLE

Four friends make a photo album. They each put 8 photos in the album. How many photos are in the photo album?

$4 \times 8 = ?$

$4 \times 4 = 16$ $4 \times 4 = 16$

You might break apart the 8 into 4 and 4.

Add the products: $16 + 16 = 32$.

So, $4 \times 8 = 32$. There are 32 photos in the album.

Tony has 6 boxes of toy cars. Each box has 8 cars in it.

1 Write a multiplication equation for this story.

.... $\times$ .... = ?

2 To help you find 6×8, you might break apart the 8 into 5 and 3. Write the two multiplication equations this would give you.

$6 \times$ .... = ...

$6 \times$ .... = ...

3 Add the two products in problem 2. How many toy cars does Tony have?

Use the array at the right to solve problems 4–6.

4 Armando drew the array to solve a problem.
   What multiplication problem is he trying to solve?

   .... × .... = ?

5 Draw a line on the array to break apart a factor.
   Explain how you can use your simpler problems
   to solve the problem.

6 Describe another way you can break apart Armando's array to solve
   the problem.

7 Which choice shows a way to break apart 3 × 8?

   Ⓐ 3 × 2 and 6 × 6

   Ⓑ 3 × 6 and 6 × 2

   Ⓒ 3 × 3 and 4 × 4

   Ⓓ 3 × 6 and 3 × 2

Develop Multiplying with 9

Read and try to solve the problem below.

> The grocery store has 8 boxes of oranges.
> There are 9 oranges in each box.
> How many oranges are there in all?

TRY IT

 Math Toolkit
- counters
- cups
- 1-centimeter grid paper
- multiplication models
- number lines

DISCUSS IT

Ask your partner: Do you agree with me? Why or why not?

Tell your partner: At first, I thought . . .

Explore different ways to understand multiplying with 9.

> The grocery store has 8 boxes of oranges. There are 9 oranges in each box. How many oranges are there in all?

MODEL IT
You can make an array and break apart the columns to make simpler problems.

You can break apart the 9 columns in 8 × 9.

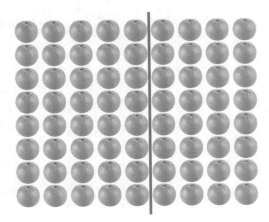

MODEL IT
You can make an array and break apart the rows to make simpler problems.

You can also break apart the 8 rows in 8 × 9.

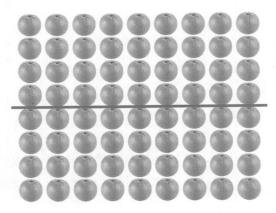

CONNECT IT

Now you will use the problem from the previous page to help you understand how to multiply with 9.

1 How is 9 broken apart in the first **Model It**?

2 Fill in the blanks to show how you can use the two simpler problems to find the product.

(8 × ....) + (8 × ....) =

.... + ... = ...

3 How is 8 broken apart in the second **Model It**?

4 Fill in the blanks to show how you can use the two simpler problems to find the product.

(.................. × 9) + (.................. × 9) =

.... + ... = ...

5 Would finding 8 × 9 by breaking apart the 9 or by breaking apart the 8 be easier for you? Or would they be about the same? Explain.

6 REFLECT

Look back at your **Try It**, strategies by classmates, and **Model Its**. Which models or strategies do you like best for multiplying with 9? Explain.

....

....

....

....

APPLY IT

Use what you just learned to solve these problems.

7 Break each array in a different way to find 7 × 9. Write the equations for each model. Show your work.

7 × 9 = ...

8 Find 9 × 9. Show your work.

9 × 9 = ...

9 A sports game has 4 planned time-outs. Sammy fills 9 bags of popcorn to sell during every time-out. Choose the expression that shows how many bags of popcorn Sammy fills.

Ⓐ (4 × 5) + (4 × 4)

Ⓑ (2 × 6) + (2 × 3)

Ⓒ (3 × 6) + (1 × 3)

Ⓓ (4 × 9) + (9 × 4)

Practice Multiplying with 9

**Study the Example showing how to break apart the factor 9 to multiply.
Then solve problems 1–5.**

EXAMPLE

Eloise buys a sheet of stickers. She counts 5 rows of 9 stickers. How many stickers are on the sheet?

$5 \times 9 = ?$

You can break apart 9 into $4 + 5$.

Multiply 5×4 and 5×5.

Then add the products: $20 + 25 = 45$.

So, $5 \times 9 = 45$. There are 45 stickers on the sheet.

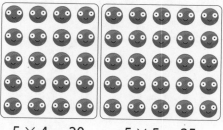

$5 \times 4 = 20$ $5 \times 5 = 25$

Solve problems 1–3 to find how many are in 6 groups of 9.

1. Use what you know about 5×9 above to break apart this 6×9 array into two groups. Draw to show the two groups.

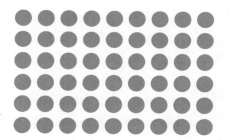

2. Write the multiplication equation you can use for each group in problem 1.

3. Add the products in problem 2 to find 6×9.

4   Draw a line to the pair of multiplication equations that can be used to solve each multiplication problem. Write the missing product for each equation.

$2 \times 9 =$ ....

$4 \times 5 =$ ....

$4 \times 4 =$ ....

$3 \times 9 =$ ....

$7 \times 3 =$ ....

$7 \times 6 =$ ....

$4 \times (5 + 4) =$ ....

$2 \times 2 =$ ....

$2 \times 7 =$ ....

$7 \times (3 + 6) =$ ....

$3 \times 4 =$ ....

$3 \times 5 =$ ....

$8 \times 9 =$ ....

$8 \times 8 =$ ....

$8 \times 1 =$ ....

5   Break apart the array. Then write equations to show how you can use the parts to find 9×9.

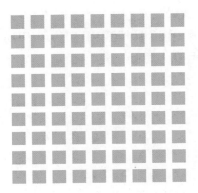

Refine Multiplying with 7, 8, and 9

Complete the Example below. Then solve problems 1–8.

EXAMPLE

Rumi sets up a model car display at the toy store. He has 7 shelves to use. He fits 8 cars on each shelf. How many model cars does Rumi display?

Look at how you could show your work using an array.

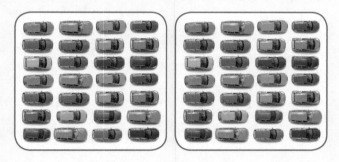

$7 \times 4 = 28$ $7 \times 4 = 28$ $28 + 28 = ?$

Solution ....

The student broke apart the 8 and added the products together.

PAIR/SHARE
Could you break apart the 7 to solve this problem?

APPLY IT

1 Joe has 8 shelves with 9 books on each shelf. How many books does Joe have altogether? Show how to break apart one of the numbers to make the problem easier to solve.

You can break apart the number 9 many different ways.

PAIR/SHARE
How did you and your partner decide how to break apart one of the numbers?

Solution ....

2 Miles is not sure how to find 5 × 8. He tells you that he knows the multiplication facts for 5, so he knows 8 × 5. Show how Miles can use 8 × 5 to find 5 × 8. Show your work.

Do you have to break apart the factor 8 to use multiplication facts for 5?

Solution ....

PAIR/SHARE
How could you have broken apart 8?

3 Athena finds 9 × 7 by breaking apart the 7 into 3 and 4. Which of the following expressions can Athena use?

Ⓐ (9 × 5) + (9 × 2)

Ⓑ (4 × 7) + (5 × 7)

Ⓒ (9 × 3) + (9 × 4)

Ⓓ (7 × 3) + (7 × 4)

Brayden chose Ⓓ as the correct answer. How did he get that answer?

Athena broke apart the 7. What will she do with the 9?

PAIR/SHARE
Will Brayden and Athena get the same answer?

4 Tucker finds 5 × 7 by breaking it apart as shown below.

$$(3 \times 7) + (\underline{\quad} \times 7)$$

What number belongs in the blank?

Ⓐ 1

Ⓑ 2

Ⓒ 4

Ⓓ 8

5 Cole has 5 packs of pencils. There are 8 pencils in each pack. He wants to know how many pencils he has in all. The model below shows how he breaks apart one number in the problem.

 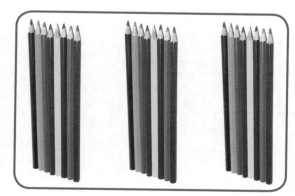

Which expression shows how Cole solves the problem?

Ⓐ (2 × 8) + (3 × 8)

Ⓑ (5 × 3) + (5 × 5)

Ⓒ (2 × 5) + (3 × 5)

Ⓓ (2 × 8) + (2 × 8)

6 Use the array shown to find 8 × 8. First, draw circles to break the array into two groups. Then fill in the blanks to show how you broke the array apart.

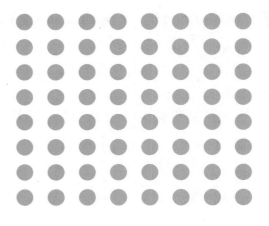

$8 \times 8 = 8 \times (\text{\dots} + \text{\dots})$

$= (8 \times \text{\dots}) + (8 \times \text{\dots})$

$= \text{\dots} + \text{\dots}$

$= \text{\dots}$

7 Is each expression equivalent to the product of 6 and 9?

	Yes	No
(6 × 3) + (6 × 3)	Ⓐ	Ⓑ
(6 × 4) + (6 × 5)	Ⓒ	Ⓓ
6 × (6 + 3)	Ⓔ	Ⓕ
9 × (2 + 4)	Ⓖ	Ⓗ
(3 × 9) + (3 × 9)	Ⓘ	Ⓙ

8 MATH JOURNAL

There are 9 rows in Mrs. Mitchell's flower garden. Each row has 9 flowers planted in it. How many flowers are planted in the garden? Use an equation to show one way to break apart one of the factors and solve the problem. Explain your thinking.

☑ SELF CHECK Go back to the Unit 2 Opener and see what you can check off.

Use Order and Grouping to Multiply

Dear Family,

This week your child is learning to use order and grouping to multiply.

He or she might solve a problem like the one below.

Sam has 5 pencil boxes. Each box has 3 packs of pencils. Each pack has 2 pencils. How many pencils does Sam have?

- One way to solve this is to first multiply to find the number of packs. There are 5 boxes with 3 packs in each: $5 \times 3 = 15$. There are 15 packs. Then multiply to find the number of pencils. There are 2 pencils in each pack: $15 \times 2 = 30$. There are 30 pencils. The parentheses in the problem below show which numbers you are multiplying first.

$$(5 \times 3) \times 2 \longrightarrow 15 \times 2 = 30$$

But what if you do not know how to find 15×2? You can try changing the order in which you multiply the numbers.

- Another way to solve this is to first multiply to find the number of pencils in one box. There are 3 packs with 2 pencils in each: $3 \times 2 = 6$. There are 6 pencils in each box. Then multiply to find the total number of pencils. There are 5 boxes: $5 \times 6 = 30$. There are 30 pencils.

$$5 \times (3 \times 2) \longrightarrow 5 \times 6 = 30$$

Invite your child to share what he or she knows about using order and grouping to multiply by doing the following activity together.

ACTIVITY CHANGING THE ORDER OF FACTORS

Do this activity with your child to multiply by changing the order of factors.

Materials 24 pennies or other small items

Do this activity with your child to see how changing the order of the factors in a multiplication fact does not change the product.

- Do the following two problems with your child.

  1. Count out 12 pennies. Work together to arrange them in an array with 3 rows of 4 pennies each. Have your child write the equation this array represents.

  2. Then arrange the other 12 pennies in an array with 4 rows of 3 pennies each. Have your child write the equation for this array.

- Discuss with your child with questions such as these:
  - *Does changing the order of the factors change the number of pennies?*
  - *Do you think this will always be true?*
  - *Does changing the order of the factors make either of the related multiplication facts easier for you?*

- Repeat with 2 rows of 6 and 6 rows of 2.

Answers: **1.** 3 × 4 = 12; **2.** 4 × 3 = 12

Explore **Using Order and Grouping to Multiply**

Previously you learned about the meaning of multiplication along with some basic facts. This lesson will help you solve multiplication problems using what you already know. Use what you know to try to solve the problem below.

> **Ava's mom buys 2 packs of 3 T-shirts. Her dad buys 3 packs of 2 T-shirts. How many T-shirts did each of Ava's parents buy?**

TRY IT

 Math Toolkit
• counters
• buttons
• cups
• 1-inch grid paper
• multiplication models
• number lines

DISCUSS IT

Ask your partner: How did you get started?

Tell your partner: I started by . . .

CONNECT IT

1 LOOK BACK

Write two multiplication equations to show how many T-shirts
Ava's mom and dad buy. How are the equations alike and different?

2 LOOK AHEAD

You have seen how the order of factors in a multiplication problem affects
the product, but what about how you group factors? Look at this problem.

Jayden buys 4 boxes of hot dogs. Each box has 2 packs.
Each pack has 5 hot dogs. How many hot dogs did she buy?

a. One way to think about this is to first find how many packs there are.
Then multiply the number in each pack, 5, by the number of packs.

4×2 packs is .... packs. $(4 \times 2) \times 5 =$ .... $\times 5 =$ ....

b. Another way to think about this is to first find how many hot
dogs are in each box. Then multiply by the number of boxes, 4.

2×5 is .... hot dogs in a box. $4 \times (2 \times 5) = 4 \times$ .... $=$ ....

c. How are $(4 \times 2) \times 5$ and $4 \times (2 \times 5)$ alike and different?

3 REFLECT

Is finding $(4 \times 2) \times 5$ or $4 \times (2 \times 5)$ easier for you? Explain.

....

....

Prepare for Using Order and Grouping to Multiply

1 Think about what you know about multiplication. Fill in each box. Use words, numbers, and pictures. Show as many ideas as you can.

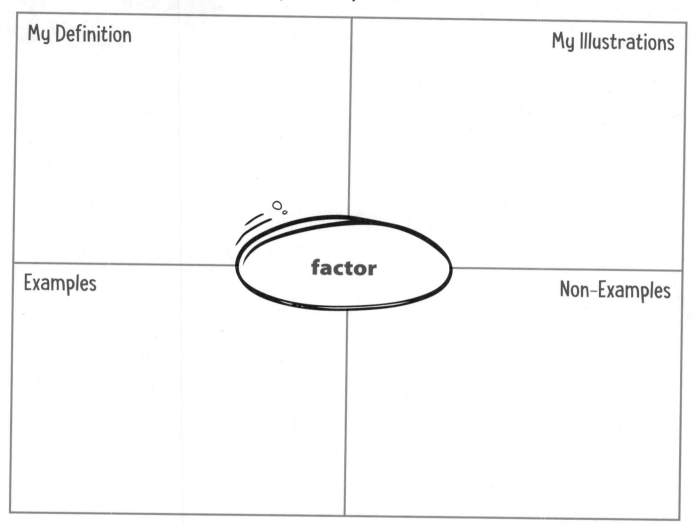

My Definition	My Illustrations
Examples	**Non-Examples**

factor

2 Gil says (3 × 2) × 4 and 3 × (2 × 4) have the same product. Do you agree? Explain.

3 Solve the problem. Show your work.

Nadia's mom buys 4 packs of 2 pens. Her dad buys 2 packs of 4 pens. How many pens did each of Nadia's parents buy?

Solution ....

4 Check your answer. Show your work.

Develop Using Order to Multiply

Read and try to solve the problem below.

> Chad reads books at the library each week for 6 weeks. He reads 3 books each week. Mia reads books at the library each week for 3 weeks. She reads 6 books each week. Who reads more books at the library, Chad or Mia?

TRY IT

 **Math Toolkit**
- counters
- buttons
- cups
- 1-inch grid paper
- multiplication models
- number lines

DISCUSS IT

Ask your partner: Why did you choose that strategy?

Tell your partner: I agree with you about . . . because . . .

Explore different ways to understand multiplying factors in any order.

> Chad reads books at the library each week for 6 weeks.
> He reads 3 books each week. Mia reads books at the library
> each week for 3 weeks. She reads 6 books each week.
> Who reads more books at the library, Chad or Mia?

PICTURE IT
You can use equal groups to help you understand the problem.

Chad

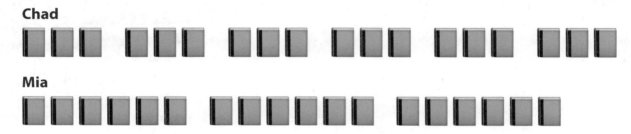

Mia

MODEL IT
You can also use arrays to help you understand the problem.

Each row in the arrays shows the number of books Chad or
Mia read each week.

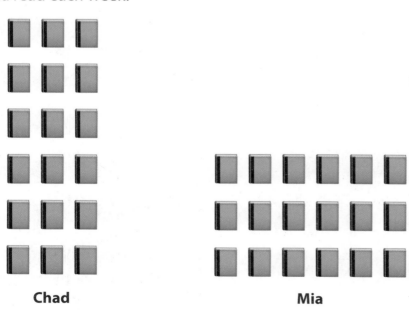

Chad   Mia

CONNECT IT

Now you will use the problem from the previous page to help you understand how to multiply factors in any order.

1 What multiplication equation could you write to find the number of books Chad reads?

2 What multiplication equation could you write to find the number of books Mia reads?

3 Who reads more books?

4 Explain how you could know that Chad and Mia read the same number of books without finding the product in each multiplication equation.

5 Your teacher tells you that $8 \times 9 = 72$. Explain how you know what 9×8 equals.

6 REFLECT

Look back at your **Try It**, strategies by classmates, and **Picture It** and **Model It**. Which models or strategies do you like best for showing that you can change the order of the factors in a multiplication problem and still get the same product? Explain.

....

....

....

....

APPLY IT

Use what you just learned to solve these problems.

7 Josie has 5 cups with 4 tokens in each cup. Ian has 4 cups with 5 tokens in each cup. Draw a model to show that Josie and Ian have the same number of tokens. Show your work.

8 Ashish and Gita each have a rock collection with the same number of rocks. Ashish has 6 shelves in his room to display all his rocks. He puts 8 rocks on each shelf. Gita has 8 shelves to display all her rocks. She puts an equal number of rocks on each shelf. How many rocks does Gita put on each shelf? Show your work.

Solution ....

9 Sara knows that 5 × 8 = 40. What other math fact does this help Sara know?

Ⓐ 5 + 8 = 13

Ⓑ 40 − 8 = 32

Ⓒ 8 × 5 = 40

Ⓓ 4 × 10 = 40

Practice Using Order to Multiply

Study the Example showing that the order of factors does not matter when you multiply. Then solve problems 1–6.

EXAMPLE

Paul has 3 groups of 2 coins. Jill has 2 groups of 3 coins. Who has more coins?

$3 \times 2 = 6$ $2 \times 3 = 6$

Paul and Jill have the same number of coins.

---

1 For each array, write how many rows there are and how many dots are in each row. Then write a multiplication equation.

.... rows

.... dots in each row

.... × .... = ...

.... rows

.... dots in each row

.... × .... = ...

> **Vocabulary**
>
> **factor** a number that is multiplied.
>
> **product** the result of multiplication.
>
> $2 \times 5 = 10$
> 2 and 5 are *factors*.
> 10 is the *product*.

2 You know that $3 \times 9 = 27$. Explain how you know what 9×3 equals.

3 Daniel colors a grid to show $4 \times 6 = 24$. Color the other grid to show $6 \times 4 = 24$.

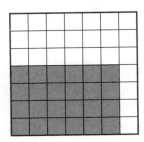

  $4 \times 6 = 24$ $6 \times 4 = 24$

4 Explain how you know there are the same number of colored squares in both grids in problem 3.

5 This array shows $4 \times 3 = 12$. Draw an array that shows $3 \times 4 = 12$.

6 Avery has 3 baskets with 9 flowers in each basket. Ralph has 9 baskets of flowers. If he has the same total number of flowers as Avery, how many flowers does Ralph have in each basket?

.... flowers

Develop Using Grouping to Multiply

Read and try to solve the problem below.

> Nykole decorates a pair of gloves with plastic jewels. She glues 3 jewels onto each finger, including thumbs. How many jewels does she use?

TRY IT

 **Math Toolkit**
- counters
- buttons
- index cards
- sticky notes
- multiplication models
- number lines

DISCUSS IT

Ask your partner: Do you agree with me? Why or why not?

Tell your partner: I am not sure how to find the answer because . . .

Explore different ways to understand grouping factors in different ways.

> **Nykole decorates a pair of gloves with plastic jewels.**
> **She glues 3 jewels onto each finger, including thumbs.**
> **How many jewels does she use?**

PICTURE IT

You can use a picture to help you understand the problem.

There are 5 fingers with 3 jewels on each: $5 \times 3 = 15$.
She has 15 jewels on each glove. There are 2 gloves.
15 jewels $\times$ 2 finds how many jewels are on both gloves altogether.

You could also multiply another way. There are 2 gloves with 5 fingers each:
$2 \times 5 = 10$. There are 10 fingers. There are 3 jewels on each finger: 10×3
also finds how many jewels she uses.

MODEL IT

You can write a multiplication problem: $2 \times 5 \times 3$.

You can use parentheses to show which two numbers you will multiply first.

$(2 \times 5) \times 3 \longrightarrow 10 \times 3 = 30$

You could also choose to multiply different numbers first.

$2 \times (5 \times 3) \longrightarrow 2 \times 15 = 30$

CONNECT IT

Now you will use the problem from the previous page to help you understand how to group factors in different ways.

1 Use parentheses to show one way to group $2 \times 5 \times 3$.

2 Use parentheses to show a different way to group $2 \times 5 \times 3$.

3 Which way would you choose to find the product? Explain why.

4 Explain how you can use grouping to make multiplying three factors easier.

5 **REFLECT**

Look back at your **Try It**, strategies by classmates, and **Picture It** and **Model It**. Which models or strategies do you like best for showing that you can change the grouping of the factors in a multiplication problem and still get the same product? Explain.

....

....

....

....

APPLY IT

Use what you just learned to solve these problems.

6 Use parentheses to show two different ways to group $7 \times 2 \times 4$. Then choose one of the ways and show the steps to finding the product. Show your work.

Solution ....

7 Use parentheses to show two different ways to group $2 \times 4 \times 3$. Then choose one of the ways and show the steps to finding the product. Show your work.

Solution ....

8 Which expressions show a possible next step to finding $3 \times 2 \times 9$?

Ⓐ 6×9

Ⓑ 6×18

Ⓒ 5×9

Ⓓ 3×11

Ⓔ 3×18

Practice Using Grouping to Multiply

Study the Example showing how to use grouping to multiply.
Then solve problems 1–9.

EXAMPLE

Leo makes bracelets. Each bracelet has 5 beads. Leo puts the bracelets in bags. Each bag has 2 bracelets. He used 3 bags. How many beads did he use?

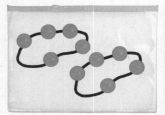 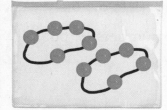 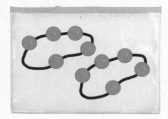

Leo wrote (5 × 2) × 3. He used parentheses to show what numbers he multiplied first.

Leo used 30 beads.

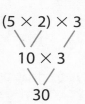

$(5 \times 2) \times 3$
10×3
30

Kelly made the bracelets shown at the right.

1. How many beads did Kelly put on each bracelet? ....

2. How many bracelets did Kelly put in each bag? ....

3. How many bags did Kelly use? ....

4. How many beads did Kelly use? ....

5. Write a multiplication equation. Use parentheses to show which numbers you will multiply first.

.... × .... × .... = ...

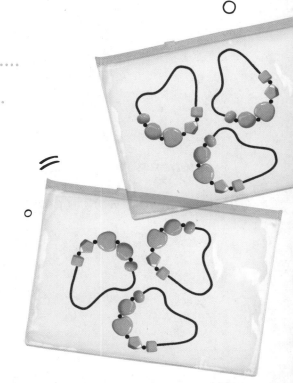

6 How would you group the numbers to find $7 \times 2 \times 4$? Why?

7 Addison and Claire chose different ways to multiply $4 \times 5 \times 3$. Addison grouped the numbers like this: $4 \times (5 \times 3)$. She found $5 \times 3 = 15$. Then she multiplied 4×15 by adding $15 + 15 + 15 + 15$ to get 60.

Explain how Claire could have grouped the numbers to multiply. Show the steps she used to find her answer.

8 Show two different ways to group $8 \times 2 \times 3$. Then find the product.

Solution ....

9 Look at your work in problem 8. Which way of grouping is easier for you? Why?

Develop Using Order and Grouping to Multiply

Read and try to solve the problem below.

> **Joelle bought 2 boxes of bananas for her ice cream shop. There are 8 bunches in each box, and there are 5 bananas in each bunch. How many bananas did Joelle buy?**

TRY IT

 **Math Toolkit**
- counters
- buttons
- cups
- index cards
- multiplication models
- number lines

DISCUSS IT

Ask your partner: Can you explain that again?

Tell your partner: At first, I thought . . .

Explore different ways to understand ordering and grouping factors in different ways.

> **Joelle bought 2 boxes of bananas for her ice cream shop. There are 8 bunches in each box, and there are 5 bananas in each bunch. How many bananas did Joelle buy?**

MODEL IT

Think of the multiplication problem you can write: $2 \times 8 \times 5$.

You can use what you have learned about multiplying in any order and grouping to help make the problem easier.

Start with $2 \times 8 \times 5$.

First, change the order of the numbers. Switch the 2 and the 8.

Now you have $8 \times 2 \times 5$.

Then group it like this: $8 \times (2 \times 5)$.

Multiply the numbers in parentheses: $2 \times 5 = \mathbf{10}$.

Then do the last multiplication: $8 \times \mathbf{10} = 80$.

MODEL IT

You can use diagrams to help you understand the problem.

The first two diagrams show two ways you can solve the problem using just grouping. The third diagram shows how you can solve the problem by changing the order of the numbers before using grouping.

$$2 \times 8 \times 5 \qquad 2 \times 8 \times 5 \qquad 8 \times 2 \times 5$$
$$16 \times 5 \qquad\quad 2 \times 40 \qquad\quad 8 \times 10$$
$$80 \qquad\qquad\quad 80 \qquad\qquad\quad 80$$

CONNECT IT

Now you will use the problem from the previous page to help you understand how to order and group factors in different ways.

1 You can order and group the factors in the multiplication expression $2 \times 8 \times 5$ in different ways. Look at the ways shown below. Fill in the missing numbers.

$(8 \times 2) \times \underline{\hspace{1cm}} = 80$ $(5 \times 2) \times \underline{\hspace{1cm}} = 80$ $\underline{\hspace{1cm}} \times (8 \times 5) = 80$

2 Multiply numbers inside parentheses first. Look back at the multiplication equations in problem 1. Multiply the numbers in the parentheses and then fill in the missing numbers below.

$(\underline{\hspace{0.8cm}}) \times \underline{\hspace{1cm}} = 80$ $(\underline{\hspace{0.8cm}}) \times \underline{\hspace{1cm}} = 80$ $\underline{\hspace{1cm}} \times (\underline{\hspace{0.8cm}}) = 80$

3 Which of the three products in problem 1 do you think is the easiest to find? Explain why you think so.

4 Explain how you can use grouping and multiplying in any order to make multiplying three numbers easier.

5 REFLECT

Look back at your **Try It**, strategies by classmates, and **Model Its**. Which models or strategies do you like best for showing that you can change the order and the grouping of the factors in a multiplication problem and still get the same product? Explain.

APPLY IT

Use what you just learned to solve these problems.

6 Change the order of the factors and use parentheses to show one way to find $3 \times 7 \times 3$. Then show the steps to finding the product. Show your work.

Solution ....

7 Change the order of the factors and use parentheses to show one way to find $4 \times 9 \times 2$. Then show the steps to finding the product. Show your work.

Solution ....

8 Which of the following does not have the same product as $8 \times (2 \times 4)$?

Ⓐ $8 \times (4 \times 2)$

Ⓑ 16×4

Ⓒ 8×6

Ⓓ $(4 \times 8) \times 2$

Practice Using Order and Grouping to Multiply

Study the Example showing how to use order and grouping to multiply. Then solve problems 1–10.

EXAMPLE

Rama changes the order and the grouping of numbers to make multiplication easier. What are two different ways Rama could multiply the numbers 4, 6, and 2?

$(2 \times 4) \times 6$ $4 \times (6 \times 2)$

8×6 4×12

48 48

Use the numbers on the number cubes, 4, 2, and 3, to answer problems 1–4.

1. Order and group the numbers. Then multiply to find the product.

   .... × .... × .... = ...

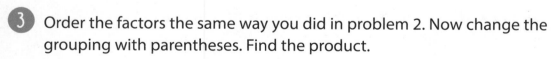

2. Order and group the numbers a different way. Then multiply to find the product.

   .... × .... × .... = ...

3. Order the factors the same way you did in problem 2. Now change the grouping with parentheses. Find the product.

   .... × .... × .... = ...

4. Which of these three products do you think is easiest to find? Explain why you think so.

5 Use the numbers 3, 5, and 2 as factors. Look at some of the ways the factors are ordered and grouped. Fill in missing numbers.

(3 × 5) × .... = 30   (5 × 2) × .... = 30   .... × (3 × 2) = 30

6 Look at problem 5. Multiply the numbers in parentheses first and then fill in the numbers below.

(........) × .... = 30   (........) × .... = 30   .... × (........) = 30

7 Which of the three products in problem 5 is easiest to find? Why do you think so?

8 Multiply the factors 9, 2, and 2. Choose an order and use parentheses to show one way to find the product.

Solution ....

9 Explain why you chose to order and group the factors the way you did in problem 8.

10 Multiply the factors 4, 2, and 5. Choose an order and use parentheses to show one way to find the product. Then show the steps to find the product.

Solution ....

Refine Using Order and Grouping to Multiply

Complete the Example below. Then solve problems 1–8.

EXAMPLE

There are 5 rows of tables in the cafeteria. Each row has 8 tables. Maria knows that 8×5 is 40. How can she use this to figure out how many tables there are?

Look at how you could show your work using arrays.

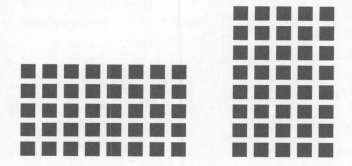

Solution ....

....

The first array shows 5×8. The second array is the same array turned on its side. It shows 8×5.

PAIR/SHARE
If two arrays have the same total, how can they show two different multiplication facts?

APPLY IT

1 There are 2 classes of third graders. In each class, there are 3 rows of desks, with 7 desks in each row. Write a multiplication expression to find the number of desks in both classes together. Show how to group the factors to find the product. Then write the answer. Show your work.

Which two numbers have a product that would be easy to multiply by in your head?

PAIR/SHARE
How would solving the problem be different if you grouped the factors another way?

Solution ....

2 AJ needs to find $3 \times 8 \times 2$. Show one way to find the product. Use parentheses to show how you grouped the numbers. Show your work.

I think it would be easiest if you changed the order of the factors before you grouped them.

Solution ....

PAIR/SHARE
How did you decide which two numbers to multiply first?

3 Matt knows $4 \times 6 = 24$. What other math fact does this help Matt remember?

Ⓐ $6 + 4 = 10$

Ⓑ $8 \times 3 = 24$

Ⓒ $24 - 6 = 18$

Ⓓ $6 \times 4 = 24$

Sadie chose Ⓐ as the correct answer. How did she get that answer?

What have you learned about the order of factors in multiplication?

PAIR/SHARE
Does Sadie's answer make sense?

4 Jackson knows 9 × 7 = 63. He needs to solve the equation .... × 9 = 63. What number goes in the blank?

Ⓐ 5

Ⓑ 6

Ⓒ 7

Ⓓ 8

5 Which of the following is NOT true?

Ⓐ 3 × 6 × 3 = 6 × 3 × 3

Ⓑ 3 × 6 × 3 = 9 × 3

Ⓒ 3 × 6 × 3 = 6 × 9

Ⓓ 3 × 6 × 3 = 3 × 18

6 Dan has 2 photo albums. Each photo album has 8 pages. Dan can fit 4 pictures on each page. How many pictures can Dan fit in the albums?

7 Lyn's mom puts pictures on her refrigerator in rows. There are 3 rows of pictures. There are 7 pictures in each row. Which expressions or arrays could be used to find the total number of pictures?

Ⓐ 3 × 7

Ⓑ 7 × 3

Ⓒ 7 × 7 × 7

Ⓓ

Ⓔ

8 **MATH JOURNAL**

How does knowing that (3 × 2) × 9 = 54 help you know what 3 × (9 × 2) equals?

✓ **SELF CHECK** Go back to the Unit 2 Opener and see what you can check off.

Use Place Value to Multiply

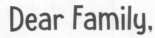
Dear Family,

This week your child is learning about using place value to multiply.

Place value can help you understand how to multiply a two-digit multiple of 10, such as 40, by a one-digit number, such as 3.

You can use base-ten blocks to understand this problem. These base-ten blocks show 3 groups of 40.

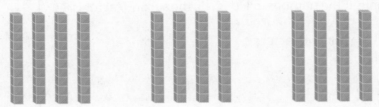

3 groups of 4 tens is 3 × 4 tens, or 12 tens.
12 tens is the same as 120.

Another way to think about this problem, without the base-ten blocks, is to rewrite the problem. Think about 40 as 4 × 10. Then:

$$3 \times 40 = 3 \times (4 \times 10)$$

When you multiply, you can change the grouping without changing the answer:

3 × (4 × 10) is the same as (3 × 4) × 10.
3 × 4 is 12, and 12 × 10 is 120.
So, again, 3 × 40 = 120.

Invite your child to share what he or she knows about using place value to multiply by doing the following activity together.

ACTIVITY USING PLACE VALUE TO MULTIPLY

Do this activity with your child to use place value to multiply.

Materials 2 number cubes

Play a game with your child to practice multiplying with a multiple of 10. The winner of each round is the player with the greater product.

- Each player rolls one number cube. The first roll gives you each your first factor. For example, if the number rolled is a 5, the first factor is 5.

- Roll again and multiply 10 by the number on the cube. This is your second factor. For example, if the number rolled is a 3, the second factor is 30.

- Find the product of your two factors.
  For example, to find 5×30:
  $$5 \times (3 \times 10)$$
  $$(5 \times 3) \times 10$$
  15×10 is 15 tens, which equals 150.

- The player with the greater product wins the round.

- Play five rounds for best out of five.

Explore Using Place Value to Multiply

In previous lessons you learned multiplication facts. In this lesson you will learn how to use these facts to help you multiply one-digit numbers and multiples of 10. Use what you know to try to solve the problem below.

> **There are 4 stacks of books on a table. Each stack has 20 books. How many books are there in all?**

TRY IT

Math Toolkit
- base-ten blocks
- hundred charts
- number lines
- multiplication models

DISCUSS IT

Ask your partner: Why did you choose this strategy?

Tell your partner: I knew . . . so I . . . .

CONNECT IT

1 LOOK BACK

Explain how you found how many books there are in all.

2 LOOK AHEAD

Multiplication can be used to find the total when there are two or more groups with the same number in each group. You have learned some multiplication facts. These facts can help you multiply with tens.

Think about 4 × 20, shown by the base-ten blocks below. Look at different ways to find this total.

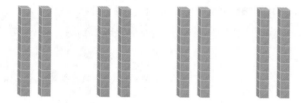

a. You can skip-count by ten 8 times to find the product:

10, 20, 30, 40, ..., ..., ..., ...

b. You can skip-count by twenty .... times:

20, 40, 60, ...

c. You can count on by groups of tens:

2 tens, 4 tens, 6 tens, 8 tens. 8 tens is ....

3 REFLECT

Do you think skip-count and counting on would work well with greater numbers, such as 8 × 80? Explain.

....

....

....

Prepare for Using Place Value to Multiply

1 Think about what you know about multiplication. Fill in each box. Use words, numbers, and pictures. Show as many ideas as you can.

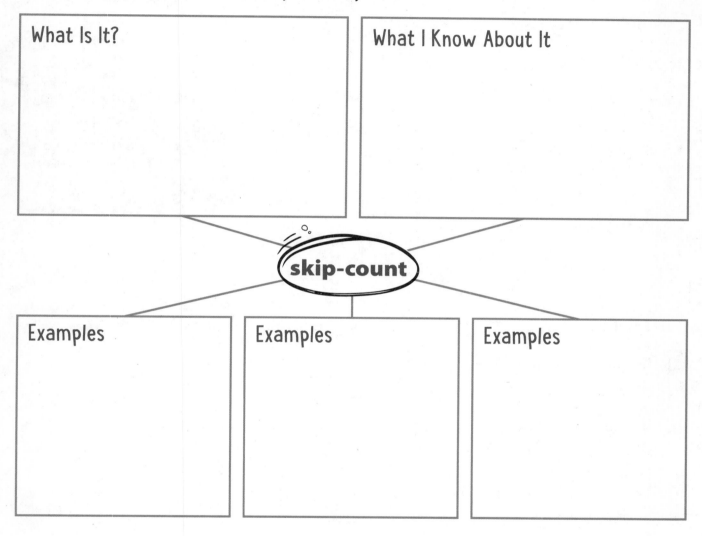

What Is It?

What I Know About It

skip-count

Examples

Examples

Examples

2 How would you use skip-counting to find 6 × 50? Explain.

3 Solve the problem. Show your work.

Travis fills 6 gift bags with prizes. Each bag holds 30 prizes. How many prizes does Travis use?

Solution ....

4 Check your answer. Show your work.

Develop Multiplying with Tens

Read and try to solve the problem below.

> A sports store orders 4 boxes of baseball caps. Each box has 40 caps. How many baseball caps does the store order?

TRY IT

 **Math Toolkit**
- base-ten blocks
- number lines
- 1-centimeter grid paper
- multiplication models

DISCUSS IT

Ask your partner: Do you agree with me? Why or why not?

Tell your partner: I started by . . .

Explore different ways to understand multiplying with tens.

> A sports store orders 4 boxes of baseball caps.
> Each box has 40 caps. How many baseball caps
> does the store order?

PICTURE IT

You can use base-ten blocks to help understand the problem.

4 boxes of baseball caps

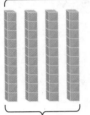 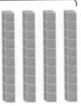

40 caps in
each box

4 groups of 4 tens is 4 × 4 tens, or 16 tens.

16 tens is 160.

MODEL IT

You can also use factors and grouping to multiply with tens.

Start with the factors from the problem:	4 × 40
You can write 40 as 4 × 10:	4 × (4 × 10)
You can change the grouping when you multiply:	(4 × 4) × 10
Multiply 4 × 4:	16 × 10

16 tens is 160.

CONNECT IT

Now you will use the problem from the previous page to help you understand how to multiply with tens.

Below are three equal multiplication expressions from the previous page.

$$4 \times 40 \qquad 4 \times 4 \times 10 \qquad 16 \times 10$$

1 You can break apart 16 into 10 plus another number. Write the number in the blank: $16 \times 10 = (10 + \underline{}) \times 10$

2 You can multiply 10 by both numbers in the parentheses in problem 1. Write these numbers in the blanks: $= (\underline{} \times 10) + (\underline{} \times 10)$

3 Write the products in the blanks: $= \underline{} + \underline{}$

4 Add the products and write the sum in the blank: $= \underline{}$

5 How can you find the product of 40×4?

6 Explain how to find the product of a given number and a multiple of 10.

7 REFLECT

Look back at your **Try It**, strategies by classmates, and **Picture It** and **Model It**. Which models or strategies do you like best for multiplying with tens? Explain.

....

....

....

....

APPLY IT

Use what you just learned to solve these problems.

8 Multiply 60 × 8. Show your work.

Solution ....

9 There are 40 nickels in a roll of nickels. Tao has 7 rolls of nickels. How many nickels does she have in all? Show your work.

Solution ....

10 Multiply 7 × 30. Show your work.

Solution ....

Practice Multiplying with Tens

Study the Example showing how you can use place value to help you multiply with tens. Then solve problems 1–8.

EXAMPLE

Hobbit's Hobby Store has 4 shelves of glue. Each shelf has 30 bottles of glue. How many bottles of glue are on the shelves?

You can use place value and grouping.

4×30
$4 \times (3 \times 10)$
$(4 \times 3) \times 10$
$12 \times 10 = 120$

There are 120 bottles of glue on the shelves.

30 bottles on each shelf

4 groups of 3 tens or 12 tens
12 tens is 120.

The hobby store has 3 boxes of wheels. There are 50 wheels in each box. How many wheels does the hobby store have?

1 You can write 50 as .... × 10.

2 $3 \times (5 \times 10)$ is one way to group the factors. Use parentheses to show another way to group the factors.

$3 \times 5 \times 10$

3 $3 \times 5 \times 10 = $ .... × 10

4 The hobby store has .... wheels.

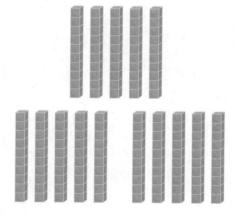

5 Draw a line to match each problem with another way to write it.

5 × 60	(4 × 3) × 10
6 × 40	10 × (5 × 4)
50 × 4	(5 × 6) × 10
6 × 30	(6 × 3) × 10
40 × 3	(6 × 4) × 10

6 Write the multiplication equation that the base-ten model shows.

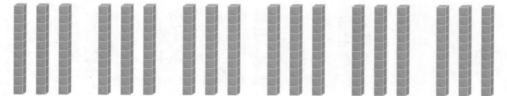

Solution ....

7 Fill in the blanks to show how to find 4 × 70.

4 × 70 = 4 × (.................... × 10)

= (4 × ....) × 10

= 28 × 10 = ...

4 × 70 = ...

8 Complete the equation below.
Show your work.

6 × 20 = ...

Refine Using Place Value to Multiply

Complete the Example below. Then solve problems 1–9.

EXAMPLE

Robin plants 9 rows of flowers. Each row has 30 flowers. How many flowers does Robin plant in all?

Look at how you could show your work by changing the grouping when you multiply.

$$9 \times 30 = 9 \times (3 \times 10)$$
$$= (9 \times 3) \times 10$$
$$= 27 \times 10$$

Solution ....

9×30 is 9 groups of 3 tens, or 27 tens.

PAIR/SHARE
How could you use skip-counting to solve this problem? Which way of solving makes more sense?

APPLY IT

1 Manu drives 50 miles each day. How many miles does he drive in 5 days? Show your work.

How many groups of 5 tens are there?

PAIR/SHARE
How did you and your partner choose the way to solve this problem?

Solution ....

2 Multiply 6 × 90. Show your work.

> How can you rewrite 90 so you can multiply with 10?

Solution ....

PAIR/SHARE
How can you check that your answer is correct?

3 Raymond can type 40 words each minute. How many words can he type in 8 minutes?

Ⓐ 32 words

Ⓑ 48 words

Ⓒ 320 words

Ⓓ 360 words

Gina chose Ⓑ as the correct answer. How did she get that answer?

> What multiplication fact can you use to solve the problem?

PAIR/SHARE
How can the digit in the ones place help you decide if an answer makes sense?

4 What is the product of 6 × 30?

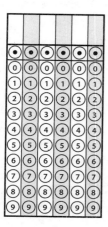

5 There are 60 toothpicks in a jar. There are 3 jars in 1 box. How many toothpicks are in 2 boxes?

Ⓐ 120

Ⓑ 180

Ⓒ 360

Ⓓ 480

6 Which multiplication expressions are ways to show 240?

Ⓐ 40 × 6

Ⓑ 4 × 60

Ⓒ 30 × 8

Ⓓ 80 × 3

Ⓔ 2 × 40

Lesson 9 Use Place Value to Multiply **223**

7 A notebook has 80 sheets of paper. How many sheets of paper do 7 such notebooks have? Show your work.

.... sheets of paper

8 At a pet store, there are 20 fish in each tank. How many fish are in 8 tanks? Show your work.

There are .... fish in 8 tanks.

9 MATH JOURNAL

Explain how you can use what you know about multiplication facts and place value to multiply 8 × 80.

☑ SELF CHECK Go back to the Unit 2 Opener and see what you can check off.

Understand the Meaning of Division

Dear Family,

This week your child is exploring the meaning of division.

When you **divide**, you separate a group of objects into smaller, equal-sized groups.

You can use **division** to find the number in each group. Consider the problem below.

Betsy has 6 stickers. She puts the same number of stickers on 3 different pages. How many stickers are on each page?

The picture shows that 6 stickers grouped equally onto 3 pages is 2 stickers on each page.

So, 6 ÷ 3 = 2.

Other times you know how many objects you want in each group, and you use division to find how many groups you can make. Consider the problem below.

Betsy has 15 flowers she wants to group into bunches of 5. How many bunches of flowers can she make?

If she puts 15 flowers into bunches of 5, she makes 3 bunches.

So, use the **division equation** 15 ÷ 5 = 3.

Invite your child to share what he or she knows about the meaning of division by doing the following activity together.

ACTIVITY EXPLORE THE MEANING OF DIVISION

Do this activity with your child to understand the meaning of division.

Materials 12 of one kind of item, such as socks, spoons, or coins

Help your child understand the meaning of division with this activity.

- Collect 12 of one item, such as socks.

- Have your child show 12 ÷ 3 by dividing the 12 items into 3 equal groups. One way to approach this is to think about "dealing" the socks into 3 piles, one at a time, until all the socks are gone.

  1. Ask your child to tell what he or she did. You child might say: *I put 12 socks into 3 equal groups. Each group got 4 socks.*

  2. Then ask your child to write or say the division equation.

  3. Gather up all the items. Then have your child divide the 12 items into groups with 4 in each group. Ask him or her to tell how many groups were formed and write or say the division equation.

- Repeat the exercise, dividing the 12 items into 6 equal groups and then dividing into groups with 2 items each. Each time, have your child describe what he or she did and write or say the division equation.

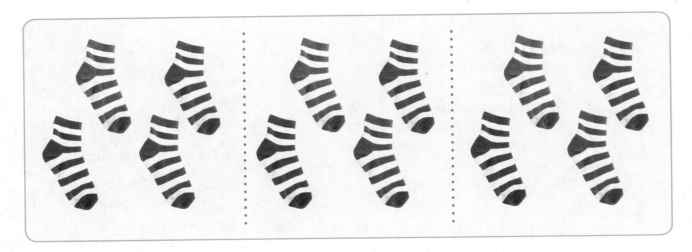

Answers:
 1. Your child might say: *I put 12 socks into 3 equal groups. Each group has 4 socks.*
 2. 12 ÷ 3 = 4
 3. 3 groups; 12 ÷ 4 = 3

Explore the Meaning of Division

What is going on when you divide numbers?

Learning Target

- Interpret whole-number quotients of whole numbers, e.g., interpret 56 ÷ 8 as the number of objects in each share when 56 objects are partitioned equally into 8 shares, or as a number of shares when 56 objects are partitioned into equal shares of 8 objects each.

SMP 1, 2, 3, 4, 5, 6

MODEL IT

Complete the models below.

1 Imagine Jake has 8 cookies. Draw cookies on the plates below to show how to **divide** the cookies into 2 equal groups.

2 Jake divided 8 by 2. How much is 8 divided by 2?

3 One way to use **division** is to *find how many in each group*. Fill in the blanks to complete the **division equation** for the problem.

There are .... in all.

There are .... equal groups.

There are .... in each group.

.... ÷ .... = ...

The ÷ means "divided by."

DISCUSS IT

- How did you know the number of cookies on each plate was equal?
- I think finding equal groups shows division because . . .

MODEL IT

Complete the models below.

4 Now imagine Rosi has 10 cookies. She wants to put 2 cookies on each plate. Draw 10 cookies in groups of 2 on plates.

5 Rosi divided 10 by 2. How much is 10 divided by 2?

6 Another way to use **division** is to *find the number of groups*. Fill in the blanks to complete the **division equation** for the problem.

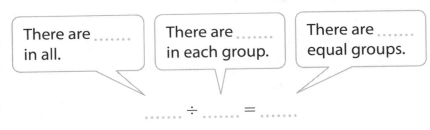

There are .... in all.

There are .... in each group.

There are .... equal groups.

.... ÷ .... = ...

> **DISCUSS IT**
> • How did you know how many plates to draw?
> • I think the total is always in front of the division sign in a division equation because . . .

7 REFLECT

How is finding the number of groups in a division problem like finding the number in each group? How is it different?

....

....

....

....

....

Prepare for Exploring the Meaning of Division

1 Think about what you know about division. Fill in each box. Use words, numbers, and pictures. Show as many ideas as you can.

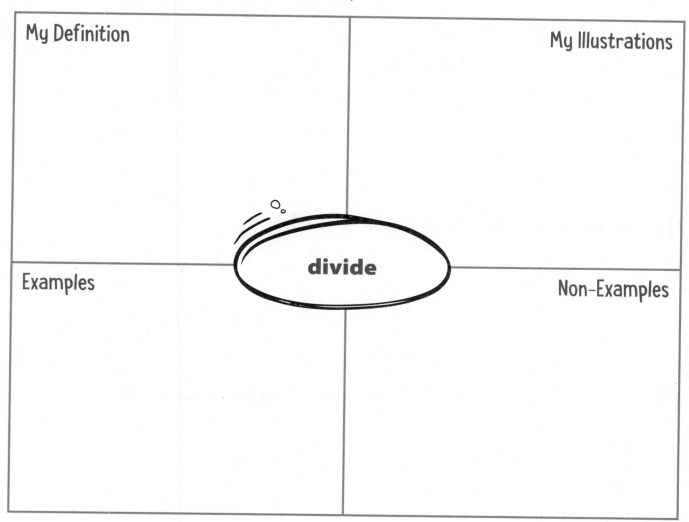

My Definition	My Illustrations
Examples	Non-Examples

2 Oscar draws a diagram to help find 12 ÷ 3. Explain how his diagram helps him solve the division problem.

  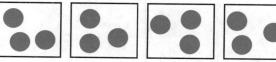

Solve.

3 Rance has 12 crackers. He wants to put 4 crackers on each plate.
Draw 12 crackers in groups of 4 on plates.

4 How many plates will Rance need? How do you know?

5 Fill in the blanks to complete the division equation for the problem.

There are ....
in all.

There are ....
in each group.

There are ....
equal groups.

.... ÷ .... = ...

Develop Understanding of Division Models

MODEL IT: EQUAL GROUPS

Try these two problems.

1 Marc has 24 oranges to put in bags. He decides to put 6 oranges in each bag.

a. Draw a model to show how many bags he needs.

b. Write the division equation for your model.

c. Use words to describe the total number of oranges, number in each group, and number of groups.

2 Marc changes his mind. He decides to put all 24 oranges in 6 bags. He puts the same number of oranges in each bag.

a. Draw a model to show how many oranges he puts in each bag.

DISCUSS IT

• What does the 6 show in your model for problem 1? What does the 6 show in your model for problem 2?

• I think the same division equation can be shown with two different models of equal groups because . . .

b. Write the division equation for your model.

c. Use words to describe the total number of oranges, number of groups, and number in each group.

MODEL IT: ARRAYS

Use arrays to model division.

3 Draw an array to show $20 \div 5 = 4$. Use words to describe your array.

4 Draw a different array to show $20 \div 5 = 4$. Use words to describe your array.

DISCUSS IT

- How did you decide on the number of rows or how many in each row in your two arrays?

- I think the same division equation can be shown with two different arrays because . . .

CONNECT IT

Complete the problems below.

5 How can drawings of equal groups, arrays, equations, and words all be used to describe what a division problem means?

6 Use any model to show and find $42 \div 7$. Write a division equation and explain what each number in the equation tells you.

Practice Using Division Models

Study how the Example represents a division equation with equal groups. Then solve problems 1–7.

EXAMPLE

Draw a picture and use words to represent the division equation **15 ÷ 3 = 5**.

There are **15** apples in **3** baskets. Each basket has **5** apples.

Use the picture of frogs on logs to answer problems 1–4.

1 How many frogs are there in all? ....

2 How many logs are there? ....

3 How many frogs are on each log? ....

4 Write a division equation about the 8 frogs in 4 equal groups.

.... ÷ .... = ...

5 A class has 20 students. The teacher divides them into groups of 4 to play tennis. How many groups are there? Draw a picture.

Solution ....

6 Parker says that this array of 18 rectangles shows the division problem 6 ÷ 3. What is his mistake?

7 Write a word problem that could be solved using the division equation 30 ÷ 5 = 6.

Refine Ideas About the Meaning of Division

APPLY IT

Complete these problems on your own.

1 EXPLAIN

Maddy draws this array of stars to show 8 ÷ 4.
What did she do wrong?

2 CREATE

Write a story problem that can be solved using the division
equation 16 ÷ 2 = 8.

3 COMPARE

David and Mitch each buy a box of pears at the grocery store.
Look at how each box divides the pears into equal groups.

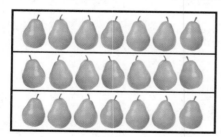 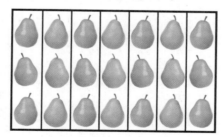

What is the same about the two boxes of pears?

What is different about the way the boxes divide the pears
into groups?

PAIR/SHARE

Discuss your solutions for
these three problems with
a partner.

Use what you have learned to complete problem 4.

4 Cory has 20 crayons. He wants to give the same number of crayons to each of his friends.

Part A Write a problem about Cory's crayons that can be solved using division.

Part B Find the solution to your problem using pictures or an array. Then write the division equation that shows the solution to your problem.

5 MATH JOURNAL

Find 45 ÷ 9 by describing two ways you can model it using equal groups. Then tell how 9 means something different in each model.

Understand How Multiplication and Division Are Connected

Dear Family,
This week your child is exploring how multiplication and division are related.

Multiplication and division can both describe problems where there are equal groups. Either one can be used to solve a problem like the one below.

Lola buys 16 apples. She puts the same number of apples in 4 bags. How many apples does she put in each bag?

You know the total (16 apples) and the number of groups (4 bags). You need to find the number in each group.

A multiplication equation for the problem is:

$$4 \times ? = 16$$

$$4 \times 4 = 16$$

A division equation for the problem is:

$$16 \div 4 = ?$$

$$16 \div 4 = 4$$

Lola puts 4 apples in each bag.

Invite your child to share what he or she knows about how multiplication and division are related by doing the following activity together.

ACTIVITY MULTIPLICATION AND DIVISION

Do this activity with your child to explore how multiplication and division are connected.

Materials 12 to 20 of one small item, such as pennies, toothpicks, or toy bricks

Do this activity with your child to demonstrate how multiplication and division are related.

- Collect a set of small items such as toothpicks. Act out problems like the one below.

- Count out 10 toothpicks. Ask your child to consider the question: *How many toothpicks will be in each pile if I put these 10 toothpicks into 2 equal piles?*

1. Ask him or her to write both a multiplication equation and a division equation for the problem.

2. Have your child group the toothpicks into 2 equal groups to find how many are in each and fill in the value for ? in the equations they wrote.

- Repeat but invite your child to give you a problem. Write a multiplication equation and a division equation and have your child check your work.

- After three or four examples, see if your child can talk to you about how multiplication and division are alike. Look for an understanding that both operations can represent equal groups.

Answers: **1.** $2 \times ? = 10$ and $10 \div 2 = ?$; **2.** $2 \times 5 = 10$ and $10 \div 2 = 5$

Explore How Multiplication and Division Are Connected

How are multiplication and division related?

Learning Target
• Understand division as an unknown-factor problem.
SMP 1, 2, 3, 4, 5, 6, 7

MODEL IT

Solve the problems below.

1. **a.** Draw an array of 4 rows of 3 pennies to the right.

   b. Write a multiplication equation for your array.

   c. Now break your array into 4 equal groups. Write a division equation for this array.

   d. What three numbers do both equations use? Tell what each number represents.

2. The result of division is called the **quotient**. Circle the quotient in your division equation in problem 1c. Circle the same number in your multiplication equation in problem 1b. Did you circle a factor or the product in your multiplication equation?

DISCUSS IT

• How do you and your partner think the multiplication and division equations are alike and different?

• I think multiplication and division are related because . . .

MODEL IT
Complete the problems below.

3 Nick buys 20 stickers. He puts the same number of stickers on each of 5 pages in his scrapbook. Draw the stickers Nick puts on the pages. Write a division equation and a multiplication equation for this problem.

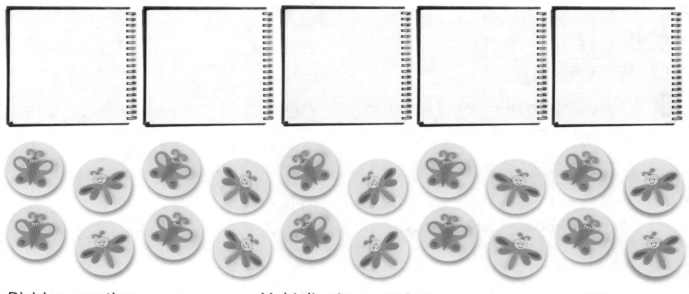

Division equation:

Multiplication equation:

....

....

4 Explain how you could use a multiplication equation to find 20 ÷ 5.

DISCUSS IT

• What numbers are used in both the multiplication and division equations in problem 3? What do the numbers mean?

• I think I can use multiplication to help me divide because . . .

5 REFLECT

How is division doing the reverse of multiplication?

....

....

....

Prepare for Exploring How Multiplication and Division Are Connected

1 Think about what you know about division. Fill in each box. Use words, numbers, and pictures. Show as many ideas as you can.

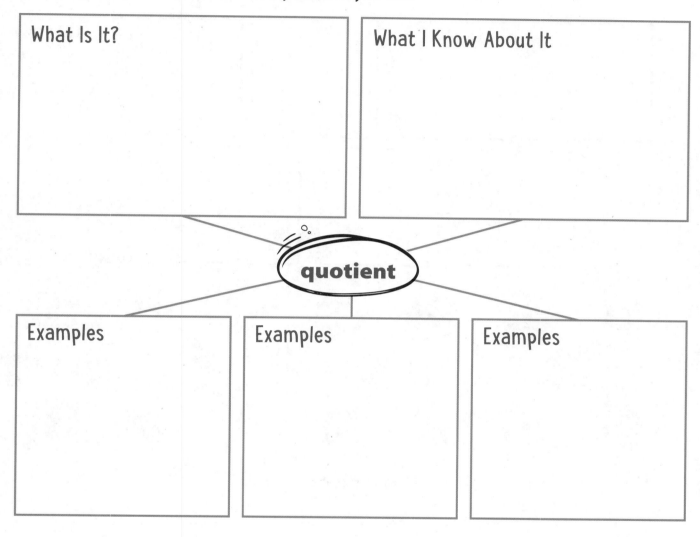

What Is It?

What I Know About It

quotient

Examples

Examples

Examples

2 Write a multiplication equation and a division equation for the array.

Lesson 11 Understand How Multiplication and Division Are Connected   **241**

Solve.

3 Yuki has 21 flowers. She puts the same number of flowers on each of 7 pages in her scrapbook to dry them. Draw the flowers Yuki puts on the pages. Write a division equation and a multiplication equation for this problem.

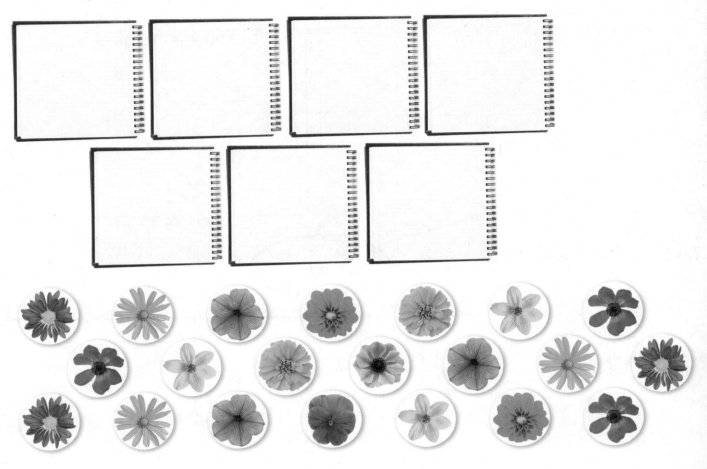

Division equation:

....

Multiplication equation:

....

4 Explain how you could use a multiplication equation to find 21 ÷ 7.

5 How is multiplication doing the reverse of division?

Develop Understanding of How Multiplication and Division Are Connected

MODEL IT: MULTIPLICATION AND DIVISION SITUATIONS

Read the following problem. Then try problems 1–3.

A pet store has 18 hamsters. The shop owner wants to put 3 hamsters in each cage. How many cages does the shop owner need for all the hamsters?

1 Draw a model using equal groups or an array to show the problem.

2 **a.** Write a division equation for the problem. Use a ? for the unknown number.

b. Write a multiplication equation for the problem. Use a ? for the unknown number.

3 The shop owner needs .... cages.

MODEL IT: MULTIPLICATION AND DIVISION FACTS

Find the value of ? to complete each fact.

 4 $24 \div 3 = ?$

$3 \times ? = 24$

$? = \text{................}$

 5 $? \times 9 = 54$

$54 \div ? = 9$

$? = \text{................}$

DISCUSS IT

• How did you find the missing number in each fact?

• I can think of a division fact as a multiplication problem because . . .

CONNECT IT

Complete the problems below.

6 How can you use the three numbers in a division equation to write the related multiplication equations?

7 Use the numbers 7, 8, and 56 to write two multiplication equations and two division equations.

Practice How Multiplication and Division Are Connected

Study how the Example shows one way to relate multiplication and division. Then solve problems 1–12.

EXAMPLE

Marta bakes **15** muffins. She puts an equal number of muffins in **3** baskets.

She thinks, **3** times what number equals **15**?

$3 \times ? = 15$

$3 \times 5 = 15$

So, Marta puts **5** muffins in each basket.

1 Draw an array of 15 muffins in 3 rows.

2 How many muffins did you put in each row? ....

3 Fill in the blanks to write a division equation for the array you drew.

.... ÷ .... = ...

Use the array to complete the equations.

4 $2 \times$ .... $= 12$ and $12 \div 2 =$ ....

5 $6 \times$ .... $= 12$ and $12 \div 6 =$ ....

> ### Vocabulary
>
> **divide** to separate into equal groups and find the number in each group or the number of groups.
>
> **array** a set of objects arranged in equal rows and equal columns.

Use the numbers 3, 6, and 18 to write the equations for problems 6–8.

6 There are 18 fish. Each bowl holds 6 fish.

Write an equation that shows the number of bowls.

.... = ...

7 There are 18 fish. An equal number of fish are in 3 bowls.

Write an equation that shows the number of fish in each bowl.

.... = ...

8 There are 3 bowls. 6 fish are in each bowl.

Write two different equations that show the total number of fish.

.... = ...

.... = ...

This array shows that 6 × 7 = 42. Use this fact to complete the equations in problems 9–12.

9 6 × 7 = ...   7 × 6 = ...

10 6 × .... = 42   42 = ... × 6

11 42 ÷ 6 = ...   42 ÷ .... = 6

12 .... = 42 ÷ 7   7 = 42 ÷ ....

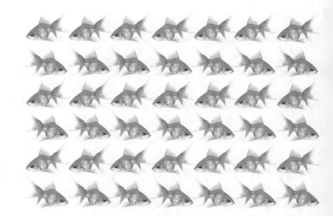

Refine Ideas About How Multiplication and Division Are Connected

APPLY IT

Complete these problems on your own.

1 IDENTIFY

Ed plants the same number of flowers in each pot at the right. Write two multiplication equations and two division equations that this picture shows.

2 EXPLAIN

Yasmin sees $63 \div ? = 7$ and thinks, "There are 63 things in all that are divided into groups. There are 7 in each group." Explain how Yasmin can use multiplication to help her find the number of groups.

3 ANALYZE

Marissa has 4 boxes of markers with 6 markers in each box. She wrote the following equations:

$$4 \times 6 = 24 \qquad 6 \times 4 = 24 \qquad 24 \div 4 = 6 \qquad 24 \div 6 = 4$$

Circle the number in each equation that shows the total number of markers. Put a box around the number in each equation that shows the number of groups. Underline the number in each equation that shows the number in each group.

PAIR/SHARE

Discuss your solutions for these three problems with a partner.

Use what you have learned to complete problem 4.

 Look at the division equation $15 \div 5 = ?$.

Part A Write a multiplication equation you can use to solve this division problem. Use a ? for the unknown number.

Part B Draw a model that could help you solve the division problem. Then solve the problem.

$15 \div 5 =$ ....

5 MATH JOURNAL

Write a story problem that can be modeled by the equation $35 \div 7 = ?$. Explain how you can use multiplication to solve this problem. Then solve the problem.

Multiplication and Division Facts

Dear Family,

This week your child is learning about multiplication and division fact families.

Fact families for multiplication and division are groups of related equations that use the same numbers. Here is one example:

$$3 \times 7 = 21 \qquad 7 \times 3 = 21 \qquad 21 \div 3 = 7 \qquad 21 \div 7 = 3$$

Knowing about fact families can help sometimes when you are trying to solve a problem. If you know the answer to any one of these, you know the answer to all of them.

$$30 \div 5 = \square \qquad 30 \div \square = 5 \qquad 5 \times \square = 30 \qquad \square \times 5 = 30$$

You might remember that $5 \times 6 = 30$. Then you also know $30 \div 5 = 6$, $30 \div 6 = 5$, and $6 \times 5 = 30$.

Your child may use a **multiplication table** to help learn multiplication facts.

This multiplication table shows all the facts up to 10×10. The numbers that are circled show that $5 \times 6 = 30$.

Invite your child to share what he or she knows about multiplication and division fact families by doing the following activity together.

×	1	2	3	4	5	6	7	8	9	10
1	1	2	3	4	5	6	7	8	9	10
2	2	4	6	8	10	12	14	16	18	20
3	3	6	9	12	15	18	21	24	27	30
4	4	8	12	16	20	24	28	32	36	40
5	5	10	15	20	25	30	35	40	45	50
6	6	12	18	24	30	36	42	48	54	60
7	7	14	21	28	35	42	49	56	63	70
8	8	16	24	32	40	48	56	64	72	80
9	9	18	27	36	45	54	63	72	81	90
10	10	20	30	40	50	60	70	80	90	100

ACTIVITY FACT FAMILY

Do this activity with your child to explore multiplication and division facts.

Materials scissors, index cards (optional), pencil (optional)

Play this game to practice recognizing facts that are in the same family.

Create fact family cards by cutting out the facts below or by writing the facts on index cards.

- Each player chooses one of the single-number cards (42 or 56) and places it faceup in front of him or her. Shuffle the fact cards. Place them facedown in two rows with four cards in each row.

- Players take turns flipping over two cards.

  - If *both* the cards are in the same fact family as the player's number card, then the player keeps the cards.

  - If either of the cards is *not* in the same fact family as the player's number card, then the player flips the cards back over.

- The first player to find the four cards that make a fact family that goes with his or her number card wins.

- Create a new game. Choose two numbers from 1 to 10 and use the multiplication table to write two new fact families on index cards or slips of paper.

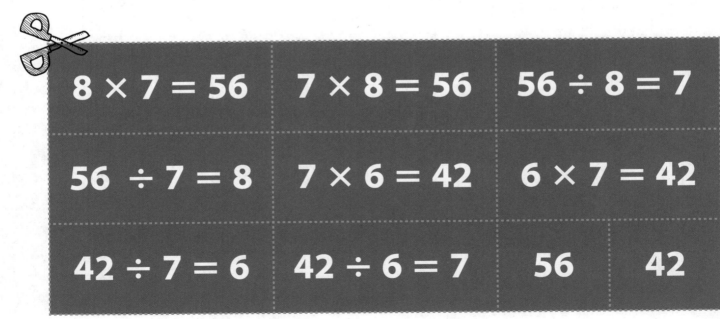

$8 \times 7 = 56$	$7 \times 8 = 56$	$56 \div 8 = 7$
$56 \div 7 = 8$	$7 \times 6 = 42$	$6 \times 7 = 42$
$42 \div 7 = 6$	$42 \div 6 = 7$	56 42

Explore Multiplication and Division Facts

You learned that multiplication and division are related. In this lesson you will see how multiplication can help you with division facts. Use what you know to try to solve the problem below.

> **Kenny has 24 marbles. He puts the same number of marbles into each of 3 bags. How many marbles are in each bag?**

TRY IT

 Math Toolkit
- connecting cubes
- counters
- buttons
- cups
- multiplication models
- number lines

DISCUSS IT

Ask your partner: How did you get started?

Tell your partner:
I knew . . . so I . . .

CONNECT IT

1 LOOK BACK

How many marbles are in each bag? Explain how you can prove you are right.

2 LOOK AHEAD

Fact families for multiplication and division are groups of related equations. All the equations, or facts, use the same numbers.

If you know one fact in a family, you can find all the others.

a. Say you need to solve $\square \div 9 = 6$. You can write the facts in this family to find one that you might know. Use the array to help you complete this fact family.

$6 \times 9 =$ ....

$9 \times 6 =$ ....

.... $\div 6 = 9$

.... $\div 9 = 6$

b. Look back at the problem on the previous page. Write the complete fact family using the three numbers for this situation.

....

....

3 REFLECT

How are the multiplication facts in the fact families above alike? How are they different? How are the division facts alike and different?

....

....

....

Prepare for Multiplication and Division Facts

1 Think about what you know about multiplication and division. Fill in each box.
Use words, numbers, and pictures. Show as many ideas as you can.

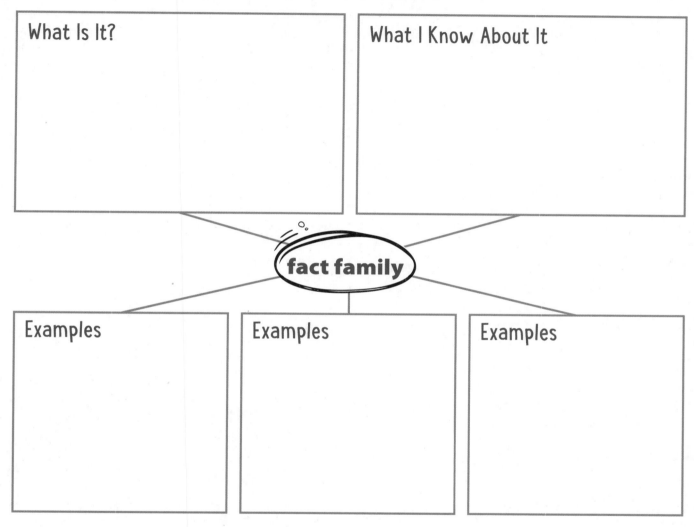

What Is It?

What I Know About It

fact family

Examples

Examples

Examples

2 How can you use fact families to help find 40 ÷ 8? Explain.

3 Solve the problem. Show your work.

Jada has 28 muffins. She puts the same number of muffins into each of 4 boxes. How many muffins are in each box?

Solution ....

4 Check your answer. Show your work.

Develop **Working with Division Facts**

Read and try to solve the problem below.

> Jo knows nickels are worth 5 cents, and she needs 40 cents altogether. She wants to find how many nickels she needs. Jo writes:
>
> $40 \div 5 = \square$
>
> **How many nickels does Jo need?**

TRY IT

 Math Toolkit
- counters
- buttons
- cups
- 1-centimeter grid paper
- multiplication models
- number lines

DISCUSS IT

Ask your partner: Why did you choose this strategy?

Tell your partner: I started by . . .

Explore different ways to find the unknown number in a division fact.

> **Jo knows nickels are worth 5 cents, and she needs 40 cents altogether. She wants to find how many nickels she needs. Jo writes:**
>
> **40 ÷ 5 = ☐**
>
> **How many nickels does Jo need?**

MODEL IT

You can use a number line to help you understand the problem.

Skip-count by **fives** to find the answer. Start at 0 and jump by fives until you get to 40.

MODEL IT

You can use fact families and multiplication facts you know.

Here are the facts in this family:

$$5 \times \boxed{} = 40 \qquad \boxed{} \times 5 = 40 \qquad 40 \div \boxed{} = 5 \qquad 40 \div 5 = \boxed{}$$

Write the multiplication facts for 5:

$1 \times 5 = 5$	$2 \times 5 = 10$	$3 \times 5 = 15$	$4 \times 5 = 20$	$5 \times 5 = 25$
$6 \times 5 = 30$	$7 \times 5 = 35$	$8 \times 5 = 40$	$9 \times 5 = 45$	$10 \times 5 = 50$

Look for the fact that has the numbers you know from the fact family, 5 and 40. Use that fact to fill in the unknown numbers above.

CONNECT IT

Now you will use the problem from the previous page to help you understand how to use fact families to find an unknown number in a division fact.

1 Mo wants to know how many nickels he needs to make 45 cents. He writes $45 \div \square = 5$. What other division fact can he write to model this problem?

2 Write the two multiplication facts that are in the same fact family. Use $\square$ for the unknown number.

3 Look at the list of multiplication facts for 5 on the previous page. Which fact will help Mo answer his division problem? How many nickels does Mo need?

4 Explain how you know which multiplication fact you can use to help you find the unknown number in a division fact.

5 REFLECT

Look back at your **Try It**, strategies by classmates, and **Model Its**. Which models or strategies do you like best for finding unknown numbers in multiplication and division facts? Explain.

....

....

....

....

APPLY IT

Use what you just learned to solve these problems.

6 Use the number line to solve $24 \div 4 = \square$.
Show your work.

Solution ....

7 Write the unknown product. Then complete this fact family.

$2 \times 3 = $ ....

....

....

....

8 Write two multiplication facts Brice can use to solve $\square \div 3 = 7$.

Practice Working with Division Facts

Study the Example showing how a drawing can help you understand division facts. Then solve problems 1–9.

EXAMPLE

Here is an array of 15 fish.

There are 3 rows with 5 fish in each row.

The fact family describes the array in different ways.

3 × 5 = 15   15 ÷ 5 = 3

5 × 3 = 15   15 ÷ 3 = 5

Write one of the facts from the list above that can help you solve problems 1–3.

1 How many fish are there altogether?

2 15 fish swim in 3 equal rows. How many fish are in each row?

3 15 fish swim in rows of 5 fish. How many rows of fish are there?

4 You know that 4 × 9 = 36. Write the whole fact family.
Use the numbers 4, 9, and 36.

.... × .... = ...

.... × .... = ...

.... ÷ .... = ...

.... ÷ .... = ...

5 Sienna draws 18 squares in two equal groups of 9. Which division equation does her drawing show?

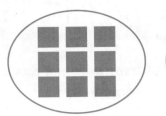

Ⓐ $9 \div 3 = 3$

Ⓑ $18 \div 6 = 3$

Ⓒ $18 \div 2 = 9$

Ⓓ $6 \div 2 = 3$

6 Write two different division equations about the array.

.... ÷ .... = ...

.... ÷ .... = ...

Chee has 24 trading cards. He gives away all his cards to friends. He gives 8 cards to each friend.

7 Use the number line to show how you can find how many friends Chee gave cards to.

Solution ....

8 Write two different division facts for the story.

.... and ....

9 Write the multiplication facts that belong to the same fact family.

.... and ....

Develop Using a Multiplication Table

Read and try to solve the problem below.

Complete the facts.

$2 \times \square = 10$ $24 \div 6 = \square$ $\square \times 6 = 48$ $\square \div 1 = 8$

TRY IT

 Math Toolkit
- connecting cubes
- counters
- multiplication tables
- 1-centimeter grid paper
- multiplication models
- number lines

 **DISCUSS IT**

Ask your partner: Do you agree with me? Why or why not?

Tell your partner: The strategy I used to find the answer is . . .

Explore different ways to use a multiplication table to complete multiplication and division facts.

> **Complete the facts.**
>
> $2 \times \square = 10$ $24 \div 6 = \square$ $\square \times 6 = 48$ $\square \div 1 = 8$

PICTURE IT
You can use a multiplication table to find the numbers in multiplication and division fact families.

A **multiplication table** shows both multiplication and division fact families.

×	1	2	3	4	5	6	7	8	9	10
1	1	2	3	4	5	6	7	8	9	10
2	2	4	6	8	10	12	14	16	18	20
3	3	6	9	12	15	18	21	24	27	30
4	4	8	12	16	20	24	28	32	36	40
5	5	10	15	20	25	30	35	40	45	50
6	6	12	18	24	30	36	42	48	54	60
7	7	14	21	28	35	42	49	56	63	70
8	8	16	24	32	40	48	56	64	72	80
9	9	18	27	36	45	54	63	72	81	90
10	10	20	30	40	50	60	70	80	90	100

MODEL IT
Use the table above to complete the fact family.

The multiplication table shows the three numbers that belong in the fact family for $2 \times \square = 10$. Look at the row for 2. Go across to find 10. Then look up to the top of that column to find the third number in the fact family. Fill in the blanks below.

$2 \times \underline{\hspace{1.5in}} = 10$ $10 \div 2 = \underline{\hspace{1.5in}}$

$\underline{\hspace{1.5in}} \times 2 = 10$ $10 \div \underline{\hspace{1.5in}} = 2$

CONNECT IT

Now you will use the problem from the previous page to help you understand how to use a multiplication table to complete a multiplication or division fact.

1 Look at the multiplication table. What are the three numbers in the fact family for $24 \div 6 = \square$?

Now fill in the blank: $24 \div 6 =$ ....

2 What are the three numbers in the fact family for $\square \times 6 = 48$?

Now fill in the blank: .... $\times 6 = 48$

3 What are the three numbers in the fact family for $\square \div 1 = 8$?

Fill in the blank: .... $\div 1 = 8$

4 Explain how you can use a multiplication table to find the three numbers in any fact family.

5 REFLECT

Look back at your **Try It**, strategies by classmates, and **Picture It** and **Model It**. Which models or strategies do you like best for completing multiplication and division facts? Explain.

....

....

....

....

....

APPLY IT

Use what you just learned to solve these problems.

6 Use the multiplication table to write the equations in the fact family that includes 42 and 6. Show your work.

×	1	2	3	4	5	6	7	8	9	10
1	1	2	3	4	5	6	7	8	9	10
2	2	4	6	8	10	12	14	16	18	20
3	3	6	9	12	15	18	21	24	27	30
4	4	8	12	16	20	24	28	32	36	40
5	5	10	15	20	25	30	35	40	45	50
6	6	12	18	24	30	36	42	48	54	60
7	7	14	21	28	35	42	49	56	63	70
8	8	16	24	32	40	48	56	64	72	80
9	9	18	27	36	45	54	63	72	81	90
10	10	20	30	40	50	60	70	80	90	100

Solution ....

7 Fill in the blank.

$56 \div$ .... $= 8$

8 Jan and Jon pick 18 apples. They share them equally. Which facts could be used to find the number of apples each person gets?

Ⓐ $6 \times 3 = 18$

Ⓑ $2 \times 9 = 18$

Ⓒ $18 \div 2 = 9$

Ⓓ $18 \div 3 = 6$

Ⓔ $18 \div 9 = 2$

Practice Using a Multiplication Table

Study the Example showing how a multiplication table can help you solve multiplication and division problems. Then solve problems 1–6.

EXAMPLE

You can use the multiplication table to multiply or divide.

Look at the green row of products for 4. Look at the green column of products for 6.

You can see how $4 \times 6 = 24$ is related to $24 \div 4 = 6$ and related to $24 \div 6 = 4$.

×	1	2	3	4	5	6	7	8	9	10
1	1	2	3	4	5	6	7	8	9	10
2	2	4	6	8	10	12	14	16	18	20
3	3	6	9	12	15	18	21	24	27	30
4	4	8	12	16	20	24	28	32	36	40
5	5	10	15	20	25	30	35	40	45	50
6	6	12	18	24	30	36	42	48	54	60
7	7	14	21	28	35	42	49	56	63	70
8	8	16	24	32	40	48	56	64	72	80
9	9	18	27	36	45	54	63	72	81	90
10	10	20	30	40	50	60	70	80	90	100

1 Write the fact family for the three numbers 6, 4, and 24.

.... × .... = ... ÷ .... = ...

.... × .... = ... ÷ .... = ...

2 Use the table or your fact family in problem 1 to fill in the unknown numbers.

$4 \times$ .... $= 24$ $24 \div 6 =$ ....

.... $\times 4 = 24$ .... $\div 4 = 6$

3 Find 21 on the table above. Use the table to fill in the unknown numbers in this fact family.

$7 \times$ .... $= 21$ $21 \div 3 =$ ....

.... $\times 7 = 21$ $21 \div$ .... $= 3$

Use the multiplication table to solve problems 4–6.

×	1	2	3	4	5	6	7	8	9	10
1	1	2	3	4	5	6	7	8	9	10
2	2	4	6	8	10	12	14	16	18	20
3	3	6	9	12	15	18	21	24	27	30
4	4	8	12	16	20	24	28	32	36	40
5	5	10	15	20	25	30	35	40	45	50
6	6	12	18	24	30	36	42	48	54	60
7	7	14	21	28	35	42	49	56	63	70
8	8	16	24	32	40	48	56	64	72	80
9	9	18	27	36	45	54	63	72	81	90
10	10	20	30	40	50	60	70	80	90	100

4 What are the three numbers in the fact family for $28 \div 4 = \square$? ....

Write the fact family.

.... × .... = ... ÷ .... = ...

.... × .... = ... ÷ .... = ...

5 What are the three numbers in the fact family for $6 \times \square = 42$? ....

Write the fact family.

.... × .... = ... ÷ .... = ...

.... × .... = ... ÷ .... = ...

6 What are the three numbers in the fact family for $\square \div 6 = 8$? ....

Write the fact family.

.... × .... = ... ÷ .... = ...

.... × .... = ... ÷ .... = ...

Refine Working with Multiplication and Division Facts

Complete the Example below. Then solve problems 1–9.

EXAMPLE

Today some students will give an oral report. The teacher is planning to have all the reports done in 15 minutes. Each student will get 3 minutes. How many students will give reports? Solve $3 \times \square = 15$.

Look at how you could show your work using a number line.

5 jumps of 3

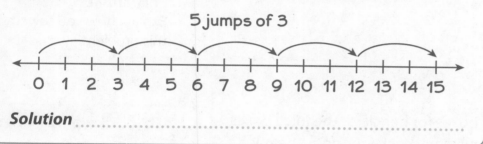

Solution ....

Each jump on the number line shows the amount of time a student gets.

PAIR/SHARE
What other equations can be used to solve this problem?

APPLY IT

1 Solve $35 \div \square = 5$. Show your work.

How can you find the third number in this fact family?

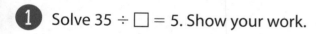

PAIR/SHARE
What are the other facts that belong to this fact family?

Solution ....

2 Solve $4 \times 9 = \square$. Show your work.

Are you looking for a factor or a product?

Solution ....

PAIR/SHARE
Explain how you solved this problem.

3 Mrs. Tobin needs 30 juice boxes for her class. The juice boxes come in packages of 6. How many packages does she need? Solve $30 \div 6 = \square$.

Ⓐ 4

Ⓑ 5

Ⓒ 6

Ⓓ 36

Pia chose Ⓓ as the correct answer. How did she get that answer?

Do you know a multiplication fact that can help you solve this problem?

PAIR/SHARE
Does Pia's answer make sense?

4 Which equation does NOT belong to the same fact family as $12 \div \square = 4$?

Ⓐ $\square \times 4 = 12$

Ⓑ $\square \times 2 = 12$

Ⓒ $4 \times \square = 12$

Ⓓ $12 \div 4 = \square$

5 Which fact can you use to solve $\square \div 5 = 4$?

Ⓐ $5 \times 5 = 25$

Ⓑ $4 \times 5 = 20$

Ⓒ $5 + 4 = 9$

Ⓓ $6 \times 4 = 24$

6 Does putting the number 8 in the box make each equation true?

	Yes	No
$9 \times \square = 64$	Ⓐ	Ⓑ
$6 \times \square = 48$	Ⓒ	Ⓓ
$56 \div \square = 8$	Ⓔ	Ⓕ
$32 \div \square = 4$	Ⓖ	Ⓗ

7 Some fact families have only one multiplication equation and one division equation. Fill in the blanks to show an example.

.... × .... = ...

.... ÷ .... = ...

8 Sasha has 32 stickers to use in her scrapbook. The scrapbook has 8 pages, and she wants to put the same number of stickers on each page. Write two multiplication facts Sasha can use to find how many stickers to put on each page. How many stickers can Sasha put on each page?

Solution ....

9 MATH JOURNAL

Draw a picture to show a fact family. Then write the fact family.

☑ SELF CHECK Go back to the Unit 2 Opener and see what you can check off.

Understand Patterns

Dear Family,
This week your child is exploring patterns.

A **pattern** is a series of numbers or shapes that follow a rule to repeat or change.

In this addition table, there is a diagonal pattern that has all 6s in it.

+	0	1	2	3	4	5	6
0	0	1	2	3	4	5	6
1	1	2	3	4	5	6	7
2	2	3	4	5	6	7	8
3	3	4	5	6	7	8	9
4	4	5	6	7	8	9	10
5	5	6	7	8	9	10	11
6	6	7	8	9	10	11	12

The table to the right shows the addends used to make these sums of 6.

The rule for this pattern has two parts:

- The addends in the first column increase by one. These addends are along the left side of the addition table.

- The addends in the second column decrease by one. These addends are across the top of the addition table.

Addend	Addend	Sum
0	6	6
1	5	6
2	4	6
3	3	6
4	2	6
5	1	6
6	0	6

Invite your child to share what he or she knows about exploring patterns by doing the following activity together.

ACTIVITY   EXPLORING PATTERNS

Do this activity with your child to understand patterns.

Materials red crayon or marker

Use the hundred chart below to explore patterns with your child.

- Have your child lightly color these numbers red: 5, 10, 15, 20, and 25.

1	2	3	4	5	6	7	8	9	10
11	12	13	14	15	16	17	18	19	20
21	22	23	24	25	26	27	28	29	30
31	32	33	34	35	36	37	38	39	40
41	42	43	44	45	46	47	48	49	50
51	52	53	54	55	56	57	58	59	60
61	62	63	64	65	66	67	68	69	70
71	72	73	74	75	76	77	78	79	80
81	82	83	84	85	86	87	88	89	90
91	92	93	94	95	96	97	98	99	100

1. Together, look for and describe patterns you see in the numbers that are colored.
2. Ask your child what the rule is for coloring the next number red.
3. Ask your child to use his or her rule to tell what the next number in the pattern will be. Have your child color all the numbers in this pattern red.

- Challenge yourselves to find other ways to describe the same pattern. There are usually several different ways to describe a pattern!

Answers:
1. Possible answers: The colored numbers form vertical lines in the hundred chart; the numbers alternate odd, even.
2. Possible answers: Color every fifth number; skip-count by fives; leave four white and color the next.
3. 30

Explore Patterns

What is a pattern?

MODEL IT

Complete the problems below.

1 A **pattern** is something that repeats. Look at the pattern of shapes below. Continue the pattern by drawing the shape that you think comes next. Explain why you drew that shape.

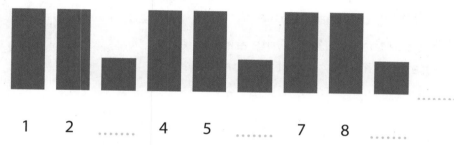

1   2   4   5   7   8   ......

2 Look at the numbers under the shapes in problem 1.

a. Write the missing numbers in the blanks under the squares. Write the number pattern below that you started for the squares.

........, ..., ..., . . .

b. What **rule** could you use to find the next number in this pattern?

MODEL IT
Complete the problems below.

3 A number chart can help you see patterns. On the hundred chart below, shade all the numbers that would be in the pattern from problem 2a on the previous page.

1	2	3	4	5	6	7	8	9	10
11	12	13	14	15	16	17	18	19	20
21	22	23	24	25	26	27	28	29	30

4 Circle the numbers 9, 18, and 27 in the chart above.

a. Describe any pattern and rule that you see. Write and circle the next number in this pattern in the correct box on the chart.

b. Will the numbers in this pattern also be shaded? Why or why not?

DISCUSS IT

- Can you and your partner find other patterns in the chart?

- I think putting numbers in a chart helps you see different patterns because . . .

5 REFLECT

How can you show something is a pattern?

....

....

....

Prepare for Exploring Patterns

1 Think about what you know about patterns. Fill in each box. Use words, numbers, and pictures. Show as many ideas as you can.

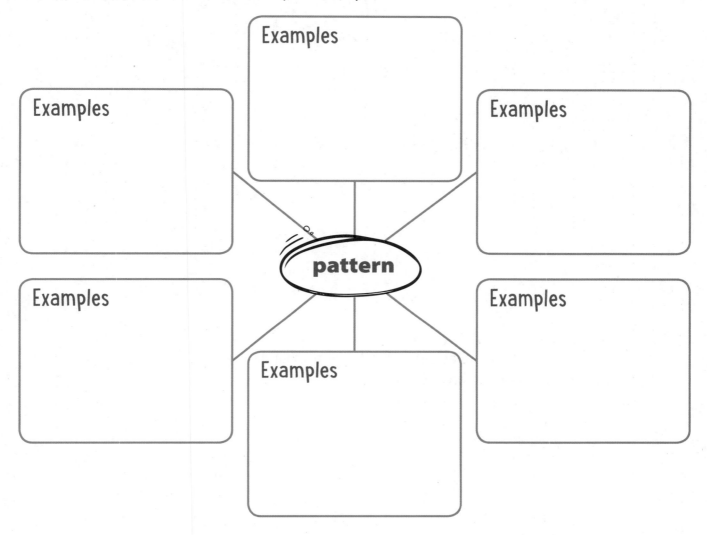

Examples

Examples

Examples

Examples

Examples

Examples

pattern

2 Look at the pattern of shapes below. Continue the pattern by drawing the shape that you think comes next. Explain why you drew that shape.

Solve.

3 On the chart below, shade all the numbers that would be in the pattern
2, 4, 6, 8, 10, …

1	2	3	4	5	6	7	8	9	10
11	12	13	14	15	16	17	18	19	20
21	22	23	24	25	26	27	28	29	30

4 What rule could you use to find the next number in this pattern?

5 Circle the numbers 8, 16, and 24 in the chart above. Describe any pattern and
rule that you see in the circled numbers. Write and circle the next number in
this pattern in the correct box on the chart.

6 Will the numbers in the pattern from problem 5 also be shaded? Why or
why not?

Develop Understanding of Patterns

MODEL IT: ADDITION PATTERNS

Use an addition table to complete these two problems.

1 **a.** Shade all the odd sums in the table.

   b. Describe any patterns you see.

   c. Look at the addends for each problem with an odd sum. Are they even or odd?

   d. Why do you think this pattern happens?

+	1	2	3	4	5	6
1	2	3	4	5	6	7
2	3	4	5	6	7	8
3	4	5	6	7	8	9
4	5	6	7	8	9	10
5	6	7	8	9	10	11
6	7	8	9	10	11	12

2 **a.** Shade all the even sums in the table.

   b. Look at the addends for each problem with an even sum. Are they even or odd?

   c. Why do you think this pattern happens?

+	1	2	3	4	5	6
1	2	3	4	5	6	7
2	3	4	5	6	7	8
3	4	5	6	7	8	9
4	5	6	7	8	9	10
5	6	7	8	9	10	11
6	7	8	9	10	11	12

DISCUSS IT

• Did you both explain the patterns in the same way?

• I can find a lot of patterns in an addition table because . . .

MODEL IT: MULTIPLICATION PATTERNS
Use the multiplication table to complete the problem.

3   **a.** Shade all the even products in the table.

    b. Describe any patterns you see.

×	1	2	3	4	5	6
1	1	2	3	4	5	6
2	2	4	6	8	10	12
3	3	6	9	12	15	18
4	4	8	12	16	20	24
5	5	10	15	20	25	30
6	6	12	18	24	30	36

    c. Look at the factors for each problem with an even product. Are they even or odd?

    d. Why do you think this pattern happens?

CONNECT IT
Complete the problems below.

4   How are multiplication and addition patterns alike? How are they different?

> ## DISCUSS IT
> • Did you and your partner explain the pattern in problem 3 in the same way?
>
> • I think I can find a lot of other patterns in a multiplication table because . . .

5   Find the two sums of 11 in the addition table on the previous page. What pattern do you see in the addends? Does this same pattern happen with other sums that show up more than once on the table? Explain.

Practice Finding Patterns

**Study how the Example shows using an addition table to find patterns.
Then solve problems 1–5.**

EXAMPLE

Add the sums in the opposite corners of each
outlined square on the addition table. What pattern
do you notice? Why do you think this happens?

+	1	2	3	4	5	6
1	2	3	4	5	6	7
2	3	4	5	6	7	8
3	4	5	6	7	8	9
4	5	6	7	8	9	10
5	6	7	8	9	10	11
6	7	8	9	10	11	12

$3 + 5 = 8$ $5 + 7 = 12$ $7 + 9 = 16$
$4 + 4 = 8$ $6 + 6 = 12$ $8 + 8 = 16$

The corner sums within a square are the same.
One set of opposite corners always matches, and
the other set always has a number 1 greater and
a number 1 less than the matching numbers,
so the sums are equal.

1 Look at the two diagonals of shaded sums on the
addition table. Describe at least two patterns you see.
Explain why one of the patterns happens.

+	1	2	3	4	5	6	7
1	2	3	4	5	6	7	8
2	3	4	5	6	7	8	9
3	4	5	6	7	8	9	10
4	5	6	7	8	9	10	11
5	6	7	8	9	10	11	12

2 Without actually adding, tell whether the sum of 583 and 278 will be odd or
even. How do you know?

3 Look at the shaded groups of three numbers on different rows of the multiplication table.

a. For each group, how does the number in the middle compare to the sum of the two end numbers?

×	0	1	2	3	4	5	6
0	0	0	0	0	0	0	0
1	0	1	2	3	4		6
2	0		4	6	8	10	12
3	0	3		9	12		18
4	0	4		12	16	20	24
5	0	5	10	15	20	25	30
6	0	6	12		24		36

b. Use the pattern from Part a to fill in the missing numbers in the table.

4 Look at the rows and columns for 0 and 1 in the multiplication table.

a. Look at the row and column for 0. Describe a pattern in the products. Explain why this pattern happens.

×	0	1	2	3	4	5	6	7	8
0	0	0	0	0	0	0	0	0	0
1	0	1	2	3	4	5	6	7	8
2	0	2	4	6	8	10	12	14	16
3	0	3	6	9	12	15	18	21	24
4	0	4	8	12	16	20	24	28	32
5	0	5	10	15	20	25	30	35	40
6	0	6	12	18	24	30	36	42	48
7	0	7	14	21	28	35	42	49	56
8	0	8	16	24	32	40	48	56	64

b. Look at the row and column for 1. Describe a pattern in the products. Explain why this pattern happens.

5 Without actually multiplying, tell whether the product of 8 × 6 will be odd or even. How do you know?

Refine Ideas About Patterns

APPLY IT

Complete these problems on your own.

1 EXPLAIN

Izzy noticed a pattern in the addition table: one diagonal that had all 4s in it. Fill in the chart below the table to show the addends.

Explain how the sum, 4, stays the same while the addends change in each line of the addition table.

+	0	1	2	3	4
0	0	1	2	3	4
1	1	2	3	4	5
2	2	3	4	5	6
3	3	4	5	6	7
4	4	5	6	7	8

Addend	Addend	Sum
0		4
	3	4
	2	4
3		4
4		4

2 EXAMINE

Jace counts to 50 by fives. Annabel counts to 50 by tens. What numbers do they both say? Explain why.

3 DETERMINE

Booth says an odd factor times an odd factor will always equal an even product. Is he correct? Explain.

PAIR/SHARE

Discuss your solutions for these three problems with a partner.

Use what you have learned to complete problem 4.

4 Look at the multiplication table below.

×	0	1	2	3	4	5	6	7	8	9
0	0	0	0	0	0	0	0	0	0	0
1	0	1	2	3	4	5	6	7	8	9
2	0	2	4	6						18
3	0		6	9	12	15	18	21	24	27
4	0	4		12		20		28		36
5	0	5		15		25		35		45

Part A Fill in the missing numbers in the table.

Part B Note the shaded products. What pattern do you notice about the factors of the products that are shaded the same color?

Part C Explain why the pattern happens.

5 MATH JOURNAL

Find and describe at least two more patterns in a multiplication table.

In this unit you learned to . . .

Skill	Lesson
Explain multiplication using equal groups and arrays.	4, 5, 6, 7
Break apart numbers to make multiplying easier, for example: 3×8 is equal to $(3 \times 4) + (3 \times 4)$.	6, 7
Use order and grouping to make multiplying easier, for example: $2 \times 6 \times 5$ is equal to $6 \times (2 \times 5)$.	8
Use place value to multiply, for example: 3×40 is equal to $3 \times 4 \times 10$.	9
Explain division using equal groups and arrays.	10
Understand division as a multiplication problem, for example: $10 \div 2 = ?$ can be shown as $2 \times ? = 10$.	11
Use multiplication and division facts up through the facts for 10.	12
Find the rule for a pattern and explain it.	13

Think about what you learned.

Use words, numbers, and drawings.

1 I am proud that I can . . .

2 I worked hardest to learn how to . . .

3 A question I still have is . . .

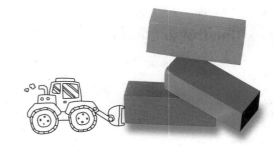

Solve Multiplication and Division Problems

SMP 1 Make sense of problems and persevere in solving them.

Study an Example Problem and Solution

Read this problem involving multiplication and division. Then look at Brandi's solution to this problem.

Seat Set-Up

Brandi is planning how to set up seats for a play.

My Notes

- Use between 80 and 100 seats.
- Make 2 seating sections.
- The number of seats in each section can be the same or different.
- Use equal rows of seats in a section.

Help Brandi set up the chairs.

- Decide the number of chairs to use.
- Tell how many seats to put in each section.
- Tell the number of rows and the number of seats in each row.

Stage

Section 1   Aisle   Section 2

Read the sample solution on the next page. Then look at the checklist below. Find and mark parts of the solution that match the checklist.

✓ PROBLEM-SOLVING CHECKLIST

- ☐ Tell what is known.
- ☐ Tell what the problem is asking.
- ☐ Show all your work.
- ☐ Show that the solution works.

a. **Circle** something that is known.

b. **Underline** something that you need to find.

c. **Draw a box around** what you do to solve the problem.

d. **Put a checkmark** next to the part that shows the solution works.

BRANDI'S SOLUTION

Hi, I'm Brandi. Here's how I solved the problem.

- **I know I need a total number of seats between 80 and 100.**

  I can find two numbers that add to 80 or 100.
  $$40 + 40 = 80 \text{ and } 50 + 50 = 100$$
  If I use more than 40 and less than 50 in each section the total will be correct.

- **I need to use numbers that can make equal rows.**

  Here are some facts that I know:
  $$4 \times 10 = 40$$
  $$6 \times 7 = 42$$
  $$5 \times 9 = 45$$

  I'm making equal rows, so I can use multiplication facts.

- **I can choose two of these products.**

  If I add the numbers, I should get a number between 80 and 100.
  $$42 + 45 = 87$$
  87 is between 80 and 100.

  I have to add the products to make sure the total works.

- **I will use 87 chairs.**

6 rows of 7 seats = 42 seats   5 rows of 9 seats = 45 seats

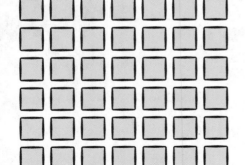   

The picture shows my thinking and helps me check my answer.

Try Another Approach

There are many ways to solve problems. Think about how you might solve the Seat Set-Up problem in a different way.

Seat Set-Up

Brandi is planning how to set up seats for a play.

My Notes

- Use between 80 and 100 seats.
- Make 2 seating sections.
- The number of seats in each section can be the same or different.
- Use equal rows of seats in a section.

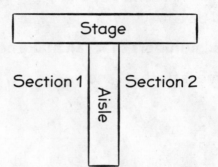

Help Brandi set up the chairs.

- Decide the number of chairs to use.
- Tell how many seats to put in each section.
- Tell the number of rows and the number of seats in each row.

PLAN IT

Answer these questions to help you start thinking about a plan.

A. What are some numbers that give you a sum between 80 and 100?

B. What are some other facts that you know that could help you solve the problem?

SOLVE IT

Find a different solution for the Seat Set-Up problem. Show all your work on a separate sheet of paper.

You may want to use the Problem-Solving Tips to get started.

PROBLEM-SOLVING TIPS

- **Tools** You may want to use . . .
  - an array.
  - equations.

- **Word Bank**

add	multiply	multiplication
array	equal	sum
product	factor	rows

- **Sentence Starters**
  - _____ a sum of _____
  - There are _____ in each _____

☑ **PROBLEM-SOLVING CHECKLIST**

Make sure that you . . .
- ☐ tell what you know.
- ☐ tell what you need to do.
- ☐ show all your work.
- ☐ show that the solution works.

REFLECT

Use Mathematical Practices As you work through the problem, discuss these questions with a partner.

- **Use Structure** What kinds of numbers are you able to make equal rows with?

- **Persevere** What is your plan for solving this problem?

Discuss Models and Strategies

Read the problem. Write a solution on a separate sheet of paper. Remember, there can be lots of ways to solve a problem!

Robot Prop

Robot #1

Brandi's play is about space creatures. She wants to make a space robot prop. Brandi has 50 pie plates. She will use the pie plates to make arms and legs for the robot.

My Robot Prop Plan

- Use up to 50 plates.
- Use the same number of plates for each arm.
- Use the same number of plates for each leg.
- Use more plates for each leg than for each arm.

How many pie plates should Brandi use for each leg and each arm?

PLAN IT AND SOLVE IT
Find a solution for the Robot Prop problem.

Make a plan for Brandi's robot.

- Tell how many plates to use for each arm and leg.

- Tell how many plates you need in all.

- Explain why your plan works.

You may want to use the Problem-Solving Tips to get started.

PROBLEM-SOLVING TIPS

- **Questions**

  - Will you try to use all of the plates?

  - Can you use multiplication facts to find some numbers to try out?

- **Sentence Starters**

- I can use _____

- I can add _____

✓ PROBLEM-SOLVING CHECKLIST
Make sure that you . . .
- ☐ tell what you know.
- ☐ tell what you need to do.
- ☐ show all your work.
- ☐ show that the solution works.

REFLECT
Use Mathematical Practices As you work through the problem, discuss these questions with a partner.

- **Use Models** How could a drawing help you find a solution?

- **Make an Argument** How do you know that the numbers you chose work?

Persevere On Your Own

Read the problem. Write a solution on a separate sheet of paper.

Space Creatures

Brandi doesn't know how many space creatures to have in the play, but she has some ideas.

Space Creatures Notes

- The creatures should march out of the spaceship in equal groups or in equal rows.
- There should be more than 20.
- There should not be more than 30.

How many space creatures should Brandi use?

SOLVE IT

Write a plan for Brandi's space creatures.

- Decide how many space creatures to use.
- Tell how many groups or rows of creatures to use. Also tell how many are in each group or row.
- Describe how the space creatures will march out of the spaceship.

REFLECT

Use Mathematical Practices After you complete the task, choose one of these questions to discuss with a partner.

- **Use Structure** How did you find numbers that can make equal groups?

- **Make an Argument** How many space creatures did you choose, and why?

Monthly Gifts

At the play, Brandi tells people they can support the theater department at the local college. Brandi asks people to sign up to make monthly gifts. She wants to raise at least $800 in 6 months from these gifts.

Here are the gift amounts.

How can Brandi raise at least $800 in 6 months?

SOLVE IT

Help Brandi find a way to raise money.

• Find how much each monthly gift raises in 6 months.

• Then find a way to raise at least $800 in 6 months.

• Tell how you know that your answer works.

REFLECT

Use Mathematical Practices After you complete the task, choose one of these questions to discuss with a partner.

• **Use Structure** How did you use basic facts to help solve this problem?

• **Reason Mathematically** What computation strategies did you use?

1 Hana likes to walk. The table shows the number of days and the number of miles she walks in a week. How many miles does Hana walk in a week?

Day	Number of Miles
Monday	3
Wednesday	3
Friday	3
Saturday	3

Write a multiplication equation that can be used to answer the question. Write your answer in the blanks.

.... × .... = ...

2 Which expressions can be used to find the product of 8, 5, and 3? Choose all the correct answers.

Ⓐ $(3 + 5) \times 8$

Ⓑ $(8 + 3) \times 5$

Ⓒ $(8 \times 5) \times 3$

Ⓓ $8 \times (3 \times 5)$

Ⓔ $3 \times (5 + 8)$

Ⓕ $5 \times (8 \times 3)$

3 Isabel breaks 9×8 into $(9 \times 3) + (9 \times 5)$ to solve the problem. What is another way Isabel could break apart 9×8? Show your work.

4 What value makes both equations true?
Record your answer on the grid.
Then fill in the bubbles.

$32 \div 8 = ?$

$8 \times ? = 32$

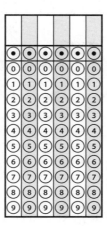

5 Kent notices a pattern in the table.

Addend	Addend	Sum
2	18	20
4	16	20
6	14	20
8	12	20
10	10	20

Describe the pattern. Write your answer in the blanks.

As one added increases by ...., the other addend decreases by ....

6 Which problem can be solved using the division equation $42 \div 6$?

Ⓐ Lizzie starts with 42 peaches. She uses some to make jam. Now she has 6 left. How many peaches does she use to make jam?

Ⓑ Lizzie buys 42 bags of peaches. Each bag has 6 peaches in it. How many peaches does Lizzie buy?

Ⓒ Lizzie buys 42 peaches. She puts them into 6 bowls with an equal number in each bowl. How many peaches are in each bowl?

Ⓓ Lizzie uses 7 peaches to make pies. She uses 6 peaches to make smoothies. How many peaches does Lizzie use in all?

7 Complete the fact family. Write your answer in the blanks.

$4 \times \text{.............} = 24$ $24 \div 6 = \text{.............}$

$4 \times 6 = \text{.............}$ $\text{.............} \div 6 = 4$

Performance Task

Answer the questions and show all your work on separate paper.

Madelyn, William, and Hannah are trying to decide how to display erasers at the school store. The erasers came in 2 packages. Each package has 24 erasers.

- William says that they can lay them out in 4 rows with 12 erasers in each row.

- Hannah thinks that they should lay them out in 7 rows with 7 erasers in each row.

- Madelyn wants to lay them out in two groups: 3 rows with 6 erasers in each row on one table, and 5 rows with 6 erasers in each row on another table.

Tell whether each person's idea will work and explain why or why not.

Checklist

Did you . . .

☐ write equations to represent the arrangements?

☐ draw diagrams?

☐ use complete sentences?

REFLECT

Use Mathematical Practices After you complete the task, choose one of the following questions to answer.

- **Persevere** How did you decide what to do first to solve this problem?

- **Model** What models helped you solve this problem?

Draw or write to show examples for each term. Then draw or write to show other math words in the unit.

divide to separate into equal groups and find the number in each group or the number of groups.

My Example

division an operation used to separate a number of items into equal-sized groups.

My Example

division equation an equation with a division symbol and an equal sign. For example, $15 \div 3 = 5$.

My Example

fact family a group of related equations that use the same numbers, but in a different order, and two different operation symbols. A fact family can show the relationship between addition and subtraction or between multiplication and division.

My Example

factor a number that is multiplied.

My Example

multiplication an operation used to find the total number of items in a given number of equal-sized groups.

My Example

multiplication equation an equation with a multiplication symbol and an equal sign. For example, $3 \times 5 = 15$.

My Example

multiplication table a table showing multiplication facts.

My Example

multiply to repeatedly add the same number a certain number of times. Used to find the total number of items in equal-sized groups.

My Example

pattern a series of numbers or shapes that follow a rule to repeat or change.

My Example

product the result of multiplication.

My Example

quotient the result of division.

My Example

rule   a set way that is followed to go from one number or shape to the next in a pattern.

My Example

My Word: _____

_____

_____

My Example

My Word: _____

_____

_____

My Example

My Word: _____

_____

_____

My Example

My Word: _____

_____

_____

My Example

My Word: _____

_____

_____

My Example

My Word: _____

_____

_____

My Example

My Word: _____

_____

_____

My Example

My Word: _____

_____

_____

My Example

My Word: _____

_____

_____

My Example

My Word: _____

_____

_____

My Example

My Word: _____

_____

_____

My Example

☑ SELF CHECK

Before starting this unit, check off the skills you know below. As you complete each lesson, see how many more skills you can check off!

I can . . .	Before	After
Understand area and find area by tiling and by multiplying.	☐	☐
Find the area of a combined rectangle or a non-rectangular shape by adding the areas of the rectangles that make up the shape.	☐	☐
Use multiplication or division to solve one-step word problems.	☐	☐
Use addition, subtraction, multiplication, or division to solve two-step word problems.	☐	☐
Solve problems using picture graphs and bar graphs.	☐	☐
Draw picture graphs and bar graphs to show data.	☐	☐

Build Your Vocabulary

REVIEW

bar graph   length
measure   picture graph
unit

Math Vocabulary

Complete the table by playing "I'm Thinking of a Word." In the first column, write the words your teacher is thinking of. Then work with a partner to complete the second column.

Write the Word	Describe the Word
1.	
2.	
3.	
4.	
5.	

Academic Vocabulary

Put a check next to the academic words you know. Then use the words to complete the sentences.

☐ collect   ☐ interesting   ☐ disagree   ☐ strategy

1 To complete the bar graph, I need to .... more data.

2 I .... with the answer. I have a different answer and can prove my solution.

3 I used addition as a .... to find the results.

4 I enjoy reading, especially when the story or article is ....

Understand Area

Dear Family,

This week your child is exploring the idea of measuring area.

Area is the amount of space a flat shape covers. In this lesson students learn that area is measured with **square units**.

1 square unit

They measure the area of a shape by exactly covering the shape with square units, using these three rules:

- All of the square units must be the same size.
- There can be no gaps between the squares.
- The squares cannot overlap each other anywhere.

Then they count to find how many square units cover the shape.

1	2	3	4
5	6	7	8
		9	10
		11	12

The area of this shape is 12 square units.

You can use smaller or larger square units to find the area of a shape. You just have to identify the size of the unit you are using.

Students will see that it takes fewer of the larger square units than the smaller square units to completely cover the same shape.

Invite your child to share what he or she knows about area by doing the following activity together.

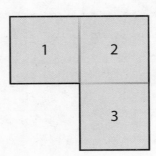

1 square unit

Do this activity with your child to understand area.

Work with your child to draw shapes that look like letters and then find their areas.

For example, the shape to the right looks like the letter C.

Use this style to draw the initial of your first name on the grid paper below.

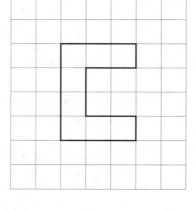

- Find the area of the initial you drew by counting the square units.

- Now make your initial another way so that it has a different area.

- Can different initials have the same area? Draw an example.

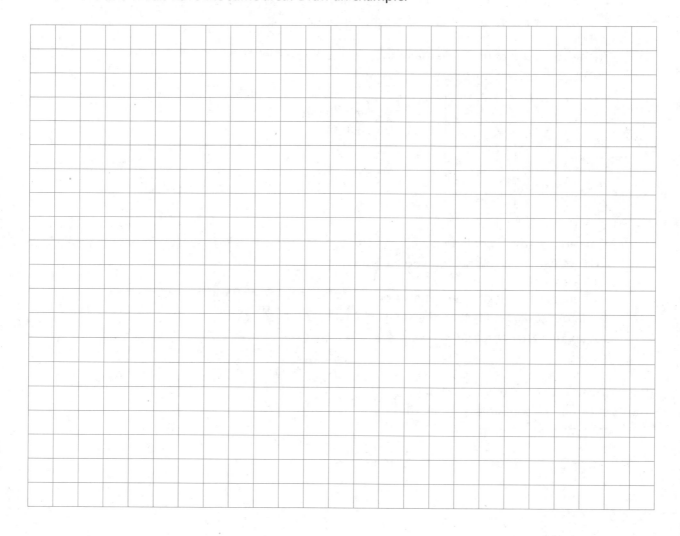

Explore Area

How can you measure the area of a shape?

MODEL IT

Complete the problems below.

1 There are different ways you can measure a rug in the shape of a rectangle.

   a. Draw a rectangular rug to the right and label its length and width.

   b. How could you measure the length and width of the rug?

2 **Area** is the amount of space a flat shape covers. The area of a rug is the amount of floor space it covers. How do you think you could measure the area of the rug to the right?

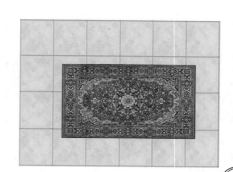

3 How are your ways of measuring in problem 1 and problem 2 different?

DISCUSS IT

• Did you and your partner come up with the same way to measure in problem 2?

• I think measuring the length or width of a rectangle is different than measuring its area because . . .

MODEL IT
Complete the problems below.

 You measure area in units that can cover space, called **square units**.

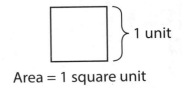

Area = 1 square unit

a. Circle the rug below that you think shows the correct way to use square units to measure its area.

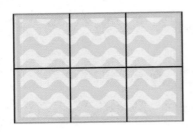 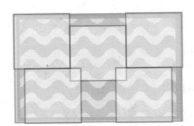

b. Explain why your choice in Part a correctly measures area.

c. What is the area of the rug in square units?

.... square units

DISCUSS IT
- Why was the other way to measure area in problem 4a wrong?
- I think square units need to be the same size when finding area because . . .

5 REFLECT

Explain how you use square units to find the area of a shape.

....

....

....

....

....

Prepare for Finding Area

1 Think about what you know about area. Fill in each box. Use words, numbers, and pictures. Show as many ideas as you can.

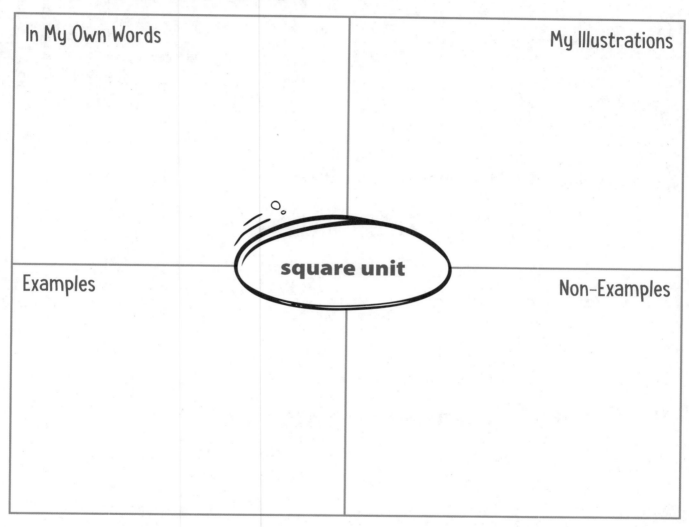

In My Own Words	My Illustrations
Examples	**Non-Examples**

square unit

2 How do you think you could measure the area of the rug to the right in square units?

Solve.

3 Circle the rug below that you think shows the correct way to use square units to measure its area.

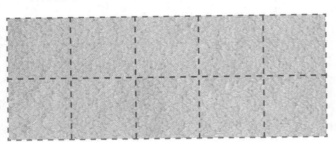 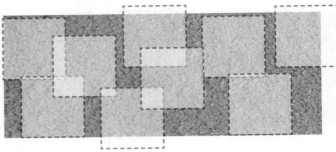

4 Explain why your choice in problem 3 correctly measures area.

5 What is the area of the rug in square units?

.... square units

MODEL IT: RECTANGULAR SHAPES

Try these two problems.

1 Look at Square *A* to the right.

a. Use an inch ruler to measure the length and width of the square unit next to Square *A*. What is the area of this square unit?

.... square inch

b. What is the area of Square *A*?

.... square inches

Square *A*

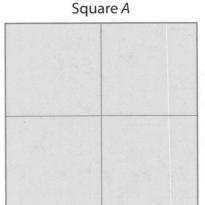

1 square unit

2 Look at Rectangle *B* below.

Rectangle *B*

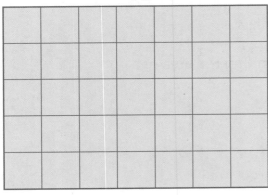

1 square unit

a. Use a centimeter ruler to measure the length and width of the square unit next to Rectangle *B*. What is the area of this square unit?

.... square centimeter

b. What is the area of Rectangle *B*?

.... square centimeters

DISCUSS IT

• How did you find the area of each shape?

• I think it would take more square centimeters than square inches to find the area of the same shape because . . .

MODEL IT: NON-RECTANGULAR SHAPES

Number and count the square units to find the area of each shape.

3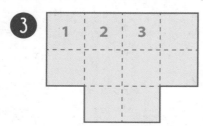

Area = ... square units

4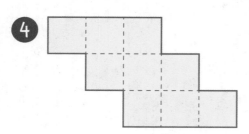

Area = ... square units

CONNECT IT

Complete the problems below.

5 How is finding the area of a rectangular shape like finding the area of a non-rectangular shape?

6 Explain how to find the area of the rectangle. Then find the area.

Practice Finding Area

**Study how the Example shows how to count square units to find area.
Then solve problems 1–7.**

EXAMPLE

The shape is covered with squares of the same size.
What is the area of this shape?

Count the square units. The area of the shape is
12 square units. You must use same-sized squares
to find the area in square units.

1	2	3	4
5	6	7	8
	9	10	
	11	12	

☐ = 1 square unit

1 Count to find each area.

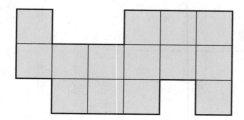

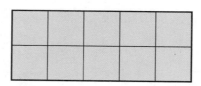

Area = ... square units   Area = ... square units

2 What is the area?

1 square inch

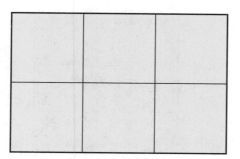

Area = ... square inches

Vocabulary

area the amount of space a flat shape covers.

square unit the area of a square with side lengths of 1 unit.

3 What is the area of this rectangle?

☐ = 1 square centimeter

4 Ria says that the area of Rectangle *A* is 9 square units. Do you agree? Explain.

Rectangle *A*

5 Fill in the blanks.

Rectangle *B* has .... rows of squares.

There are .... squares in each row.

Rectangle *B*

6 How can you skip-count to find the area of Rectangle *B*? Write the area.

7 What is the area of Rectangle *C*? How does this compare to the area of Rectangle *B*? Are the rectangles the same size? Explain.

Rectangle *C*

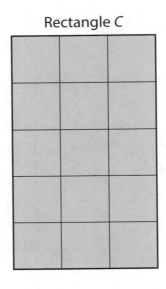

Refine Ideas About Finding Area

APPLY IT
Complete these problems on your own.

1 COMPARE

Find the area of each shape below.

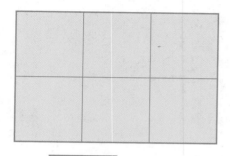

Each [ ] has an area of 1 square meter. Each [ ] has an area of 1 square foot.

Area = ...   Area = ...

2 EXAMINE

Anna says the area of this rectangle is 12 square units because each of the small rectangles is 1 unit long. Why is Anna wrong?

1	2	3
4	5	6
7	8	9
10	11	12

3 RELATE

Think about how you could find the area of this shape.

First, draw the square units.

Then number the square units to find the area of the shape.

Area = ... square units

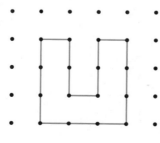

PAIR/SHARE
Discuss your solutions to these three problems with a partner.

Use what you have learned to complete problem 4.

4 Use a ruler and the dot grid below to complete the problems.

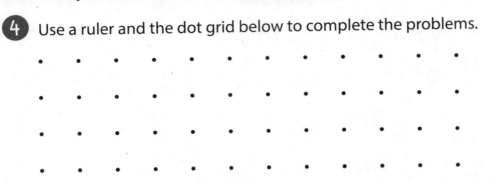

Part A Draw a rectangle with an area of 8 square units on the grid. Label it with an *A*.

Part B Draw a rectangle with an area greater than 8 square units on the same grid. Label it with a *B*.

Part C How did you know how to draw your rectangle *B* with an area that is greater than 8 square units?

5 MATH JOURNAL

Explain how you can find the area of a rectangle drawn on a dot grid.

Multiply to Find Area

Dear Family,

This week your child is learning to multiply to find the area of a rectangle.

Previously, your child learned that **area** is the number of square units that cover a shape and then just counted the squares to find the area.

When the shape is a rectangle, you can use multiplication to find the number of square units that cover the shape.

In this rectangle, there are 5 rows, each with 3 square units.
 5 × 3 = 15 tells how many square units in all.

There are 3 columns, each with 5 square units.
 3 × 5 = 15 tells how many square units in all.

The area of this rectangle is 15 square units.

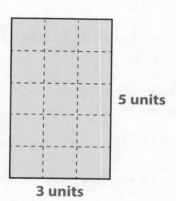

5 units

3 units

To find the area of *any* rectangle, multiply the length by the width (or the width by the length).

4 × 2 = 8
2 × 4 = 8

2 cm

4 cm

The area of this rectangle is 8 square centimeters.

Invite your child to share what he or she knows about multiplying to find area by doing the following activity together.

ACTIVITY MULTIPLYING TO FIND AREA

Do this activity with your child to multiply to find area.

Materials inch ruler or yardstick, calculator, pencil and paper

Practice using multiplication to find the area of different rectangular surfaces with your child.

Have a five-minute *Area Scavenger Hunt*.

Each player looks around the house for two rectangular objects with dimensions less than a foot. The goal is to find one with a "small" area and one with a "large" area.

Determine who found the larger rectangle.

• Measure the length and the width of the two larger rectangles to the nearest whole inch.

• Multiply the length and width of each rectangle to calculate the area in square units (square inches).

• Was the result what you expected?

Determine who found the smaller rectangle.

• Measure the length and the width of the two smaller rectangles to the nearest whole inch.

• Multiply the length and width of each rectangle to calculate the area in square units (square inches).

• Was the result what you expected?

Discuss with your child whether there could be another rectangle with the same area as yours but with different length and width. For example, if you know a rectangle has an area of 24 square inches, what could the length and width be?

Explore Multiplying to Find Area

You have already learned how to find the area of a rectangle by counting the number of square units that cover the rectangle. This lesson will help you find the area using multiplication. Use what you know to try to solve the problem below.

Jenny wants to find the area of the rectangle shown. But some ink spilled on it. How can she find the area if she cannot count all of the square units?

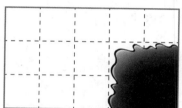

Area of [ ] = 1 square unit.

TRY IT

🧰 **Math Toolkit**
• square tiles
• counters
• grid paper
• perimeter and area tool 🖱
• multiplication models 🖱

💬 **DISCUSS IT**

Ask your partner: How did you get started?

Tell your partner: I knew ... so I ...

CONNECT IT

1 **LOOK BACK**

Explain how you found the area of Jenny's rectangle when you could not see all the squares. What is the area of Jenny's rectangle?

2 **LOOK AHEAD**

When you know the length and width of a rectangle, you do not have to count the square units to find the area. You can multiply instead.

a. Jenny's rectangle without the ink spill is an array of squares that have been pushed together. What two multiplication equations can you write to describe this array?

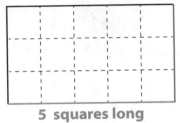

3 squares wide

5 squares long

b. Write an equation to multiply the **length** and the **width** of the rectangle. Explain how you can use length and width to find the area of a rectangle.

c. Explain how 5 × 3 gives you the same area as counting all the squares.

3 **REFLECT**

How is finding the area of a rectangle like finding the number of items in an array?

....

....

....

....

Prepare for Multiplying to Find Area

1 Think about what you know about measurement. Fill in each box. Use words, numbers, and pictures. Show as many ideas as you can.

Word	In My Own Words	Example
length		
width		
area		

2 Manny skip-counts by fours 3 times to find the area of the rectangle shown. Lee multiplies the length of the rectangle by the width. They both say the area of the rectangle is 12 square units. Explain why the two methods give the same answer.

3 Solve the problem. Show your work.

Marcos wants to find the area of the rectangle shown. But some ink spilled on it. How can he find the area if he cannot count all of the square units?

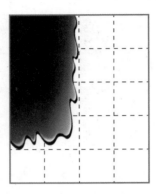

Area of ☐ = 1 square unit.

Solution ....

4 Check your answer. Show your work.

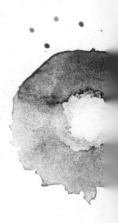

Develop Multiplying to Find Area

Read and try to solve the problem below.

What is the area of the rectangle?

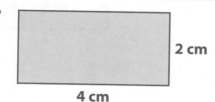

2 cm

4 cm

TRY IT

 **Math Toolkit**
- square tiles
- grid paper
- dot paper
- perimeter and area tool
- multiplication models

DISCUSS IT

Ask your partner: What strategy did you use?

Tell your partner: The strategy I used to find the answer was . . .

Explore different ways to understand multiplying to find area.

What is the area of the rectangle?

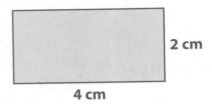

2 cm

4 cm

PICTURE IT

You can use square tiles to find area.

The model below shows the rectangle covered by 1-centimeter squares.

1	2	3	4
5	6	7	8

Area of ▢ = 1 square centimeter.

MODEL IT

You can also use a multiplication equation to find area.

The length of the rectangle is **4 centimeters**.
Using 1-centimeter squares,
4 squares will fill a row.

The width of the rectangle is **2 centimeters**.
Using 1-centimeter squares,
2 squares will fill a column.

Multiply length and width to
find the area of the rectangle.

Area = 4 × 2

CONNECT IT

Now you will use the problem from the previous page to help you understand how to multiply to find area.

1 How many 1-centimeter squares fit along the length of the rectangle? ....

What is the length of the rectangle? .... centimeters

2 How many 1-centimeter squares fit along the width of the rectangle? ....

What is the width of the rectangle? .... centimeters

3 What does the problem ask you to find?

4 The unit of measurement for the length and width of the rectangle is centimeters. What is the unit of measurement for the area?

5 Complete the equation below to find the area of the rectangle.

length	×	**width**	=	**area**

.... centimeters × .... centimeters = ... square centimeters

6 The area of the rectangle is .... square centimeters.

7 Explain how you can use square tiles or multiplication to find the area of a rectangle.

8 REFLECT

Look back at your **Try It**, strategies by classmates, and **Picture It** and **Model It**. Which models or strategies do you like best for mulitplying to find the area of a rectangle? Explain.

....

....

....

APPLY IT

Use what you just learned to solve these problems.

9 What is the area of the square? Show your work.

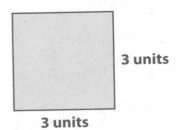

3 units

3 units

Solution ....

10 Sheigh has a rectangle that is 5 centimeters long. The area of the rectangle is 10 square centimeters. What is the width of the rectangle? Show your work.

Solution ....

11 A rectangle has a length of 8 inches and a width of 6 inches. What is the area of the rectangle? Show your work.

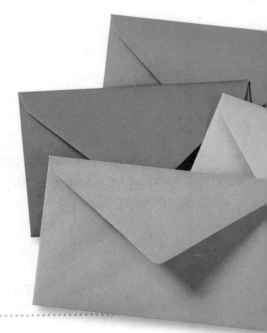

Solution ....

Practice Multiplying to Find Area

**Study the Example showing how to multiply to find area.
Then solve problems 1–9.**

EXAMPLE

A rectangle has a length of 4 centimeters and a width of 3 centimeters. What is the area?

Fill the rectangle with 1-centimeter squares. There are 4 squares in a row and 3 rows.

You can multiply to find the total number of squares: $4 \times 3 = 12$.

The area is 12 square centimeters.

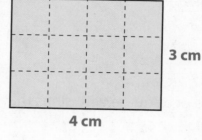

3 cm

4 cm

---

1 What is the area of this rectangle? Write an equation.

length   ×   width   =   area

.... units × .... units = ... square units

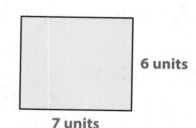

6 units

7 units

---

2 A rectangle has a length of 8 inches and a width of 7 inches. What is the area of the rectangle?

---

3 A square has sides that are 4 centimeters long. What is the area? Write an equation.

4   Write an equation to find the area of Rectangle A. Then write the area.

Equation ....

Area ....

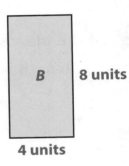

A   9 units

3 units

5   A rectangle has a length of 6 centimeters and a width of 5 centimeters. What is the area of the rectangle? Show your work.

6   What is the area of a square with sides that are 8 centimeters long? Show your work.

7   What is the area of Rectangle B? Show your work.

B   8 units

4 units

8   Lena draws a square with an area that is greater than the area of Rectangle B. What are two possible side lengths of Lena's square? Explain.

9   Pablo draws Rectangle P. He says that the area is greater than 50 square units. What could the unknown side length be? Explain.

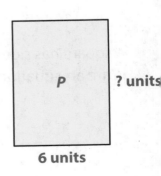

P   ? units

6 units

Develop Solving Word Problems About Area

Read and try to solve the problem below.

> Tyler's rectangular bedroom floor is 9 feet wide and 9 feet long.
> Suki's rectangular bedroom floor is 8 feet wide and 10 feet long.
> Whose bedroom floor has a greater area?

TRY IT

 Math Toolkit
- square tiles
- grid paper
- dot paper
- perimeter and area tool
- multiplication models

DISCUSS IT

Ask your partner: Can you explain that again?

Tell your partner: I agree with you about . . . because . . .

Explore different ways to understand solving word problems about area.

> **Tyler's rectangular bedroom floor is 9 feet wide and 9 feet long.**
> **Suki's rectangular bedroom floor is 8 feet wide and 10 feet long.**
> **Whose bedroom floor has a greater area?**

PICTURE IT

You can use models to help you multiply to find area.

The models below show the length and width of Tyler's and Suki's bedroom floors.

Tyler's Bedroom Floor

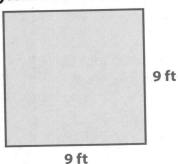

9 ft

9 ft

Suki's Bedroom Floor

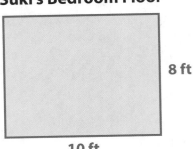

8 ft

10 ft

MODEL IT

You can also use multiplication equations to find area.

Use words to describe the measurements of each bedroom floor.

Tyler's room:

The **length** of the floor is **9** feet.
The **width** of the floor is **9** feet.

Suki's room:

The **length** of the floor is **10** feet.
The **width** of the floor is **8** feet.

Multiply **length** and **width** to find the area of each floor.

Tyler's floor: Area = **9 × 9**

Suki's floor: Area = **10 × 8**

CONNECT IT

Now you will use the problem from the previous page to help you understand how to solve word problems about area.

1 What does the problem ask you to find?

2 What units are used to measure the length and width of the floors?

3 What unit should you use to record the area of each floor?

4 Complete the equation below to find the area of Tyler's bedroom floor.

length × **width** = **area**

.... feet × .... feet = ... square feet

The area of Tyler's bedroom floor is .... square feet.

5 Complete the equation below to find the area of Suki's bedroom floor.

length × **width** = **area**

.... feet × .... feet = ... square feet

The area of Suki's bedroom floor is .... square feet.

6 So, ... has the bedroom floor with the greater area.

7 Explain how you know that the areas of the bedroom floors must have the label "square feet."

8 REFLECT

Look back at your **Try It**, strategies by classmates, and **Picture It** and **Model It**. Which models or strategies do you like best for solving word problems about area? Explain.

....

....

APPLY IT

Use what you just learned to solve these problems.

9 Fran found the area of a rectangle by multiplying 5 units and 4 units. Draw Fran's rectangle. Label the length and the width. What is the area of the rectangle? Show your work.

Solution ....

10 Kayla draws the rectangle shown. James draws a rectangle that has the same area as Kayla's rectangle, but it has different side lengths. What are possible side lengths for James's rectangle? Show your work.

2 units

9 units

Solution ....

11 Jan has a rectangular photo that is 7 inches long and 5 inches wide. How much space will this photo cover in Jan's photo album? Show your work.

Solution ....

Practice Solving Word Problems About Area

Study the Example showing how to solve a word problem about area. Then solve problems 1–6.

EXAMPLE

Ana's garden is 7 feet long and 7 feet wide. Noah's garden is 8 feet long and 6 feet wide. Which garden has a lesser area?

You can draw a model. Then multiply length and width to find the area of each garden.

Ana: 7 × 7 = 49 square feet
Noah: 8 × 6 = 48 square feet

Noah's garden has a lesser area.

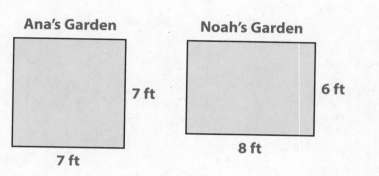

Ana's Garden — 7 ft, 7 ft

Noah's Garden — 6 ft, 8 ft

1 Roberto's desk is in the shape of a rectangle that is 4 feet long and 2 feet wide. What is the area of Roberto's desktop? Fill in the blanks.

   length   ×   **width**   =   **area**

   _____ feet × _____ feet = _____ square feet

2 Show how to find the area of this rug.

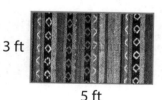

3 ft

5 ft

3 Vera buys a rug like the one in problem 2. Vera's rug is square. It has sides that are 4 feet long. Does Vera's rug cover more or less area than the rug in problem 2? Explain.

4 Aiden prints a rectangular photo that is 4 units wide and 6 units long. Bella prints a square photo. It is 5 units on each side. Draw the photos and label the side lengths. Write the area for each.

5 Draw and label a rectangle that has a lesser area than the area of a square that is 3 units on each side. Write the area of the rectangle.

6 Ron buys a rectangular rug for his room. The rug is 8 feet long and 5 feet wide. The floor in his room is shaped like a square that is 10 feet long and 10 feet wide. How much of the floor in Ron's room will NOT be covered by the rug? Show your work.

Solution

Refine Multiplying to Find Area

Complete the Example below. Then solve problems 1–8.

EXAMPLE

Ms. Cruz is putting carpet in the living room. The length and width of the room is shown below. How many square feet of carpet does Ms. Cruz need to cover the whole floor?

Living Room

8 ft

9 ft

Look at how you could show your work using multiplication.

length × width = area

9 feet × 8 feet = 72 square feet

Solution ....

> The student multiplies the length and the width to find the area.

APPLY IT

1 Marcia finds the area of a square. The length of one side of the square is 5 centimeters. What is the area of the square? Show your work.

> The sides of a square are all the same length.

Solution ....

2 Ms. Clark is building a rectangular patio that is 4 yards long and 3 yards wide. She has enough bricks to cover an area of 14 square yards. Does Ms. Clark have enough bricks to build the patio? Explain. Show your work.

I think there are at least two different steps you need to do to solve this problem.

Solution ....

....

PAIR/SHARE
How could you use a picture to solve this problem?

3 What is the area of the rectangle shown below?

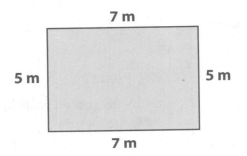

7 m

5 m   5 m

7 m

To find the area of the rectangle, do you add or multiply?

Ⓐ 35 square meters

Ⓑ 24 square meters

Ⓒ 12 square meters

Ⓓ 7 square meters

Bobby chose Ⓑ as the correct answer. How did he get that answer?

PAIR/SHARE
Do you need the measure of each side of the rectangle labeled to solve the problem? Why or why not?

4 Mr. Frank is putting tile on a bathroom wall above the tub. The model shows the length and width of the wall. How many square feet of tile does he need to cover the wall?

Ⓐ 49 square feet

Ⓑ 42 square feet

Ⓒ 26 square feet

Ⓓ 13 square feet

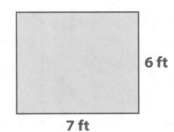

6 ft

7 ft

5 Which shape below has an area of 12 square feet?

Ⓐ 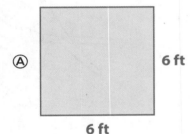 6 ft

6 ft

Ⓑ 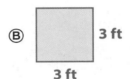 3 ft

3 ft

Ⓒ 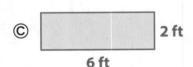 2 ft

6 ft

Ⓓ 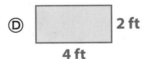 2 ft

4 ft

6 The area of a rectangular patio is 24 square yards. Which measurements could be the length and width of the patio?

Ⓐ length: 8 yards, width: 4 yards

Ⓑ length: 5 yards, width: 5 yards

Ⓒ length: 6 yards, width: 3 yards

Ⓓ length: 6 yards, width: 4 yards

Ⓔ length: 8 yards, width: 3 yards

Lesson 15 Multiply to Find Area   **333**

7 Rita is making a quilt. It is made with 45 square blocks of fabric and is 9 blocks long.

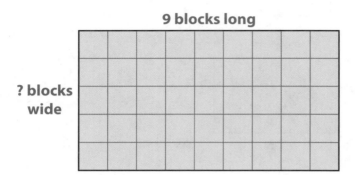

9 blocks long

? blocks wide

Complete the equation below to show how many blocks wide the quilt is. Use numbers from the ones listed below.

| 4 | 5 | 6 | 9 | 45 |

 ×  = ...

8 MATH JOURNAL

Draw a rectangle. Label its length and width. Then explain how to find the area of your rectangle. Use a multiplication equation in your explanation.

☑ SELF CHECK Go back to the Unit 3 Opener and see what you can check off.

Add Areas

Dear Family,

This week your child is learning to find the area of a shape that is not a rectangle by adding up the areas of rectangles inside the shape.

There are several ways to find the area of this "T" shape.

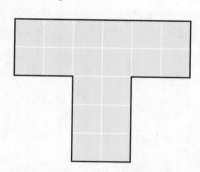

For example, you can add 2 × 6 plus 3 × 2:

2 × 6 plus 3 × 2 = 12 + 6 = 18

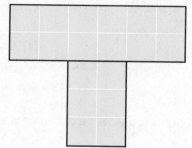

Or you can add 2 × 2 plus 2 × 2 plus 5 × 2:

2 × 2 plus 2 × 2 plus 5 × 2 = 4 + 4 + 10 = 18

So, the area of the shape is 18 square units.

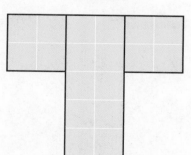

The more complicated the shape, the more fun it can be to find different ways to break it up into rectangles.

Invite your child to share what he or she knows about adding areas by doing the following activity together.

ACTIVITY ADDING AREAS

Do this activity with your child to practice breaking apart a shape into rectangles to find its area.

First, invite your child to draw an interesting shape in the grid below. For example, the shape might look like the one at the right, or it might be more complex.

Then work together to find the area of the shape by breaking the shape apart into two or more rectangles. Find the area of each rectangle and add the areas.

Now, draw the same shape but break it apart in a different way.

Talk together about whether there are other ways you can break apart your shape into rectangles. Will you always get the same area?

Explore Adding Areas

Previously, you learned how to count squares and how to use multiplication to find the areas of rectangles with whole-number sides. Use what you know to try to solve the problem below.

Ayana makes a poster that is 3 feet long and 2 feet wide. Raul makes a poster that is 3 feet long and 1 foot wide. They hang the posters on their classroom wall, as shown. What is the total area of the wall covered by the posters?

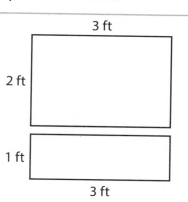

3 ft

2 ft

1 ft

3 ft

TRY IT

Math Toolkit

• square tiles
• grid paper
• dot paper
• perimeter and area tool
• multiplication models

DISCUSS IT

Ask your partner: Do you agree with me? Why or why not?

Tell your partner: I knew . . . so I . . .

CONNECT IT

1 LOOK BACK

Explain how you can find the area of the wall covered by both posters.

2 LOOK AHEAD

A combined rectangle is a rectangle composed of more than one rectangle. You can find the area of a combined rectangle in different ways.

Look at this rectangle made of two rectangles.

a. Complete these equations to show how you can find the total area by adding the areas of the two smaller rectangles:

Rectangle A: .... × .... = ...
            inches   inches   square inches

Rectangle B: .... × .... = ...
            inches   inches   square inches

Rectangle A + B: .... + ... = ...
       square inches   square inches   square inches

b. Think of the two rectangles as one rectangle. Complete the equation to show how you can find the total area by multiplying side lengths.

Rectangle: .... × .... = ...
        inches   inches   square inches

3 REFLECT

Why do you think both strategies give the same total area for the rectangle?

....

....

....

Prepare for Adding Areas

1 Think about what you know about area. Fill in each box. Use words, numbers, and pictures. Show as many ideas as you can.

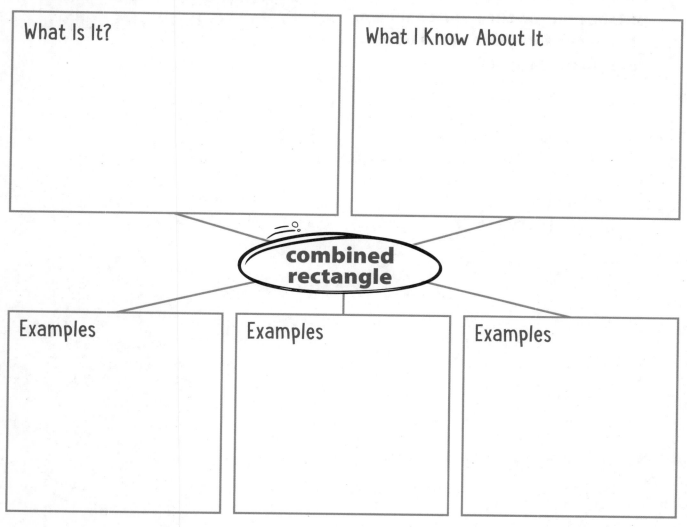

| What Is It? | What I Know About It |

combined rectangle

| Examples | Examples | Examples |

2 Did Lola and Eric each create a combined rectangle from rectangles *A* and *B* below? Explain.

3 in. | A | 3 in. | B
3 in. | 1 in.

Lola   Eric

3 in. | A | B
4 in.

A | 4 in.
B
3 in.

3 Solve the problem. Show your work.

Kelsie has a floor mat that is 4 feet long and 3 feet wide. Greg has a floor mat that is 3 feet long and 2 feet wide. They put the mats on the floor, as shown. What is the total area of the floor covered by the mats?

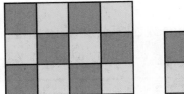 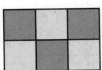

Solution ....

....

4 Check your answer. Show your work.

Develop Finding Areas of Combined Rectangles

Read and try to solve the problem below.

Mrs. Chang's vegetable garden is shown. It is shaped like a rectangle. She grows tomatoes in one part. She grows corn in the other part. What is the area of the garden?

3 ft

5 ft   4 ft

TRY IT

 Math Toolkit
- square tiles
- grid paper
- dot paper
- perimeter and area tool
- multiplication models

DISCUSS IT

Ask your partner: How did you get started?

Tell your partner: I am not sure how to find the answer because . . .

Explore different ways to understand adding areas.

Mrs. Chang's vegetable garden is shown. It is shaped like a rectangle. She grows tomatoes in one part. She grows corn in the other part. What is the area of the garden?

3 ft

5 ft   4 ft

PICTURE IT

You can find the area of a large rectangle by splitting it into two smaller rectangles.

Use square units to find the area of each small rectangle. Then add the two areas to find the area of the large rectangle.

Tomatoes   Corn

1	2	3	4	5	1	2	3	4
6	7	8	9	10	5	6	7	8
11	12	13	14	15	9	10	11	12

Each square unit has an area of 1 square foot.

15 square units + 12 square units = ?

MODEL IT

You can find the area of a rectangle by multiplying the length and the width.

The length of the rectangle is
5 feet + 4 feet, or **9 feet**.

The width of the rectangle is **3 feet**.

9 × 3 = ?

3 ft

5 ft   4 ft

CONNECT IT

Now you will use the problem from the previous page to help you understand how to add areas.

1 Look at **Model It**. The equation $9 \times 3 = ?$ is used to find the area. Explain what each factor stands for in the equation.

2 The picture of the garden in **Model It** shows the length broken into two lesser numbers. What are these two numbers? ....

3 You can use these numbers to find the areas of the two parts of the garden.

.... $\times 3 =$ .... $\times 3 =$ ....

4 You can add the areas of the two parts to find the area of the whole garden.

.... $+$ .... $=$ ....

The area of the garden is .... square feet.

5 Explain how you can find the area of a rectangle by adding the areas of the two smaller rectangles it is made from.

6 REFLECT

Look back at your **Try It**, strategies by classmates, and **Picture It** and **Model It**. Which models or strategies do you like best for finding the area of combined rectangles? Explain.

....

....

....

....

APPLY IT

Use what you just learned to solve these problems.

7 What is the area of the figure to the right?
Show your work.

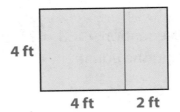

4 ft

4 ft   2 ft

Solution ....

8 How many 1-meter-square tiles will it take to cover the figure below?
Show your work.

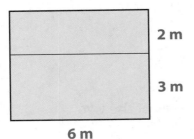

2 m

3 m

6 m

Solution ....

9 What is the area of this figure?

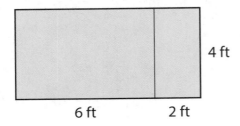

4 ft

6 ft   2 ft

Ⓐ 12 square feet
Ⓒ 20 square feet

Ⓑ 18 square feet
Ⓓ 32 square feet

Practice Finding Areas of Combined Rectangles

Study the Example showing how to find the area of combined rectangles. Then solve problems 1–6.

EXAMPLE

The diagram shows how Ms. Rigby covers her bulletin board with colored paper. What is the area of the whole bulletin board?

You can count the square units. There are 32 squares.

You can multiply the length and the width.
Length = 2 feet + 6 feet, or 8 feet
Width = 4 feet
$8 \times 4 = 32$

1	2	3	4	5	6	7	8
9	10	11	12	13	14	15	16
17	18	19	20	21	22	23	24
25	26	27	28	29	30	31	32

4 ft

2 ft   6 ft
Area = 32 square feet

Use the bulletin board from the Example to answer problems 1 and 2.

1 Write an equation for the area of each colored section of the bulletin board.

red section:

blue section:

2 Add the areas of the two sections. How does this area compare to the answer in the Example?

3 Baxter's dog run has a small covered section and a large open section. What is the total area of the dog run?

Baxter's Dog Run

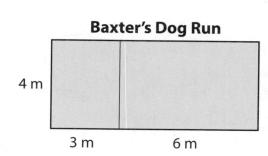

4 m

3 m   6 m

4 Joaquin makes two paintings on small cards. The diagram shows how he hangs them together on the wall. Fill in the blanks.

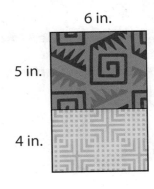

6 in.

5 in.

4 in.

a. The gray area is .... square inches.

b. The red area is .... square inches.

c. The total area is .... square inches.

5 Show how to find the area of Figure *A*.

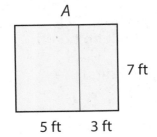

A

7 ft

5 ft   3 ft

6 Mila and her mom are tiling the playroom floor with two colors of tiles. They have 70 dark blue tiles and 30 light blue tiles. Each tile is 1 square foot. The diagram shows Mila's plan.

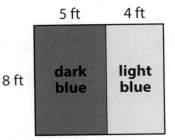

5 ft   4 ft

8 ft   dark blue   light blue

a. Show how to find the total area that they are tiling.

b. Will Mila's plan work with the tiles she has? Explain.

Develop Finding Areas of Non-Rectangular Shapes

Read and try to solve the problem below.

> **Elsa uses 1-inch-square tiles to build the shape shown. What is the area of Elsa's shape?**

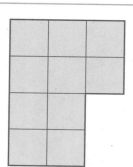

TRY IT

 Math Toolkit
- 1-inch tiles
- 1-inch grid paper
- dot paper
- perimeter and area tool
- multiplication models
- number lines

DISCUSS IT

Ask your partner: Can you explain that again?

Tell your partner: I agree with you about . . . because . . .

Explore different ways to understand finding area of non-rectangular shapes.

Elsa uses 1-inch-square tiles to build the shape shown.
What is the area of Elsa's shape?

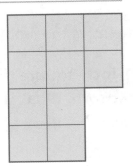

PICTURE IT

You can find the area of a shape by counting the number of square units that cover the shape.

There are 10 square units. Each square unit has an area of 1 square inch.

1	2	3
4	5	6
7	8	
9	10	

MODEL IT

You can find the area of a shape by breaking it apart into smaller shapes.

One Way:
You can break apart Elsa's shape into two smaller shapes like this:

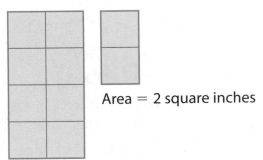

Area = 2 square inches

Area = 8 square inches

Another Way:
You can break apart Elsa's shape into two different smaller shapes like this:

Area = 6 square inches

Area = 4 square inches

CONNECT IT

Now you will use the problem from the previous page to help you understand how to find the area of non-rectangular shapes.

1 **Model It** shows two ways to break apart Elsa's shape. Look at the first way. For each smaller shape, write a multiplication equation to show its area.

.... × .... = ... × .... = ...

Write an addition equation to show the total area of Elsa's shape.

.... + ... = ...

The total area of Elsa's shape is .... square inches.

2 Look at the second way to break apart Elsa's shape. For each smaller shape, write a multiplication equation to show its area.

.... × .... = ... × .... = ...

Write an addition equation to show the total area of Elsa's shape.

.... + ... = ...

The total area of Elsa's shape is .... square inches.

How does this total area compare to the total area you found in problem 1?

3 Mike breaks apart a shape into two smaller shapes. Rick breaks apart the same shape into two different shapes. Explain how you know that the total area of Mike's two shapes is the same as the total area of Rick's two shapes.

4 **REFLECT**

Look back at your **Try It**, strategies by classmates, and **Picture It** and **Model It**. Which models or strategies do you like best for finding the area of non-rectangular shapes? Explain.

....

....

....

APPLY IT

Use what you just learned to solve these problems.

5 What is the total area of this shape? Show your work.

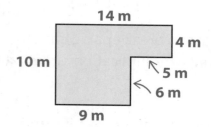

Solution ....

6 What is the area of this shape? Show your work.

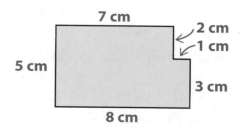

Solution ....

7 Opal draws this model of a picnic table. What is the total area of the picnic table? Show your work.

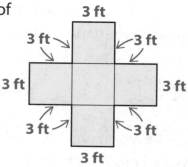

Solution ....

Practice Finding Areas of Non-Rectangular Shapes

Study the Example showing how to find the area of shapes that are not rectangles. Then solve problems 1–10.

EXAMPLE

Mr. Carey makes this shape with 1-inch tiles.
He asks his students to find the area.
Two students share their work.

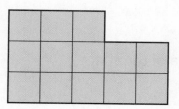

Renata's Way

1	2	3		
4	5	6	7	8
9	10	11	12	13

Marco's Way

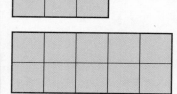

3 square inches

+

10 square inches

---

1 Marco breaks the shape into two rectangles. Outline two rectangles to show Marco's way.

2 Write multiplication equations to show the area of each rectangle you outlined in problem 1.

.... inches × .... inches = ... square inches

.... inches × .... inches = ... square inches

3 Write an addition equation to show the total area of the shape.

.... square inches + ... square inches = ... square inches

4 Sara breaks the shape into two rectangles in a different way. Outline two rectangles to show Sara's way. Then show how to find the total area.

Marco's Way

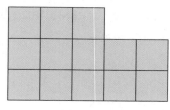

Sara's Way

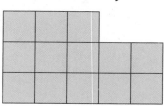

Use the top shape to answer problems 5–7.

5 Shade the rectangle in this shape that is 5 inches long and 2 inches wide. What is the area of this rectangle?

6 What is the area of the rectangle that is not shaded?

7 What is the total area of the shape?

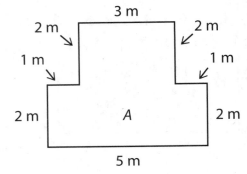

8 Draw a line to break Shape *A* into 2 rectangles. Then find the total area.

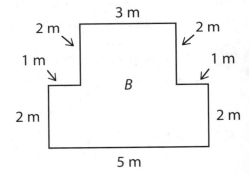

9 Draw lines to break Shape *B* into 3 rectangles. Then find the total area.

10 Draw lines to show two different ways to break this shape into rectangles. Then find the total area.

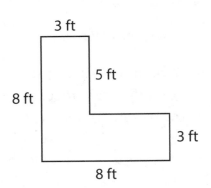

Refine Adding Areas

Complete the Example below. Then solve problems 1–7.

EXAMPLE

Miguel draws this shape in his notebook.

What is the area of Miguel's shape?

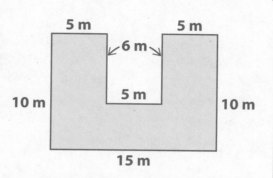

Look at how you could show your work by breaking apart the shape into 3 rectangles.

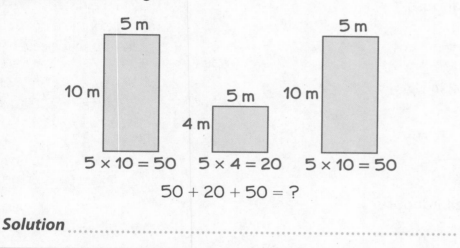

$5 \times 10 = 50$ $5 \times 4 = 20$ $5 \times 10 = 50$

$50 + 20 + 50 = ?$

Solution ....

> The student breaks apart the shape into 3 smaller rectangles and then adds the areas of these shapes to find the area of Miguel's shape.

PAIR/SHARE
What is another way you can break apart the shape?

APPLY IT

1 What is the area of the shape below?

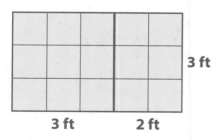

3 ft

3 ft   2 ft

Solution ....

> There are at least two ways I could solve this.

PAIR/SHARE
Compare the way you and your partner solved the problem.

2 Seth uses 1-inch-square tiles to build the shape shown below.

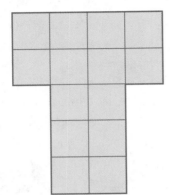

What is the total area of Seth's shape?

Solution ....

3 Kale draws a model of a birdhouse.

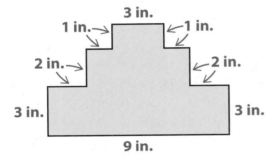

What is the total area of the birdhouse?

Ⓐ 30 inches

Ⓑ 30 square inches

Ⓒ 40 inches

Ⓓ 40 square inches

Sue chose Ⓒ as the correct answer. How did she get that answer?

How can counting help you solve this problem?

PAIR/SHARE
How else could you solve this problem?

Is area the distance around a shape or the amount of space the shape covers?

PAIR/SHARE
Does Sue's answer make sense?

4 Mrs. Ambrose draws the model below of her new patio and rock garden.

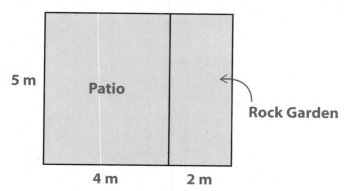

5 m   Patio   Rock Garden

4 m   2 m

What is the total area of Mrs. Ambrose's new patio and rock garden?

Ⓐ 22 meters

Ⓑ 22 square meters

Ⓒ 30 meters

Ⓓ 30 square meters

5 At the right are two rectangles that are joined together.

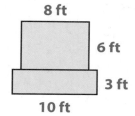

8 ft

6 ft

3 ft

10 ft

Would joining each rectangle below to the two rectangles above make a shape that has an area of 98 square feet?

	Yes	No
8 ft 3 ft	Ⓐ	Ⓑ
10 ft 2 ft	Ⓒ	Ⓓ
5 ft 4 ft	Ⓔ	Ⓕ
9 ft 2 ft	Ⓖ	Ⓗ

6 Find the unknown measurements in the shape below. Then break apart the shape into two rectangles to find its area.

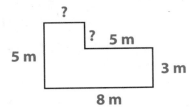

The area is .... square meters.

7 **MATH JOURNAL**

Draw your own shape made up of at least 2 rectangles. Label the dimensions of your shape. Find the total area. Then explain how you found the area.

✓ **SELF CHECK** Go back to the Unit 3 Opener and see what you can check off.

Solve One-Step Word Problems Using Multiplication and Division

Dear Family,

This week your child is solving one-step word problems using multiplication and division.

For example, he or she might see a problem like this one.

> *Tom created a patio using square tiles side-by-side with no gaps. He used 24 square tiles and made 6 rows. Tom used the same number of squares in each row. How many squares did he put in each row?*

One way to make sense of a problem like this is to make a grid showing rows of tiles with the same number in each row. Draw 1 tile in each row, until all 24 tiles are used. Then count to see how many tiles are in each row.

Or you can use multiplication or division equations to find the number of squares in each row, since all the rows are equal groups.

$$6 \times ? = 24 \quad \text{or} \quad 24 \div 6 = ?$$

However you solve the problem, you find that Tom put 4 squares in each row.

Invite your child to share what he or she knows about solving one-step word problems using multiplication and division by doing the following activity together.

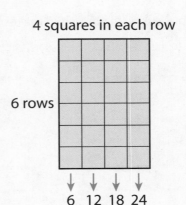

4 squares in each row

6 rows

6 12 18 24

ACTIVITY ONE-STEP WORD PROBLEMS

Do this activity with your child to practice solving one-step word problems with multiplication and division.

Materials 40 small objects (pennies, buttons, paper clips)

- Using some of the objects, ask your child to create an array.

- Take turns making up and solving word problems about the array.

- Each time, have your child say an equation to describe the problem.

- Ask your child to say whether he or she used multiplication or division to solve the problem.

For example, suppose your child makes the following array.

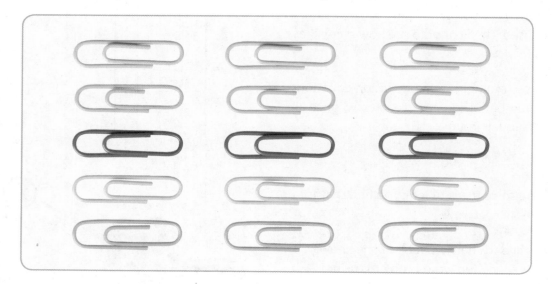

Here are two possible problems about the array. Ask your child to say an equation for each problem.

1. *Nigel has 15 cookies. He puts them in equal groups onto 5 plates. How many cookies are on each plate?*

2. *Paul pasted 15 stickers in his scrapbook. He put 3 stickers in each row. How many rows of stickers did he make?*

Answers: **1.** 15 ÷ 5 = 3 or 5 × 3 = 15; **2.** 15 ÷ 3 = 5 or 3 × 5 = 15

Explore Solving One-Step Word Problems Using Multiplication and Division

You have learned about different ways to show multiplication and division. In this lesson you will learn how to solve multiplication and division word problems. Use what you know to try to solve the problem below.

> **Write a word problem about this array that you could solve with multiplication or division. Then write an equation to represent your problem.**

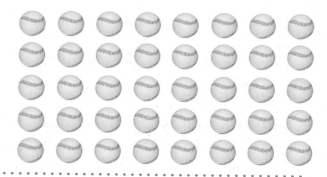

TRY IT

Math Toolkit
• counters
• buttons
• cups
• 1-centimeter grid paper
• multiplication models
• number lines

DISCUSS IT

Ask your partner: How did you get started?

Tell your partner: I started by . . .

CONNECT IT

1 LOOK BACK

Explain how you decided what word problem to write to match the array of baseballs.

2 LOOK AHEAD

Often you can write either a multiplication or a division equation to solve a problem. Look at the problems below. Write a multiplication equation and a division equation you could use to solve each problem about bananas. Use a ? in your equations to show the unknown number.

a. Two bunches have a total of 12 bananas. Each bunch has the same number of bananas. How many bananas are in each bunch?

b. Each bunch has 6 bananas. If there are 12 bananas, how many bunches are there?

3 REFLECT

How are the multiplication and divison equations alike in problem 2b?

....

....

....

....

Prepare for Solving One-Step Word Problems

1 Think about what you know about solving word problems. Fill in each box. Use words, numbers, and pictures. Show as many ideas as you can.

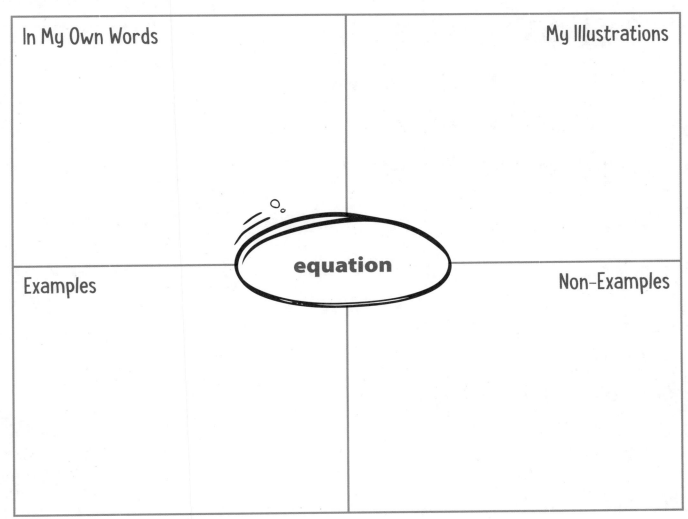

In My Own Words	My Illustrations

equation

Examples	Non-Examples

2 Write a multiplication equation and a division equation you could use to solve the following problem. Use a ? in your equations to show the unknown number.

There are a total of 24 tangerines in 3 boxes. Each box has the same number of tangerines. How many tangerines are in each box?

3 Solve the problem. Show your work.

Write a word problem about this array that you could solve with multiplication or division. Then write an equation to represent your problem.

Solution ....

4 Check your answer. Show your work.

Develop Solving Problems About Equal Groups

Read and try to solve the problem below.

A store has 24 saltwater fish. The store has 4 tanks for the fish. Each tank has an equal number of fish. How many fish are in each tank?

TRY IT

 **Math Toolkit**
- counters and buttons
- cups
- index cards
- multiplication models
- number lines

DISCUSS IT

Ask your partner: Can you explain that again?

Tell your partner: I knew . . . so I . . .

Explore different ways to understand solving word problems about equal groups.

> **A store has 24 saltwater fish. The store has 4 tanks for the fish. Each tank has an equal number of fish. How many fish are in each tank?**

PICTURE IT

You can use a drawing to show and solve problems about equal groups.

Make 4 groups of 1 fish each. Add 1 fish at a time to each group until there are 24 fish.

 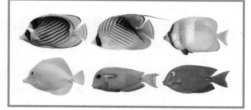

There are 4 tanks with ? fish in each tank.

MODEL IT

You can also use words to show and solve problems about equal groups.

Make notes about the problem.

> 24 fish in all. 4 groups, or tanks.

> ? fish in each group.

Use multiplication or division to find the number of fish in each group.

> $4 \times ? = 24$ or

> $24 \div 4 = ?$

CONNECT IT

Now you will use the problem from the previous page to help you understand how to solve word problems about equal groups.

1 What does 24 in the problem stand for?

What does 4 stand for?

2 What is the unknown number in the problem?

3 Use the letter *f* to stand for the unknown number. Write a division equation that can be used to solve the problem. Then write a related multiplication equation.

4 What is the solution? Explain how you found your answer.

5 Suppose the problem is changed to the one below.

> There are 24 fish. The store manager wants to put 6 fish in each tank. How many tanks will there be?

Write both a multiplication and division equation. Then solve the problem.

6 REFLECT

Look back at your **Try It**, strategies by classmates, and **Picture It** and **Model It**. Which models or strategies do you like best for solving problems about equal groups? Explain.

....

....

....

....

APPLY IT

Use what you just learned to solve these problems. Use a drawing of equal groups or an equation with a letter for the unknown number to show your work.

7 Jenna has 30 photos of her friends. She puts 6 photos on each page in her album. How many pages does Jenna use? Show your work.

Solution

8 There are 9 drawing kits on a table in the art room. Each kit has 4 pencils. How many pencils are there in all? Show your work.

Solution

9 Tom has 21 apples and 3 baskets. If Tom puts the same number of apples in each basket, how many apples will be in each basket? Show your work.

Solution

Practice Solving Problems About Equal Groups

Study the Example that shows how a drawing can help you understand problems about equal groups. Then solve problems 1–8.

EXAMPLE

24 students sign up for an Irish folk dancing class.
There are 4 students in each group. How many groups are there?

Draw a picture.

  24 students
  4 in each group
  n groups

Write an equation.

  $24 \div 4 = n$
  $n = 6$

There are 6 groups of students.

18 students take hula dance classes. There are 6 students in each class. How many classes are there?

1   Make a drawing for this problem. Use ☺ for each student. Make groups to show the classes.

2   Complete the multiplication and division equations for this problem. Write the value of n.

  $18 \div$ .... $= n$ $n \times$ .... $= 18$ $n =$ ....

3   How many hula dance classes are there? ....

There are 2 classes for Mexican folk dance. There are 8 students in each class. How many students take Mexican folk dance class?

4 What is the unknown that you need to find out?

5 Write an equation for the problem. Use *n* to stand for the number you need to find out. Solve the problem.

Equation ....

.... students take Mexican folk dance class.

15 students take modern dance lessons. There are 3 students in each group. How many groups of students are there?

6 Write an equation for the problem. Then solve.

Equation ....

There are .... groups of students.

7 If 15 more students sign up for modern dance, how many groups would there be?

Equation ....

There would be .... groups of students.

8 How can you use the answer to problem 6 to find the answer to problem 7?

Develop Solving Problems About Arrays

Read and try to solve the problem below.

A clothing store uses stacking crates for storing jeans. The manager orders 42 crates. Six crates will fit in one row along the wall. How many rows of crates will there be?

TRY IT

 Math Toolkit
- counters
- square tiles
- grid paper
- sticky notes
- multiplication models
- number lines

DISCUSS IT

Ask your partner: Do you agree with me? Why or why not?

Tell your partner: I do not understand how . . .

Explore different ways to understand solving word problems about arrays.

> A clothing store uses stacking crates for storing jeans. The manager orders 42 crates. Six crates will fit in one row along the wall. How many rows of crates will there be?

PICTURE IT

You can use a drawing to show and solve problems about arrays.

Use an array. Show a row of 6. Add rows of 6 until you get to 42.

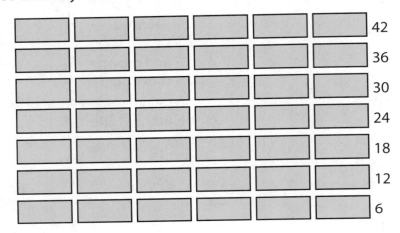

MODEL IT

You can also use words to show and solve problems about arrays.

Make notes about the problem.

42 crates in all.

6 crates in each row.

? rows

Use multiplication or division to find the number of rows.

$? \times 6 = 42$

or

$42 \div 6 = ?$

CONNECT IT

Now you will use the problem from the previous page to help you understand how to solve word problems about arrays.

1 What do the numbers in the problem stand for?

2 What is the unknown number in the problem?

3 Use the letter *r* to stand for the unknown number. Write a division equation that can be used to solve the problem. Then write a related multiplication equation.

4 Show and explain how to solve the problem.

5 Explain how you can use an array to solve this problem.

> There are 24 crayons in a box. There are 8 crayons in each row. How many rows of crayons are there?

6 REFLECT

Look back at your **Try It**, strategies by classmates, and **Picture It** and **Model It**. Which models or strategies do you like best for solving problems about arrays? Explain.

APPLY IT

Use what you just learned to solve these problems. Use an array or an equation with a letter for the unknown number to show your work.

7 Grace's garden has 4 rows of tomatoes with 8 plants in each row. How many tomato plants are in Grace's garden? Show your work.

Solution ....

8 There are 20 children in gym class. The teacher lines up the children in 4 equal rows for a game. How many children are in each row? Show your work.

Solution ....

9 There are 54 flowers in the garden. There are 9 flowers in each row. How many rows of flowers are there? Show your work.

Solution ....

Practice Solving Problems About Arrays

Study the Example that shows how an array can help you solve multiplication and division problems. Then solve problems 1–6.

EXAMPLE

The art teacher wants to hang 18 drawings on the hall wall. She hangs 6 drawings in each row. How many rows of drawings are there?

18 drawings
6 in each row
n rows

$18 \div 6 = n$　and　$n \times 6 = 18$

$18 \div 6 = 3$　and　$3 \times 6 = 18$

There are 3 rows of drawings.

$$\begin{array}{r} 6 \\ 6 \\ +\ 6 \\ \hline 18 \end{array}$$

In the art room, there are 20 easels. The easels are arranged in 4 equal rows. How many easels are in each row?

1 Draw an array to show the 20 easels in 4 rows. Put the same number in each row.

2 Complete the division equation to solve the problem. n stands for the unknown.

$20 \div$ .... $= n$, so $n =$ ....

3 How many easels are in each row? ....

4   The art room has 5 shelves of paint jars. There are 9 paint jars on each shelf. How many paint jars are in the art room? Show your work.

Solution

5   There are 54 frames on the wall in an art store. The frames are in 6 equal rows. How many frames are in each row? Show your work.

Solution

6   A store has 3 shelves with the same number of drawing pads on each shelf. There are 30 drawing pads in all. How many drawing pads are on each shelf? Show your work.

Solution

Develop Solving Problems About Area

Read and try to solve the problem below.

> For an art project, Sean uses colored squares of paper to tile a rectangle that has an area of 48 square inches. Each piece of paper is 1 square inch. He makes 6 rows. How long is the rectangle?

TRY IT

Math Toolkit
- 1-inch tiles
- 1-inch grid paper
- sticky notes
- multiplication models
- perimeter and area tool

DISCUSS IT

Ask your partner: Why did you choose that strategy?

Tell your partner: The strategy I used to find the answer was . . .

Explore different ways to understand solving word problems about area.

> For an art project, Sean uses colored squares of paper to tile a rectangle that has an area of 48 square inches. Each piece of paper is 1 square inch. He makes 6 rows. How long is the rectangle?

PICTURE IT

You can use a drawing to show and solve problems about area.

Draw a picture.

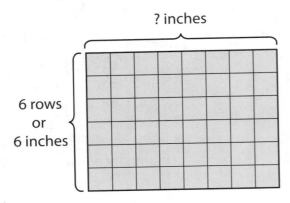

? inches

6 rows
or
6 inches

Area = 48 square inches

MODEL IT

You can also use an equation to solve problems about area.

Make notes about the problem.

The rectangle has an area of 48 square inches.

6 rows means the rectangle is 6 inches wide.

The rectangle is ? inches long.

Use multiplication or division to find how long the rectangle is.

$$6 \times ? = 48$$

or

$$48 \div 6 = ?$$

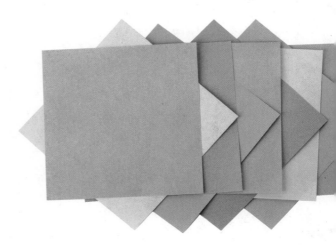

CONNECT IT

Now you will use the problem from the previous page to help you understand how to solve word problems about area.

1 What is the unknown in this problem?

2 Write a division equation using the letter ℓ to stand for the unknown number. Then write a related multiplication equation.

3 Show and explain how to solve the problem.

4 How could you use the multiplication fact $6 \times 7 = 42$ to find the solution to this problem?

5 Suppose Sean's rectangle has an area of 56 square inches and he makes 7 rows. Explain how you could use multiplication and division to find the length of this rectangle.

6 **REFLECT**

Look back at your **Try It**, strategies by classmates, and **Picture It** and **Model It**. Which models or strategies do you like best for solving multiplication and division problems about area? Explain.

APPLY IT

Use what you just learned to solve these problems. Use a drawing of square tiles or an equation with a letter for the unknown number to show your work.

7 A walkway is made of square patio blocks. Each block is 1 square meter. There are 2 rows of blocks with 9 blocks in each row. What is the area of the walkway? Show your work.

Solution ....

8 Michael uses tiles with an area of 1 square foot each to build a rectangular patio with an area of 35 square feet. He uses 5 tiles in each row. How many rows of tiles are there? Show your work.

Solution ....

9 Ayla uses 30 square pieces of fabric to make a quilt. Each square is 1 square foot. Her finished quilt has 5 rows, and she used the same number of squares in each row. How long is her quilt?

Which equations could be used to solve this problem?

Ⓐ $5 \times s = 30$

Ⓑ $30 \times 5 = s$

Ⓒ $30 = s \times 5$

Ⓓ $5 \times 30 = s$

Ⓔ $30 \div 5 = s$

Practice Solving Problems About Area

Study the Example that shows how to use drawings and equations to help you solve multiplication and division problems about area. Then solve problems 1–6.

EXAMPLE

Mrs. Milton tiles her patio floor with 1-square-foot tiles. The floor has an area of 21 square feet. She makes 3 equal rows of tiles. How many tiles are in each row?

21 square feet = 21 tiles
3 equal rows
n tiles in each row

3 rows

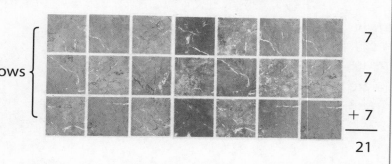

7

7

+ 7
___
21

$21 \div 3 = n$ and $3 \times n = 21$
$21 \div 3 = 7$ and $3 \times 7 = 21$

There are 7 tiles in each row.

Mr. Salton paves the entrance to his house with 1-square-foot stone tiles. The area of the entrance is 42 square feet. He puts 7 tiles in each row. How many rows of tiles are there?

1 Make a drawing at the right to show the rows of tiles.

2 Complete the division equation to solve the problem. Use *n* to stand for the unknown number.

$42 \div$ .... $= n$, so $n =$ ....

3 How many rows of stone tiles are there? ....

4 A rectangular quilt is made from 36 squares that each have an area of
1 square foot. One side of the quilt is 9 feet long. How long is the other side?
Show your work.

Solution ....

5 There are 7 rows of squares on a game board.
There are 9 squares in each row. How many
squares are on the game board? Show your work.

Solution ....

6 Each square on the game board in problem 5 has sides that are 2 inches long.
How long is the side with 7 squares? How long is the side with 9 squares?
Show your work.

The side with 7 squares is .... inches long.

The side with 9 squares is .... inches long.

Refine Solving One-Step Word Problems Using Multiplication and Division

Complete the Example below. Then solve problems 1–9.

EXAMPLE

Troy has 18 homework problems to do. He has 3 days to finish the homework. If he does the same number of problems each day, how many problems will he do in a day?

Look at how you could show your work using a drawing.

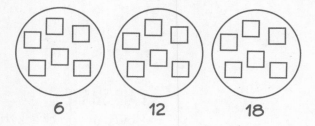

6   12   18

Solution ....

This problem can be solved using 3 × ? = 18 or 18 ÷ 3 = ?.

APPLY IT

1 Mr. Rivera is posting 28 student papers on the bulletin board. He posts the papers in 4 rows, with an equal number of papers in each row. How many papers does Mr. Rivera put in each row? Show your work.

What does 28 stand for in the problem?

Solution ....

2 There are 54 players at a baseball clinic. The coach puts them into teams of 9 players. How many teams are there? Show your work.

What fact do you know that includes both numbers in the problem?

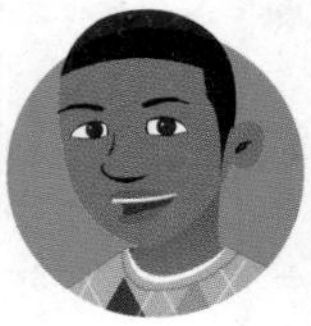

PAIR/SHARE
How can you check that your answer is correct?

Solution ....

3 Mai eats 3 servings of fruit each day. How many servings of fruit does she eat in a week? [1 week = 7 days]

Ⓐ 10 servings

Ⓑ 18 servings

Ⓒ 21 servings

Ⓓ 24 servings

Harry chose Ⓐ as the correct answer. How did he get that answer?

Should you multiply or divide to solve the problem?

PAIR/SHARE
How did you figure out how Harry got his answer?

4 There are 8 socks in the dryer.
How many pairs of socks is this?

5 Dana forms a rectangle with 15 square sticky notes.
She puts 5 notes in each row.
How many rows does she make?

Ⓐ 3

Ⓑ 5

Ⓒ 10

Ⓓ 20

6 Jasmine has 42 balloons. She gives an equal number of balloons to 6 children.
Can each equation be used to find the number of balloons Jasmine gives
each child?

	Yes	No
$42 \times 6 = \square$	Ⓐ	Ⓑ
$6 \times \square = 42$	Ⓒ	Ⓓ
$6 \div \square = 42$	Ⓔ	Ⓕ
$42 \div 6 = \square$	Ⓖ	Ⓗ

Lesson 17 Solve One-Step Word Problems Using Multiplication and Division

7 Which problems can be solved using $12 \div 4 = \square$?

Ⓐ Brandon has 12 cookies. He gives the same number of cookies to each of his 4 friends. How many cookies does each friend get?

Ⓑ Zoe has 12 folders. She wants to put 4 papers in each folder. How many papers does she need?

Ⓒ Michael rides his bike 4 miles a day. How many days will it take him to ride 12 miles?

Ⓓ Lilah has 12 tomatoes. She always uses 4 tomatoes to make a salad. How many salads can she make?

Ⓔ Jacob has 12 flowers. He gives 4 flowers to his friends. How many flowers does Jacob have left?

8 Catrina uses green tiles to make a square on her kitchen floor that has an area of 25 square feet. How long is each side of the green square? Show your work.

Each side of the green square is .... feet long.

9 MATH JOURNAL

Missy wants to hang 12 pictures on her bedroom wall. She hangs 3 pictures in each row. How many rows of pictures are there? Explain two ways to find the answer.

 SELF CHECK Go back to the Unit 3 Opener and see what you can check off.

Dear Family,

This week your child is solving two-step word problems using any mix of the four operations and estimating to check the answer.

Here is a problem your child might see.

> Jenny has 152 peaches, and she uses 8 peaches to make one pie. If she first gives 72 peaches to her neighbor, how many pies can she make with the peaches she keeps for herself?

When solving two-step problems, it is particularly helpful to make a diagram.

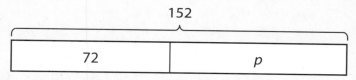

The diagram shows that Jenny started with 152 peaches, gave 72 to her neighbor, and kept p peaches for herself.

In this problem, the first step is to subtract to find out how many peaches Jenny kept. $152 - 72 = 80$, so Jenny kept 80 peaches.

The second step is to figure out how many groups of 8 peaches Jenny can make from her 80 peaches. Since there are equal groups, write a multiplication or division equation to find how many equal groups (g).

$8 \times g = 80$ or $80 \div 8 = g$

$80 \div 8 = 10$, so Jenny can make 10 pies.

The problem can also be solved by combining the two steps into one equation: $(152 - 72) \div 8 = 10$.

Invite your child to share what he or she knows about solving two-step word problems using the four operations by doing the following activity together.

Do this activity with your child to practice solving two-step word problems.

Work with your child to make up a real-world problem this diagram could represent.

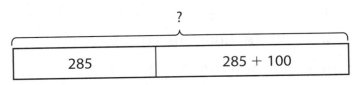

?	
285	285 + 100

- For example, you might make up a problem like the following.

    Mia drives 285 miles on Saturday. On Sunday she drives 100 more miles than she drove on Saturday. How many miles does Mia drive in all over the weekend?

- Work with your child to solve the problem. Possible solution methods are shown below.

- Change the numbers and try creating a new problem to match the new numbers.

Possible solution methods:
Add to find out how many miles Mia drives on Sunday.
285 + 100 = 385, so the number of miles for Sunday is 385.
Then add the miles for Saturday to the miles for Sunday:
285 + 385 = 670.

You could also combine the steps to write just one equation:

$m = 285 + (285 + 100)$

$m = 285 + 385$

$m = 670$

Mia drives 670 miles in all.

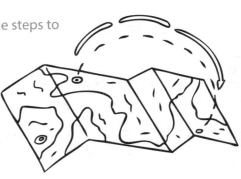

Explore Solving Two-Step Word Problems Using the Four Operations

In this lesson you will learn how to solve two-step word problems using any of the four **operations**—addition, subtraction, multiplication, and division. Use what you know to try to solve the problem below.

> **The Shirt Shack has 438 T-shirts at the end of the day. Then they receive a delivery of new shirts in which:**
> - **the shirts come in 4 different colors (green, gray, orange, purple).**
> - **there are 8 shirts of each color.**
>
> **How many T-shirts does the store have now?**

TRY IT

Math Toolkit
- base-ten blocks
- 1-centimeter grid paper
- sticky notes
- multiplication models
- number lines

DISCUSS IT

Ask your partner: How did you get started?

Tell your partner: At first I thought . . .

CONNECT IT

① LOOK BACK

Explain how you found how many T-shirts the store has now.

② LOOK AHEAD

You can use equations to solve two-step word problems. You can use an equation for each step or combine both steps in one equation. Look at the following problem:

> A hat store has 45 hats. They sell 20 hats. The rest of the hats sit on 5 shelves with the same number of hats on each shelf. How many hats are on each shelf?

a. Complete two equations to solve the problem.

Hats to start −	**Hats sold**	= **Hats left**

$$\text{.............} - \text{.............} = \ell$$
$$\text{.............} = \ell$$

Hats left ÷	**Shelves**	= **Hats on each shelf**

$$\text{.............} \div \text{.............} = h$$
$$\text{.............} = h$$

b. Complete one equation to solve the problem.

(Hats to start −	**Hats sold)** ÷	**Shelves**	= **Hats on each shelf**

$$(\text{.............} - \text{.............}) \div \text{.............} = h$$
$$\text{.............} \div \text{.............} = h$$
$$\text{.............} = h$$

③ REFLECT

How are solving a problem with two equations and with one equation alike and different?

....

....

Prepare for Solving Two-Step Word Problems Using the Four Operations

1 Think about what you know about solving word problems. Fill in each box. Use words, numbers, and pictures. Show as many ideas as you can.

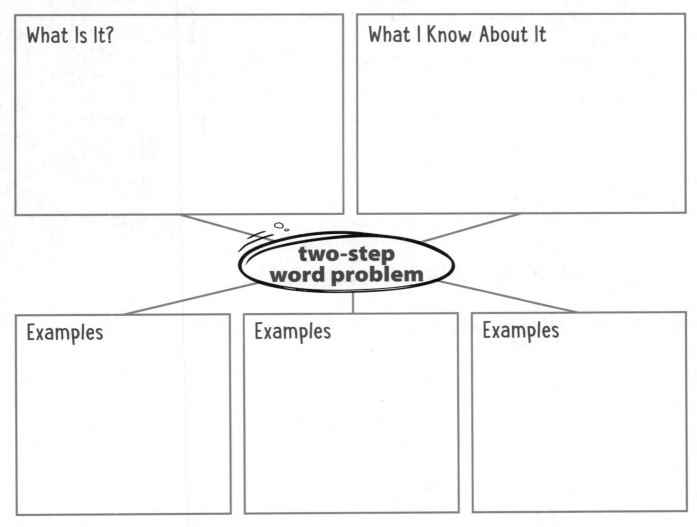

What Is It?

What I Know About It

two-step word problem

Examples

Examples

Examples

2 Is the following problem a two-step word problem? Explain.

A store has 40 suits. They sell 16 suits. The rest of the suits are hung on 4 racks with the same number of suits on each rack. How many suits are on each rack?

3 Solve the problem. Show your work.

Chanel has 356 beads. Then she receives a package with more beads in which:
- **the beads come in 6 different colors (red, orange, yellow, green, blue, purple).**
- **there are 9 beads of each color.**

How many beads does Chanel have now?

Solution ....

4 Check your answer. Show your work.

Develop Solving Two-Step Word Problems Using Two Equations

Read and try to solve the problem below.

Sam has a box with 12 cans of paint. There are 3 other cans of paint on a table. He puts all of the paint cans together on the table in rows of 5. How many rows of paint cans does Sam make?

TRY IT

 Math Toolkit
- counters
- 1-centimeter grid paper
- sticky notes
- multiplication models
- number lines

DISCUSS IT

Ask your partner: Why did you choose that strategy?

Tell your partner: The strategy I used to find the answer was . . .

Explore different ways to understand solving two-step word problems using two equations.

> Sam has a box with 12 cans of paint. There are 3 other cans of paint on a table. He puts all of the paint cans together on the table in rows of 5. How many rows of paint cans does Sam make?

PICTURE IT
You can use a drawing to show two-step word problems.

15 cans of paint in rows of 5 cans.

3 cans already on the table.

12 cans added to the table.

MODEL IT
You can also use words and numbers to model two-step problems.

   12 cans in a box
+   3 cans on the table
   15 cans in all

15 cans ÷ 5 cans in each row = ? rows

CONNECT IT

Now you will use the problem from the previous page to help you understand how to solve two-step word problems using two equations.

1 How do you find the total number of cans of paint that Sam has?

Let c be the total number of cans. Write an equation to find c.

2 How does Sam arrange the paint cans?

3 How can you find the number of rows?

Let r equal the number of rows. Write an equation to find r that includes c and r.

4 How can you find the value of c? What is the value of c?

Write the equation from problem 3 using the value of c. How many rows of paint cans does Sam make?

5 Explain how you can use multiplication to check that your answer is correct.

6 REFLECT

Look back at your **Try It**, strategies by classmates, and **Picture It** and **Model It**. Which models or strategies do you like best for solving two-step word problems? Explain.

....

....

....

....

....

APPLY IT

Use what you just learned to solve these problems. Write an equation for each step in the problem. Use letters for the unknown numbers.

7 Demarco has 4 five-dollar bills. Then his grandfather gives him 1 ten-dollar bill. How much money does Demarco have now? Show your work.

Solution ....

8 There are 40 water bottles that are divided equally between 5 teams. Each team has 4 players. Each player gets an equal number of water bottles. How many water bottles does each player get? Show your work.

Solution ....

9 Vegetable plants are sold in packs of 4. A container holds 2 packs of plants. There are 10 containers on one shelf. How many plants are on the shelf? Show your work.

Solution ....

Practice Solving Two-Step Word Problems Using Two Equations

Study the Example showing how to solve two-step problems using two equations. Then solve problems 1–10.

EXAMPLE

Sally buys 6 bags of round beads to make bracelets. There are 4 round beads in each bag. She also buys 5 heart-shaped beads. How many beads does Sally buy?

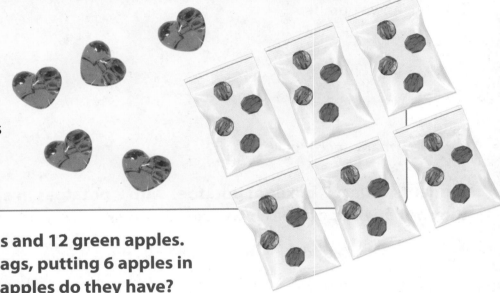

Round beads:
    6 groups of 4
    $r = 6 \times 4 = 24$

All beads:
    round beads + heart beads
    $a = r + 5; 24 + 5 = 29$

Sally bought 29 beads.

Students collect 12 red apples and 12 green apples. They put all the apples into bags, putting 6 apples in each bag. How many bags of apples do they have?

1 Write an equation that shows how many apples they collect.

2 They collect .... apples.

3 Write an equation that shows how many bags of apples the students have.

4 The students have .... bags of apples.

5 Draw a model to check your work.

A store has 4 baskets of soccer balls with 8 balls in each basket. They sell 10 balls. How many balls are left?

6 Draw a model for the problem. Label the model.

7 Write an equation for each step of the problem. Use letters for the unknown numbers.

8 How many soccer balls are left? ....

Students collect 7 boxes of potatoes with 8 potatoes in each box. Then they put all the potatoes into bags. There are 8 potatoes in each bag.

9 How many bags do the students need for the potatoes? Show your work.

They need .... bags.

10 Later the students collect 24 more potatoes. How many bags do they need for all the potatoes? Show your work.

They need .... bags.

Develop Solving Two-Step Word Problems Using One Equation

Read and try to solve the problem below.

Third graders at Brown Elementary School are raising money for the school library.
• The goal is to raise $250.
• They raise $9 each day for 8 days in a row.
How much more money, *m*, is needed to reach the goal? To solve this problem, write an equation for each step. Or write one equation that includes both steps.

TRY IT

 Math Toolkit
• base-ten blocks
• counters
• cups
• 1-centimeter grid paper
• multiplication models
• number lines

DISCUSS IT

Ask your partner: Do you agree with me? Why or why not?

Tell your partner: I do not understand how . . .

Explore different ways to understand how to solve two-step word problems using one equation.

> **Third graders at Brown Elementary School are raising money for the school library.**
> - **The goal is to raise $250.**
> - **They raise $9 each day for 8 days in a row.**
> How much more money, *m*, is needed to reach the goal? To solve this problem, write an equation for each step. Or write one equation that includes both steps.

PICTURE IT

You can use a diagram to show a two-step word problem.

250

| 9 | 9 | 9 | 9 | 9 | 9 | 9 | 9 | *m* |

MODEL IT

Use the diagram above to help write an equation for a two-step word problem.

The students raise $9 each day for 8 days. So, they have already raised **8 × 9** dollars.

They need a total of **250** dollars. They need to raise *m* more dollars.

The **amount already raised** plus *m* should equal **250**.

Write this as one equation.

$$(8 \times 9) + m = 250$$

CONNECT IT

Now you will use the problem from the previous page to help you understand how to solve two-step word problems using one equation.

$$(8 \times 9) + m = 250$$
$$72 + m = 250$$

1 What operation is done first? .... Why?

2 How can you find the unknown addend, m?

3 Why could you subtract 72 from 250 to find m?

4 What is m, and what does it stand for?

5 Explain how you can use addition to check your answer.

6 REFLECT

Look back at your **Try It**, strategies by classmates, and **Picture It** and **Model It**. Which models or strategies do you like best for solving two-step word problems? Explain.

....

....

....

....

Lesson 18 Solve Two-Step Word Problems Using the Four Operations

APPLY IT

Use what you just learned to solve these problems.

7 Nima is training for a bike race. During the first three weeks in April she rides a total of 176 miles. During the last week in April, she rides 9 miles each day for 7 days.

a. Write an equation that can be used to find how many miles in all, *m*, that Nima rides in April.

b. Use your equation from Part a to find how many miles in all Nima rides in April. Show your work.

Solution ....

8 Tabitha has a bag with 24 marbles. There are 6 other marbles on the ground. She puts all of the marbles together on the ground and makes rows of 5. How many rows of marbles, *r*, does Tabitha make? Write an equation that can be used to solve the problem. Then solve the problem. Show your work.

Solution ....

9 Tim is saving money to buy a pair of hockey skates that costs $289. For the past 6 weeks, he has saved $7 each week. How much money, *h*, does Tim still need to save? Show your work.

Solution ....

Practice Solving Two-Step Word Problems Using One Equation

Study the Example showing how to solve a two-step word problem using one equation. Then solve problems 1–5.

EXAMPLE

Students in the science club raise $210 for lab equipment. They buy 7 packs of batteries for $9 each. How much money, m, do they have left? Write an equation that can be used to solve the problem. Then solve the problem.

$(7 \times 9) + m = 210$
$63 + m = 210$
$210 - 63 = m$
$m = 147$

They have $147 left.

210

| 9 | 9 | 9 | 9 | 9 | 9 | 9 | m |

---

1 Mrs. Horn needs 50 rulers for the art room. She has 7 packs with 4 rulers in each pack. How many more rulers, r, does she need? Complete the equations to solve the problem.

$(7 \times \text{.......}) + r = 50$

$\text{.......} + r = 50$

$\text{.......} - \text{.......} = r$, and $r = \text{.......}$.

50

| 4 | 4 | 4 | 4 | 4 | 4 | 4 | r |

Mrs. Horn needs .... more rulers.

2 The principal wants to buy a banner that costs $95. Five parents each donate $6 for the banner. How much more money, d, is needed? Complete the equations to solve the problem.

$(\text{.......} \times \text{.......}) + d = 95$

$\text{.......} + d = 95$

$d = \text{.......}$

95

| 6 | 6 | 6 | 6 | 6 | d |

They need .... more.

3 A camp needs 100 students to help with the 4-year-old campers. Eight students from 4 different classes have agreed to help. How many more students are needed? Write an equation that can be used to solve the problem. Then solve the problem. Show your work.

Solution ....

4 The art teacher has 75 paintbrushes. He gives 35 brushes to another teacher. He splits the rest equally among 8 students. How many brushes does he give to each student? Show your work.

Solution ....

5 Mr. Berg buys 5 number puzzles and 3 word puzzles for his students. The puzzles are $7 each. Mr. Berg uses a $60 gift card to pay for the puzzles. How much money is left on the card? Show your work.

Solution ....

Develop Estimating Solutions to Word Problems

Read and try to solve the problem below.

A zoo names an elephant Tiny.
- **On Saturday, Tiny ate 152 pounds of food.**
- **On Sunday, he ate 12 more pounds of food than he did on Saturday.**

How many pounds of food did Tiny eat that weekend? Estimate to check your answer.

TRY IT

 Math Toolkit
- base-ten blocks
- 1-centimeter grid paper
- sticky notes
- number lines

DISCUSS IT

Ask your partner: Can you explain that again?

Tell your partner: I disagree with you about this part because . . .

Explore different ways to understand how to estimate solutions to two-step word problems.

> **A zoo names an elephant Tiny.**
> - **On Saturday, Tiny ate 152 pounds of food.**
> - **On Sunday, he ate 12 more pounds of food than he did on Saturday.**
> **How many pounds of food did Tiny eat that weekend?**
> **Estimate to check your answer.**

PICTURE IT

You can use a table to show the information in a two-step word problem.

Amount of Food Tiny Ate	
Saturday	Sunday
152 pounds	152 pounds + 12 pounds

$152 + (152 + 12) = f$

MODEL IT

Estimate the solution to the two-step problem.

You can round each number to the nearest hundred and then add mentally.

    152 rounds to 200.
    12 rounds to 0.
    200 + (200 + 0) = 400

You can also round each number to the nearest ten and then add mentally.

    152 rounds to 150.
    12 rounds to 10.
    150 + (150 + 10) = 310

CONNECT IT

Now you will use the problem from the previous page to help you understand why it is useful to estimate solutions to two-step word problems.

$$152 + (152 + 12) = f$$

1 Add the numbers in parentheses. Break the numbers apart to use numbers that are easy to work with: **150 + 2 + 10 + 2 =** ....

2 What is the next step? Explain and show it.

3 How many pounds of food did Tiny eat that weekend? Compare the answer to the estimates on the previous page. Are they close?

4 Do you think the answer is reasonable? Explain why.

5 Would it be better to estimate before solving the problem or after? Does it matter? Explain.

6 REFLECT

Look back at your **Try It**, strategies by classmates, and **Picture It** and **Model It**. Which models or strategies do you like best for estimating the solution to a two-step word problem? Explain.

....

....

....

....

APPLY IT

Use what you just learned to solve these problems. Estimate to check your answers.

7 Kennedy planted 222 flowers last week. This week she planted 65 more flowers than last week. How many flowers did she plant in all? Show your work.

Solution ....

8 Joan earned $136 last week and $215 this week. She uses some of her earnings to buy a jacket. Joan has $273 left after buying the jacket. How much does she spend on the jacket? Show your work.

Solution ....

9 A bookstore has 650 copies of a new book. The first day, 281 copies are sold. At the end of the week there are only 43 copies left. How many books are sold between the first day and the end of the week? Tell why your answer is reasonable. Show your work.

Solution ....

Practice Estimating Solutions to Word Problems

Study the Example showing how to estimate the solution to a two-step word problem. Then solve problems 1–4.

EXAMPLE

The city garden has red and pink rose bushes. There are 119 red rose bushes. There are 17 fewer pink rose bushes than red rose bushes. About how many rose bushes are in the city garden?

Round to the nearest ten and solve.
119 rounds to 120, and 17 rounds to 20.
I know $120 - 20$ is 100,
so I *estimate* 100 pink rose bushes.
I know $120 + 100 = 220$,
so I *estimate* 220 rose bushes.

$$119 + (119 - 17) = b$$
$$119 + 102 = b, \text{ so } b = 221.$$

Rose Bushes	
Red	**Pink**
119	$119 - 17$
(about 120)	(about $120 - 20$, or 100)

The actual number of rose bushes in the garden is 221.
That is close to 220, so 221 is reasonable.

For the concert, 109 adult tickets are sold. 67 more student tickets are sold than adult tickets. How many tickets are sold in all?

1 Complete the table to show the information in the problem. Round to the nearest hundred.

2 Write an equation to estimate the total number of tickets sold. Then find the actual total.

_____ $= t$

_____ $= t$

About _____ tickets are sold.

Really, _____ tickets are sold.

Tickets Sold	
Adult	**Student**
(about)	(about +)

3 In the school parking lot there are 113 fewer bikes than cars. There are 185 cars. How many cars and bikes are in the parking lot?

Round to the nearest ten to estimate. Then complete the chart.

Cars	Bikes		
185	185 − 113		
(about 190)	(about 190 −	, or	)

.... + (.................. − ....) = c

c = ...

Estimate: There are about .... cars and bikes.

Actual: .... + (.................. − ....) = c

⠀⠀⠀c = ...

There are .... cars and bikes in all.

4 Sarah reads 215 pages of her book during the first week of vacation. During the second week she reads 62 more pages than in the first week. How many pages does she read in the two weeks? Round to the nearest ten to estimate. Then solve. Show your work.

Estimate: She reads about .... pages during the two weeks.

Actual: ....

⠀⠀⠀..................................

Sarah reads .... pages.

Refine Solving Two-Step Word Problems Using the Four Operations

Complete the Example below. Then solve problems 1–9.

EXAMPLE

Bridget is packing strawberries in sandwich bags to sell at her gymnastics meet. She has 140 strawberries, and she makes bags of 5. So far, Bridget has packed 105 strawberries. How many more bags of 5 strawberries can Bridget make?

Look at how you could show your work using an equation.

$$(140 - 105) \div 5 = b$$
$$35 \div 5 = b$$
$$b = ?$$

Solution ....

The student uses an equation that uses both subtraction and division.

PAIR/SHARE
Can you write a different equation to solve this problem?

APPLY IT

1 Students in Miss Kemp's class earn 1 point for each page they read. A student who earns 300 points gets a prize. Elise reads 8 pages a day for 7 days in a row. How many more points does she need to get a prize? Show your work.

What operation do you use to find how many pages Elise has read?

Solution ....

PAIR/SHARE
How can you check your answer?

2 Emry has 243 stamps from the United States in her collection. She has 58 stamps from other countries. Emry puts 129 of her stamps in a scrapbook. She solves this equation:
$243 + 58 - 129 = s$.

Emry says, "There are 172 stamps NOT in the scrapbook." Is her answer reasonable? Use estimation to check her work. Show your work.

> Could you round the numbers to the nearest ten or hundred to estimate?

Solution

PAIR/SHARE
Can you solve this problem in a different way?

3 In the morning, 134 books are checked out from the library. In the afternoon, 254 books are checked out, and 118 books are checked out in the evening. How many books in all are checked out from the library on this day?

> How can you estimate the answer?

Ⓐ 270

Ⓑ 388

Ⓒ 496

Ⓓ 506

Paolo chose Ⓑ as the correct answer. How did he get that answer?

PAIR/SHARE
How can you tell if Paolo's answer is reasonable?

4 Which equation CANNOT be used to solve the problem below?

Rosa and Brett are the only two people in a school election. Rosa gets 314 votes in the election. She gets 18 more votes than Brett. How many people voted in the election?

Ⓐ $314 + (314 - 18) = n$

Ⓑ $n = 314 + (314 - 18)$

Ⓒ $(314 - 18) + 314 = n$

Ⓓ $314 + (314 + 18) = n$

5 George estimates that 800 people voted in the election in problem 4. Which mistake could he have made?

Ⓐ George rounded 18 down to 10 instead of up to 20.

Ⓑ George rounded 314 up to 320 instead of down to 310.

Ⓒ George rounded 314 up to 400 instead of down to 300.

Ⓓ George rounded 18 up to 100 instead of down to 0.

6 A produce manager unpacks 108 bananas. There are 9 bunches of 4 bananas each. The rest are single bananas. Which pairs of equations can be used to find the number of single bananas?

Ⓐ $9 \times 4 = b$
   $108 - b = s$

Ⓑ $b = 108 \div 4$
   $b + 9 = s$

Ⓒ $4 \times 9 = b$
   $108 = s - b$

Ⓓ $108 \div 9 = b$
   $b + 4 = s$

Ⓔ $b = 9 \times 4$
   $s + b = 108$

Ⓕ $b = 9 \times 4$
   $108 + s = b$

7 Greg is packing a book order. He has already packed 3 boxes with 5 books in each box. There are 210 books left to pack. How many books are in the whole order? Show your work.

There are .... books in the whole order.

8 Gina wants to estimate the total of three bills she has to pay. The bills are for $125, $115, and $138. Gina wants to make sure that she has enough money. She wants the estimate to be greater than the total of the bills. Should she round to the nearest ten or nearest hundred? Explain.

9 MATH JOURNAL

Simone is stocking a shelf with jars of pickles. She has one box with 30 jars and another box with 18 jars. She can fit 6 jars in a row on the shelf. Write and solve one equation to find out how many rows she makes using all the jars in both boxes. Explain how you solved the problem.

 SELF CHECK   Go back to the Unit 3 Opener and see what you can check off.

Scaled Graphs

Dear Family,

This week your child is learning to solve problems using data in scaled graphs.

In a scaled picture graph, such as the one to the right, each symbol represents more than one item.

Using a **scale** of 2 or more allows more information to fit into a smaller space. Learning about scaled graphs gives your child a chance to apply the multiplication and division facts he or she has been practicing.

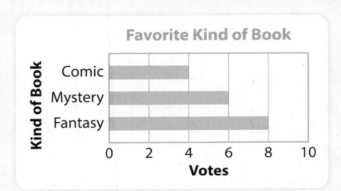

In this picture graph, the **key** tells us that each ⬛ stands for 2 votes. You multiply 2 by the number of ⬛ to find the total votes for each kind of book. You can see that Mystery has 3 × 2, or 6, votes.

Your child might see the same **data** on a scaled bar graph.

Your child may interpret either graph to answer questions such as *How many students voted for Comic?* or *How many more students voted for Fantasy than for Mystery?*

Invite your child to share what he or she knows about solving problems using scaled graphs by doing the following activity together.

ACTIVITY SOLVING PROBLEMS USING A SCALED GRAPH

Do this activity with your child to solve problems using scaled graphs.

Talk with your child about the data on this picture graph.

Soccer Goals Scored This Season	
Bears	⚽ ⚽ ⚽ ⚽ ⚽
Cheetahs	⚽ ⚽
Eagles	⚽ ⚽ ⚽ ⚽ ⚽
Falcons	⚽ ⚽ ⚽ ⚽ ⚽ ⚽
Lions	⚽ ⚽ ⚽
Tigers	⚽ ⚽ ⚽ ⚽ ⚽ ⚽ ⚽ ⚽

Key: Each ⚽ stands for 3 goals.

Discuss questions such as:
- What does this graph show?
- How many teams are shown, and what are their names?
- What does each soccer ball stand for?

Work with your child to write and solve an equation to answer the following questions.

1. How many more goals did the Eagles score than the Lions?

2. If 6 players on the Tigers scored all the team goals and each scored the same number of goals, how many did each player score?

Then ask each other more questions that require using an operation such as addition, subtraction, multiplication, or division to solve.

For real-world practice, keep an eye out for picture graphs or bar graphs in magazines, online, or elsewhere. Utility bills can be a good source of bar graphs, for example. Share these examples with your child and notice that they almost all use a scale of two or more to show the data.

Answers:
1. Possible equation: $15 - 9 = 6$; The Eagles scored 6 more goals than the Lions.
2. Possible equation: $24 \div 6 = 4$; Each player scored 4 goals.

Explore Scaled Graphs

You have had practice modeling and solving word problems. In this lesson, you will use information from graphs to solve word problems. Use what you know to try to solve the problem below.

Ron keeps track of the points scored by his teammates during a basketball game. He records his data in the picture graph shown. How many points did each teammate score?

Points Scored During the Game	
Alan	🏀
Cate	🏀 🏀 🏀
Gary	🏀 🏀 🏀 🏀 🏀
Mae	🏀 🏀 🏀 🏀

Key: Each stands for 2 points.

TRY IT

🧰 **Math Toolkit**
• counters
• buttons
• cups
• 1-inch grid paper

DISCUSS IT

Ask your partner: How did you get started?

Tell your partner:
I knew . . . so I . . .

CONNECT IT

1 LOOK BACK

How many points did each teammate score? Explain.

2 LOOK AHEAD

The data in a picture graph can also be shown on a bar graph. A bar graph for these data is shown.

The **scale** on a bar graph is the difference between any two numbers that are next to each other along the bottom or left side of the graph. These numbers are called scale numbers.

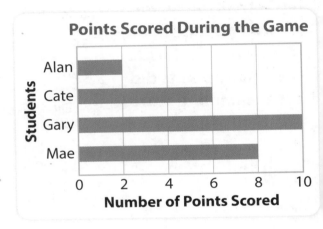

Points Scored During the Game

a. What is the scale of this bar graph? ....

b. What does the bar for Gary mean? How do you know?

c. How do the **key** for the picture graph and the scale for the bar graph compare? Explain how each helps you read a graph.

3 REFLECT

How are the picture graph and the bar graph alike and different in showing the same data?

....

....

....

....

Prepare for Scaled Graphs

1 Think about what you know about data graphs. Fill in each box. Use words, numbers, and pictures. Show as many ideas as you can.

Word	In My Own Words	Example
picture graph		
bar graph		
key		
scale		

2 Use the graphs to answer the questions.

Do You Play Soccer?

Key: Each ⚽ stands for 3 votes.

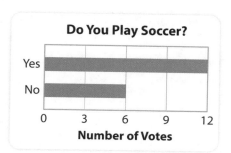

Do You Play Soccer?

a. What is the scale of the bar graph? ....

b. What does the key for the picture graph tell you?

3 Solve the problem. Show your work.

Courtney keeps track of the points scored by her teammates during a math competition. She records her data in the picture graph shown. How many points did each teammate score?

Points Scored	
Jon	★ ★
Dara	★ ★ ★ ★
Lee	★ ★ ★ ★ ★ ★
Sam	★ ★ ★

Key: Each ★ stands for 5 points.

Solution ....

....

4 Check your answer. Show your work.

Develop Reading and Interpreting Picture Graphs

Read and try to solve the problem below.

Jaime asks students in his school to choose their favorite season. The picture graph shows how students answered. How many more students chose summer than chose winter as their favorite season?

Favorite Season	
Winter	😊 😊 😊 😊
Spring	😊 😊 😊
Summer	😊 😊 😊 😊 😊 😊
Fall	😊 😊 😊 😊 😊

Key: Each stands for 5 students.

TRY IT

🧰 Math Toolkit
• counters
• sticky notes
• 1-inch grid paper

DISCUSS IT

Ask your partner: Why did you choose that strategy?

Tell your partner: A model I used was . . . It helped me . . .

Explore different ways to understand how to answer questions about picture graphs.

Jaime asks students in his school to choose their favorite season. The picture graph shows how students answered. How many more students chose summer than chose winter as their favorite season?

Favorite Season	
Winter	😊😊😊😊
Spring	😊😊😊
Summer	😊😊😊😊😊😊
Fall	😊😊😊😊😊

Key: Each 😊 stands for 5 students.

PICTURE IT
You can use pictures to understand the problem.

Remember that each 😊 stands for 5 students.

Winter

Summer

MODEL IT
You can also use number lines to help understand the problem.

Remember that each 😊 stands for **5 students.**

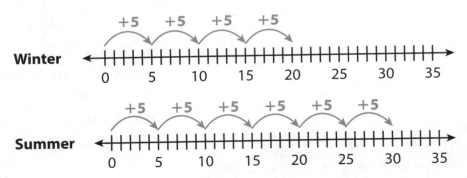

CONNECT IT

Now you will use the problem from the previous page to help you understand how to answer questions about picture graphs.

1 What does the problem ask you to find?

2 Complete the key. Each 😊 stands for .... students.

3 Complete the table.

Favorite Season	Number of 😊	×	Students for each 😊	=	Number of Students
Winter	4	×	5	=	
Summer		×	5	=	

4 How many more students chose summer than chose winter?

$30 - 20 =$ .... So, ... more students chose summer.

5 Explain why the key is important when you are solving a problem that has a picture graph.

6 REFLECT

Look back at your **Try It**, strategies by classmates, and **Picture It** and **Model It**. Which models or strategies do you like best for reading and interpreting picture graphs? Explain.

....

....

....

....

APPLY IT

Use the picture graph and what you just learned to solve problems 7–9. Show your work.

Favorite Season	
Winter	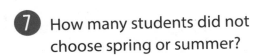
Spring	😊 😊 😊
Summer	😊 😊 😊 😊 😊 😊
Fall	😊 😊 😊 😊 😊

Key: Each 😊 stands for 5 students.

7 How many students did not choose spring or summer?

Solution

8 Use a number line to find how many students chose spring.

Spring
0   5   10   15   20   25   30   35

Solution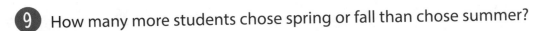

9 How many more students chose spring or fall than chose summer?

Solution

Practice Reading and Interpreting Picture Graphs

Study the Example showing how to read and interpret a scaled picture graph. Then solve problems 1–9.

EXAMPLE

Some third graders went on a field trip to the zoo. The picture graph shows their favorite animals. How many students chose giraffes?

The key shows that each picture stands for 4 students. The row for giraffes has 4 pictures.

You can add 4 four times.

4 + 4 + 4 + 4 = 16

You can multiply 4 by 4.

4 × 4 = 16

So, 16 students chose giraffes.

Favorite Zoo Animal	
Snakes	🧍🧍🧍🧍🧍🧍
Apes	🧍🧍🧍🧍🧍🧍🧍🧍
Lions	🧍🧍🧍
Giraffes	🧍🧍🧍🧍

Key: Each 🧍 stands for 4 students.

Use the picture graph above to solve problems 1–4. Show your work.

1 How many students chose lions? Draw a model to show your work. ....

2 How many students chose snakes? ....

3 How many more students chose giraffes than lions? ....

4 How many fewer students chose lions than apes? ....

Use the picture graph to solve problems 5–9. Show your work.

Students voted for their favorite animal at the petting zoo. The picture graph shows the number of students who voted for each animal.

Favorite Zoo Animal	
Goats	🖐🖐🖐🖐🖐🖐
Rabbits	🖐🖐🖐🖐🖐🖐🖐🖐🖐🖐
Llamas	🖐🖐🖐
Pigs	🖐🖐🖐🖐🖐🖐🖐🖐🖐

Key: Each 🖐 stands for 6 students.

5 How many students voted for llamas? ....

6 How many fewer students chose goats than pigs? ....

7 How many votes did goats and rabbits get altogether? ....

8 How many more students chose rabbits than llamas? ....

9 Make your own statement about the data in the picture graph. Show how you know your statement is true.

Develop Reading and Interpreting Bar Graphs

Read and try to solve the problem below.

> The Hart School wants to build a new playground. The graph shows the number of dollars each grade has raised to build the playground. Grade 3 and Grade 4 together want to raise $300. How much more money must they raise?

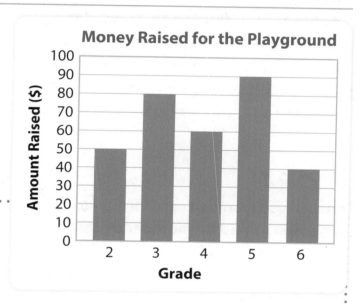

Money Raised for the Playground

TRY IT

 Math Toolkit
- base-ten blocks
- 1-inch grid paper
- sticky notes

DISCUSS IT

Ask your partner: Do you agree with me? Why or why not?

Tell your partner: I agree with you about . . . because . . .

Explore different ways to understand how to answer questions about a bar graph.

The Hart School wants to build a new playground. The graph shows the number of dollars each grade has raised to build the playground. Grade 3 and Grade 4 together want to raise $300. How much more money must they raise?

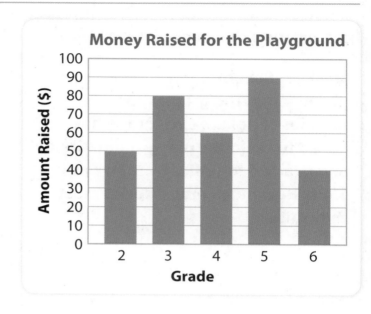

Money Raised for the Playground

y-axis: Amount Raised ($), marked 0, 10, 20, 30, 40, 50, 60, 70, 80, 90, 100
x-axis: Grade, marked 2, 3, 4, 5, 6

EXPLAIN IT

You can use words to explain how to use the graph to find the number of dollars raised by each grade.

Third Grade

Point to the Grade 3 bar. Find the top of the bar. Follow the line at the top of the bar to the left. Stop at the number on the left side of the graph. This is the number of dollars Grade 3 raised.

Fourth Grade

Point to the Grade 4 bar. Find the top of the bar. Follow the line at the top of the bar to the left. Stop at the number on the left side of the graph. This is the number of dollars Grade 4 raised.

CONNECT IT

Now you will use the problem from the previous page to help you understand how to answer questions about bar graphs.

1 What does each bar on the bar graph show?

2 What do the scale numbers along the left side of the bar graph stand for?

3 What is the difference between one scale number and the next? ....

4 Look at the Grade 3 bar. How much money did Grade 3 raise? ....

Look at the Grade 4 bar. How much money did Grade 4 raise? ....

5 What operation do you use to find out how much money was raised by

Grade 3 and Grade 4 altogether? ....

How much money did Grade 3 and Grade 4 raise altogether? ....

6 What operation do you use to find out how much more money must be raised

in order for Grade 3 and Grade 4 to together raise $300? ....

How much more money must the two grades raise? ....

7 Explain how the scale numbers of a bar graph help you to understand what the bar shows.

8 **REFLECT**

Look back at your **Try It**, strategies by classmates, and **Explain It**. Which models or strategies do you like best for reading and interpreting bar graphs? Explain.

....

....

....

Lesson 19 Scaled Graphs   **427**

APPLY IT

Use the bar graph and what you just learned to solve problems 9 and 10.

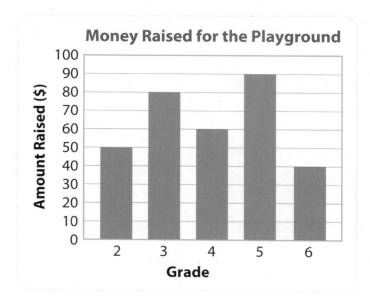

9 How much money in all have the grades raised? Show your work.

Solution ....

10 Choose the statements that are true.

Ⓐ Grade 5 needs to raise another $10 to have raised the same amount as Grade 4 and Grade 6 together.

Ⓑ Grade 3 has raised $50 more than Grade 6.

Ⓒ Grade 2 and Grade 6 together have raised more money than Grade 5.

Ⓓ Grade 2, Grade 4, and Grade 6 combined have raised $20 less than Grade 3 and Grade 5 combined.

Ⓔ Grade 2 and Grade 3 together have raised the same amount of money as Grade 5 and Grade 6 together.

Practice Reading and Interpreting Bar Graphs

**Study the Example showing how to read and interpret a bar graph.
Then solve problems 1–5.**

EXAMPLE

The bar graph shows the number of cartons of milk sold in one week. Were more cartons sold on Monday and Tuesday or on Wednesday and Thursday?

Look where the bars end. Read the scale numbers on the left side of the graph:

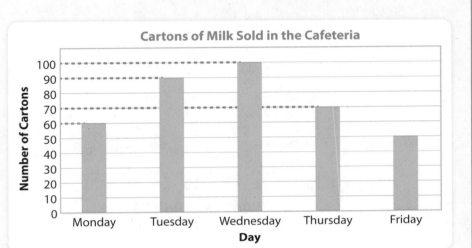

Monday = 60, Tuesday = 90, Wednesday = 100, Thursday = 70.

   60 + 90 = 150 and 100 + 70 = 170

More cartons of milk were sold on Wednesday and Thursday than on Monday and Tuesday.

Use the bar graph above to solve problems 1 and 2. Show your work.

1 How many cartons of milk were sold on the two days with the least number of cartons?

2 How many cartons of milk were sold in all that week?

Use the bar graph to solve problems 3–5. Show your work.

The bar graph shows what students in Ms. Tate's class bought for lunch one day.

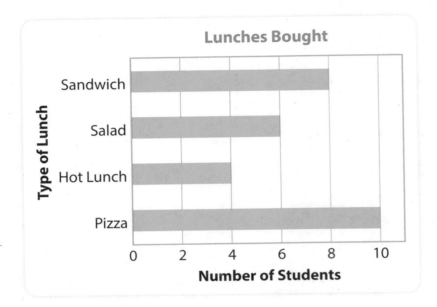

Lunches Bought

Type of Lunch

- Sandwich
- Salad
- Hot Lunch
- Pizza

Number of Students
0   2   4   6   8   10

3 Students bought the same number of pizza lunches as

.... and .... together.

4 The number of salads bought is 2 less than the

number of .... bought.

5 Make your own statement about the data in the graph. Tell how you know your statement is true.

Develop Drawing a Scaled Graph

Read and try to solve the problem below.

Nan keeps track of how many minutes she practices the guitar each day. She wants to draw a graph using the data shown. How can Nan show the data in a graph?

Time I Practice Guitar	
Monday	5 minutes
Tuesday	30 minutes
Wednesday	15 minutes
Thursday	25 minutes
Friday	20 minutes

TRY IT

 Math Toolkit
- counters
- 1-inch tiles
- 1-inch grid paper
- blank bar graphs
- blank picture graphs

DISCUSS IT

Ask your partner: Do you agree with me? Why or why not?

Tell your partner: I disagree with this part because . . .

Explore different ways to understand how to show data and make a graph.

Nan keeps track of how many minutes she practices the guitar each day. She wants to draw a graph using the data shown. How can Nan show the data in a graph?

Time I Practice Guitar	
Monday	5 minutes
Tuesday	30 minutes
Wednesday	15 minutes
Thursday	25 minutes
Friday	20 minutes

PICTURE IT

You can use number lines to help you choose a scale or a key.

The number line below has a scale of 5. The points on the number line show the number of minutes Nan practices on the different days.

Scale of 5

0 5 10 15 20 25 30 35 40

The number line below has a scale of 10. The points on the number line show the number of minutes Nan practices on the different days. Some points fall between the scale numbers.

Scale of 10

0   10   20   30   40

MODEL IT

You can use the scale or key and multiplication to help you make a graph.

Multiply to find the **scale numbers** to write on a bar graph or **how many symbols** to draw on a picture graph. Use a scale of 5.

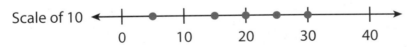

$1 \times 5 = 5$ $2 \times 5 = 10$ $3 \times 5 = 15$ $4 \times 5 = 20$

$5 \times 5 = 25$ $6 \times 5 = 30$ $7 \times 5 = 35$ $8 \times 5 = 40$

CONNECT IT

Now you will use the problem from the previous page to help you draw a bar graph and a picture graph.

1 How do you use the scale numbers to help you draw the bars on a bar graph?

2 Complete Nan's bar graph.

  a. Write the title on the graph.

  b. Write the two labels for the graph.

  c. Complete the scale numbers.

  d. Draw the remaining bars on the graph.

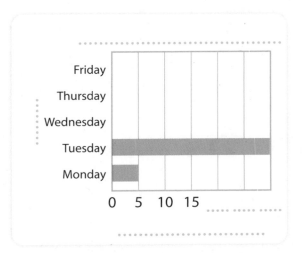

3 Use Nan's data to create a picture graph.

  a. Write the same title as for the bar graph.

  b. Choose a symbol to use.

  c. Create a key based on the scale.

  d. Draw the symbols for each day.

Friday	
Thursday	
Wednesday	
Tuesday	
Monday	

Key: Each .... stands for ....

4 REFLECT

Look back at your **Try It**, strategies by classmates, and **Picture It** and **Model It**. Which models or strategies do you like best for drawing a scaled graph? Explain.

APPLY IT

Use what you just learned to solve these problems.

Robert records the different bugs he sees in a table. Use the table to complete problems 5 and 6.

Bugs Robert Saw	
Type of Bug	**Number of Bugs**
Ant	16
Bee	4
Moth	6
Spider	12

5 Complete a picture graph using Robert's data.

Ant	
Bee	
....	
....	

Key: Each 🐝 stands for .... bugs.

6 Complete a bar graph using Robert's data.

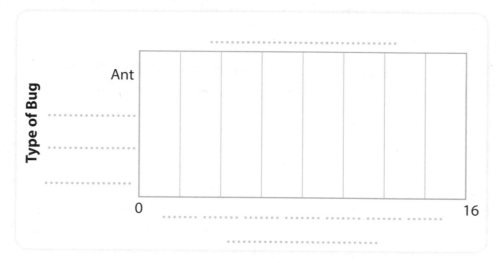

Practice Drawing a Scaled Graph

Study the Example showing how to make a scaled graph. Then solve problems 1–5.

EXAMPLE

Jess asks some students in her school which color they like best. She records the data in a table. How can she make a picture graph to show the data?

Color	Students
Blue	10
Green	5
Purple	20
Red	30
Yellow	15

$10 = 2 \times 5$
$5 = 1 \times 5$
$20 = 4 \times 5$
$30 = 6 \times 5$
$15 = 3 \times 5$

$\longrightarrow$

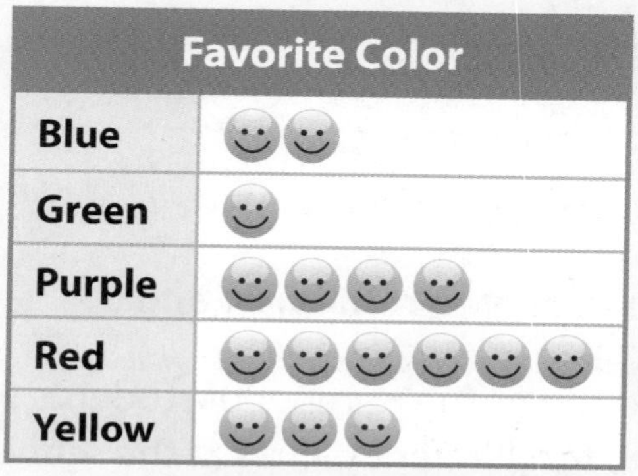

Favorite Color	
Blue	☺ ☺
Green	☺
Purple	☺ ☺ ☺ ☺
Red	☺ ☺ ☺ ☺ ☺ ☺
Yellow	☺ ☺ ☺

Key: Each ☺ stands for 5 students.

Each number has 5 as a factor. Use a scale of 5.

Use the graph above to solve problems 1 and 2. Show your work.

1 Jess wants to create a bar graph to show the same data. How can she use the scale from the picture graph?

2 Complete the bar graph at the right to show Jess's data.

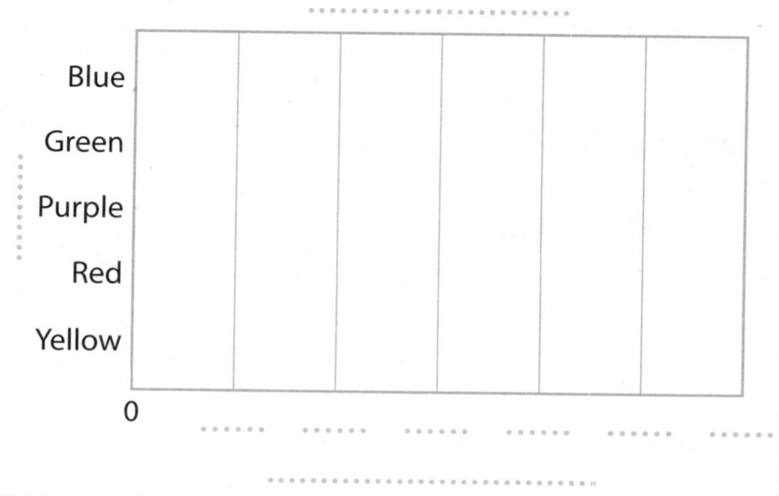

3 Pablo asks some students which sport they like best. He records the data in this table and starts to make a picture graph. Complete the picture graph below.

Sport	Number of Students
Baseball	14
Basketball	10
Biking	16
Soccer	18

Baseball	☺ ☺ ☺ ☺ ☺ ☺ ☺
Basketball	
Biking	
Soccer	

Key: Each ☺ stands for .... students.

Use the table to solve problems 4 and 5.

4 The table shows the number of students who signed up for different games at the school fair. Complete the bar graph below using the data in the table. Be sure to write a title, draw bars, and label all parts of the graph.

Games at School Fair	
Game	**Number of Students**
Balloon Toss	24
Relay Race	20
Sack Race	28
Softball Throw	12

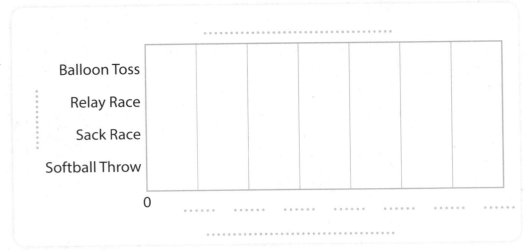

5 Explain how you decided what scale to use.

Refine Scaled Graphs

Complete the Example below. Then solve problems 1–7.

EXAMPLE

Sean records his classmates' favorite bike colors in this table. He wants to draw a scaled graph of the data. How can he decide what scale to use?

Favorite Bike Color	
Color	**Votes**
Blue	12
Green	6
Orange	3
Red	9

Look at how you could show your work using number lines.

Scale of 2
```
0   2   4   6   8   10  12  14
```

Scale of 3
```
0   3   6   9   12  15
```

Solution ....

....

> Are the numbers in the data set numbers you say when you skip-count by twos or skip-count by threes?

PAIR/SHARE
How could you multiply to solve this problem?

APPLY IT

1 Complete the bar graph using the data in Sean's table above.

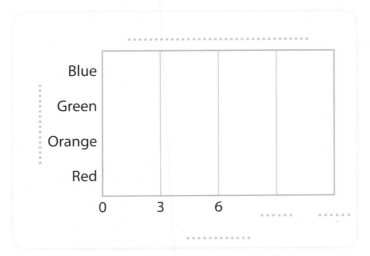

> Remember to write a title on your graph and label all the parts of your graph.

PAIR/SHARE
Take a quick look at your graph. How can you tell that it matches the data you used?

Use the bar graph below to solve problems 2 and 3.

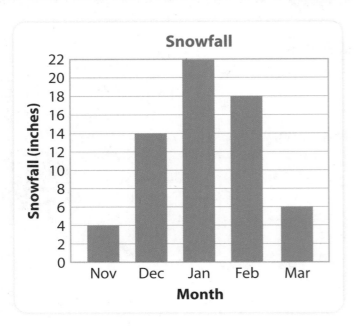

Snowfall

Snowfall (inches)

22
20
18
16
14
12
10
8
6
4
2
0

Nov   Dec   Jan   Feb   Mar

Month

2 How much more snow fell in February and March combined than fell in November and December combined? Show your work.

I think there are at least two different steps to this problem.

PAIR/SHARE
What data on the bar graph do you need to solve the problem?

Solution ....

3 Which two months combined have the same amount of snowfall as January?

Ⓐ February and March

Ⓑ December and March

Ⓒ November and December

Ⓓ November and February

Lara chose Ⓓ as the correct answer. How did she get that answer?

I think the first step is to find the snowfall for January.

PAIR/SHARE
How did you and your partner decide whether to add or subtract?

Jane makes a bar graph of the number of tickets to the school play she sells each day. Use the bar graph to solve problems 4 and 5.

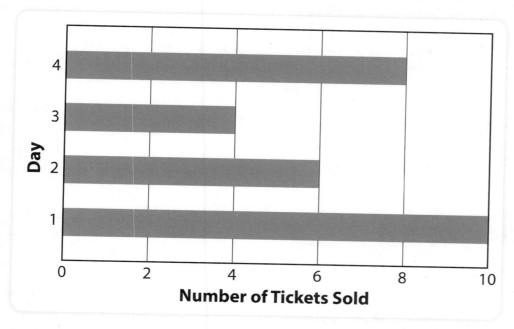

4 Tell whether each sentence is *True* or *False*.

	True	False
The scale for Jane's bar graph is 2.	Ⓐ	Ⓑ
A good title for Jane's bar graph would be "Tickets Sold for Ten Days."	Ⓒ	Ⓓ
Jane sold 1 more ticket on Day 2 and Day 4 together than on Day 1 and Day 3 together.	Ⓔ	Ⓕ
Jane sold 8 fewer tickets on Day 2, Day 3, and Day 4 combined than on Day 1.	Ⓖ	Ⓗ

5 Suppose Jane makes a picture graph of her data. She uses a ticket symbol to represent two tickets sold. How many ticket symbols does she draw to show the number of tickets sold on Day 1?

.... ticket symbols

Use the picture graph to answer problem 6.

Soccer Goals Scored This Season	
Bears	⚽ ⚽ ⚽ ⚽ ⚽
Cheetahs	⚽ ⚽
Eagles	⚽ ⚽ ⚽ ⚽ ⚽
Falcons	⚽ ⚽ ⚽ ⚽ ⚽ ⚽ ⚽
Lions	⚽ ⚽ ⚽
Tigers	⚽ ⚽ ⚽ ⚽ ⚽ ⚽ ⚽ ⚽

Key: Each ⚽ stands for 2 goals.

6 Which statements are true based on the picture graph?

Ⓐ The Eagles scored 10 goals.

Ⓑ The Lions scored 3 goals.

Ⓒ The Tigers scored as many goals as the Bears and the Lions combined.

Ⓓ The Falcons scored 2 more goals than the Eagles.

Ⓔ The Tigers and the Cheetahs scored 20 goals altogether.

7 MATH JOURNAL

People are asked their favorite Olympic winter sport. 20 say snowboarding, 10 say bobsledding, 50 say figure skating, and 30 say ski jumping. Explain how you would decide on what scale to use to show this data in a picture or bar graph.

 SELF CHECK Go back to the Unit 3 Opener and see what you can check off.

In this unit you learned to . . .

Skill	Lesson
Understand area and find area by tiling and by multiplying.	14, 15
Find the area of a combined rectangle or a non-rectangular shape by adding the areas of the rectangles that make up the shape.	16
Use multiplication or division to solve one-step word problems.	17
Use addition, subtraction, multiplication, or division to solve two-step word problems.	18
Solve problems using picture graphs and bar graphs.	19
Draw picture graphs and bar graphs to show data.	19

Think about what you learned.

Use words, numbers, and drawings.

1 The most important thing I learned was .... because . . .

2 I would like to learn more about how to . . .

3 I could use more practice with . . .

Use the Four Operations

Study an Example Problem and Solution

SMP 1 Make sense of problems and persevere in solving them.

Read this problem that involves using different operations to solve it. Then look at Sweet T's solution to this problem.

Sweet T's Tees

Sweet T wants to buy shirts for his fingerboard team. The team will have between 8 and 10 members. Everyone should get two different shirts.

- $50 set-up fee to print.
- Add $2 to the cost of each shirt to print on it.

Sweet T can spend up to $225 for shirts. It's okay to have money left over.

- Tell what kind of shirts and how many to order.
- Decide whether or not to print on the shirts.
- Give the total cost and amount of money left over.

Long Sleeve
$8 each

Short Sleeve
$6 each

Collar
$7 each

Read the sample solution on the next page. Then look at the checklist below. Find and mark parts of the solution that match the checklist.

☑ PROBLEM-SOLVING CHECKLIST

☐ Tell what is known.
☐ Tell what the problem is asking.
☐ Show all your work.
☐ Show that the solution works.

a. **Circle** something that is known.
b. **Underline** something that you need to find.
c. **Draw a box around** what you do to solve the problem.
d. **Put a checkmark** next to the part that shows the solution works.

SWEET T'S SOLUTION

- **I know that there will be 8 to 10 team members.**

  I will plan on buying for 9 members. I don't want to have too many extra shirts.

- **I can make a table to show the costs for different kinds of shirts.**

  Multiply the price of the shirt by the number to buy.

Type of Shirt	Plain	With Print
Short Sleeve	$9 \times \$6 = \$54$	$9 \times \$8 = \$72$
Collar	$9 \times \$7 = \$63$	$9 \times \$9 = \$81$
Long Sleeve	$9 \times \$8 = \$72$	$9 \times \$10 = \$90$

- **I can find the cost for the two most expensive shirts.**

  Cost of shirts: $\$81 + \$90 = \$171$

  Add set-up fee: $\$171 + \$50 = \$221$

  I think this is too close to $225.

- **I'll buy . . .**

9 collar shirts with print:	$81
9 plain short-sleeve shirts:	$54
set-up fee:	+ $50
total:	$185

- **I can subtract to find the amount left over.**

  $\$225 - \$185 = \$40$

  There will be $40 left over after buying the shirts.

Hi, I'm Sweet T. Here's how I solved this problem.

The table helps me see all of the choices.

I could buy the most expensive shirts. I would rather have money to buy other things.

This plan gives the team two different looking shirts.

Try Another Approach

There are many ways to solve problems. Think about how you might solve Sweet T's Tees problem in a different way.

Sweet T's Tees

Sweet T wants to buy shirts for his fingerboard team. The team will have between 8 and 10 members. Everyone should get two different shirts.

- $50 set-up fee to print.
- Add $2 to the cost of each shirt to print on it.

Sweet T can spend up to $225 for shirts. It's okay to have money left over.

- Tell what kind of shirts and how many to order.

- Decide whether or not to print on the shirts.

- Give the total cost and amount of money left over.

Short Sleeve $6 each

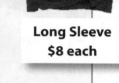

Long Sleeve $8 each

Collar $7 each

PLAN IT

Answer these questions to help you start thinking about a plan.

A. How many team members will you buy for?

B. Do you want to have any leftover money? If so, about how much?

SOLVE IT

Find a different solution for Sweet T's Tees problem. Show all your work on a separate sheet of paper.

You may want to use the Problem-Solving Tips to get started.

• PROBLEM-SOLVING TIPS •

● Models

Type of Shirt	Plain	With Print

● Word Bank

add   subtract   multiply

sum   difference   product

● Sentence Starters

• The cost to buy _____

• I need to multiply _____

☑ PROBLEM-SOLVING CHECKLIST

Make sure that you . . .

☐ tell what you know.

☐ tell what you need to do.

☐ show all your work.

☐ show that the solution works.

REFLECT

Use Mathematical Practices As you work through the problem, discuss these questions with a partner.

• **Reason Mathematically** What are all of the numbers in the problem and what do they mean?

• **Persevere** What is your plan for solving the problem?

Discuss Models and Strategies

Read the problem. Write a solution on a separate sheet of paper. Remember, there can be lots of ways to solve a problem!

Fingerboard Parts

Sweet T wants to have extra fingerboard parts. He wants members to be able to mix and match parts to make different boards.

Decks
$8 each

Available in yellow, red, pink, purple, orange, and green.

Trucks
$6 for a set of 2

Available in pink, red, blue, black, and white.

Wheels
$7 for a set of 4

Available in yellow, red, blue, black, and white.

Sweet T can spend up to $160 on fingerboard parts. What should he buy?

Trucks

Deck

Wheels

PLAN IT AND SOLVE IT
Find a solution for the Fingerboard Parts problem.

- Make a list of the parts to buy. Include the numbers of the different parts and the colors.

- Tell why you chose the parts that you did.

- Find the total cost to buy the parts. Tell how much money is left.

You may want to use the Problem-Solving Tips to get started.

PROBLEM-SOLVING TIPS

- **Questions**
  - How many of each part do you need to make one fingerboard?
  - Do you want to have more of one kind of part? Why?

- **Tools** You may want to use . . .
  - a table.
  - an organized list.

- **Sentence Starters**
- I would like to have _____
- I will buy _____

☑ **PROBLEM-SOLVING CHECKLIST**
Make sure that you . . .
☐ tell what you know.
☐ tell what you need to do.
☐ show all your work.
☐ show that the solution works.

REFLECT
Use Mathematical Practices As you work through the problem, discuss these questions with a partner.

- **Use Models** How can you use equations to help find a solution?

- **Persevere** How can you check that your solution makes sense?

Persevere On Your Own

Read the problem. Write a solution on a separate sheet of paper.

Skate Park

Sweet T has $80 left after buying items for the team. He wants to buy at least three different items for the skate park he is making. Here are the items Sweet T is looking at, along with the prices.

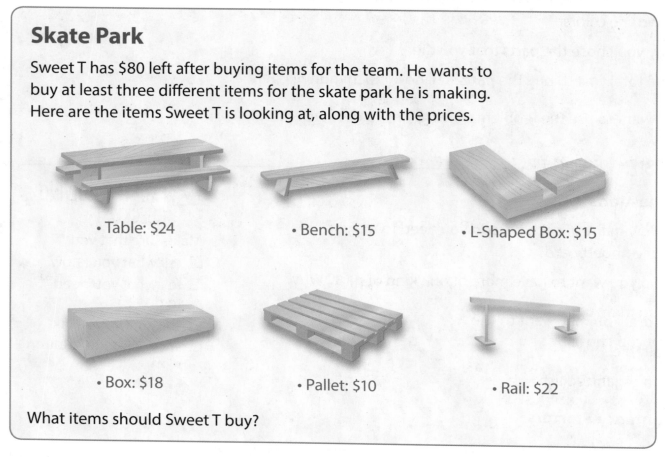

• Table: $24   • Bench: $15   • L-Shaped Box: $15

• Box: $18   • Pallet: $10   • Rail: $22

What items should Sweet T buy?

SOLVE IT

Tell which items Sweet T should buy.

• Give the total cost.

• Explain why you chose the items you did.

REFLECT

Use Mathematical Practices After you complete the task, choose one of these questions to discuss with a partner.

• **Persevere** What steps did you take to get your solution?

• **Use a Model** Which operations did you use to solve the problem?

Grip Tape

Sweet T wants to buy pieces of grip tape for the team. The tape sticks to the deck of the fingerboard to make it less slippery. Sweet T thinks that each of the 9 members of his team needs at least 4 pieces of grip tape.

Grip Tape

   1 piece for $1

      OR

   Buy 5 and get 1 piece free.

How many pieces of grip tape should Sweet T buy?

SOLVE IT

Decide how many pieces of grip tape Sweet T should buy for each team member.

- Tell why you chose this number.
- Tell the total number of pieces needed.
- Find a way to buy groups of 5 or separate pieces to get this total.
- Give the total cost.

REFLECT

Use Mathematical Practices After you complete the task, choose one of these questions to discuss with a partner.

- **Make an Argument** What reasons did you have for your decision about the number of pieces to buy?
- **Persevere** What was your first step in finding a solution? Why did you start this way?

1 The rectangle below is made of unit squares. Complete the equation to find the area of the rectangle. Write your answer in the blanks.

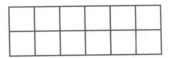

.... units × .... units = ... square units

2 Jessie buys a number of album downloads for $8 each. She also buys a T-shirt for $12. Jessie spends a total of $84. Which equation can be used to find the number of album downloads, a, that she buys?

Ⓐ $(8 \times a) + 12 = 84$

Ⓑ $8 \times (12 + a) = 84$

Ⓒ $8 + (12 \times a) = 84$

Ⓓ $(8 + 12) \times a = 84$

3 Bianca has 54 books. She puts them in a bookcase with 6 shelves. She puts the same number of books on each shelf. How many books does she put on each shelf?

Write related multiplication and division equations to find the number of books on each shelf. Use b for the unknown number.

4 Nicole uses tiling to find the total area of the two rectangles shown. Each unit square is 1 square foot.

Which expressions can be used to find the area, in square feet, of Nicole's rectangles? Choose all the correct answers.

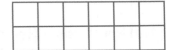

Ⓐ $5 \times (3 + 2)$

Ⓑ $(6 \times 2) + (6 \times 3)$

Ⓒ $(6 + 6) \times 5$

Ⓓ $(3 + 2) \times 6$

Ⓔ 5×6

5 Mark has 15 red balloons, 12 green balloons, 9 blue balloons, and 18 yellow balloons.

Use Mark's data to complete the picture graph.

Mark's Balloons	
Color of Balloon	**Number of Balloons**
Red	
Green	
Blue	
Yellow	

Key: Each ⬭ stands for .... balloons.

6 Kanti's school put on three music shows. Kanti sold 289 tickets for the first show, 115 tickets for the second show, and 198 tickets for the third show.

She says, "I sold 602 tickets."

Is Kanti's answer reasonable? Use estimation to check her work. Show your work.

Solution ....

....

Performance Task

Answer the questions and show all your work on separate paper.

Dan is planning to build a square porch attached to the side of his house. After the porch is built, he would like to cover the floor with 1-foot square tiles. The diagram below shows the measurements of the porch and the lawn where he plans to build. How many tiles will he need to cover the porch floor?

Side of House

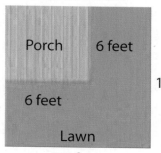

Porch   6 feet

10 feet

6 feet

Lawn

10 feet

After Dan bought all of the tiles he needed, he changed his mind about the shape of the porch. How could he change the shape of the porch, but still use the same number of tiles? Explain how you found your answer. Then draw a new model for Dan's porch showing the new shape and its side lengths.

REFLECT

Use Mathematical Practices After you complete the task, answer the following questions.

- **Persevere** How can you tell this question is about area?

- **Argue and Critique** How did you justify the measurements you chose?

Draw or write to show examples for each term. Then draw or write to show other math words in the unit.

area the amount of space inside a closed two-dimensional figure. Area is measured in square units such as square centimeters.

My Example

data a set of collected information. Often numerical information such as a list of measurements.

My Example

key tells what each symbol in a picture graph represents.

My Example

operation a mathematical action such as addition, subtraction, multiplication, or division.

My Example

scale (on a graph) the value represented by the distance between one tick mark and the next on a number line.

My Example

square unit the area of a square with side lengths of 1 unit.

My Example

My Word: _____

_____

_____

My Example

My Word: _____

_____

_____

My Example

My Word: _____

_____

_____

My Example

My Word: _____

_____

_____

My Example

My Word: _____

_____

_____

My Example

My Word: _____

_____

_____

My Example

Cumulative Practice

Name: _____

Set 1: Solve One-Step Word Problems

Solve the problems. Show your work.

1 Peter has 7 marbles. His sister gives him some more marbles. Now Peter has 15 marbles. How many marbles did Peter's sister give him?

2 Carla has 14 stickers. 7 are circles and the rest are stars. How many of Carla's stickers are stars?

3 There are 2 fewer dogs than cats. There are 8 dogs. How many cats are there?

Set 2: Solve Two-Step Word Problems

Solve the problems. Show your work.

1 Matt has 2 red crayons and 3 purple crayons. Then he buys 5 more crayons. How many crayons does Matt have now?

2 Ayah has $14. She spends $8 on a book. Then her aunt gives her $2. How much money does Ayah have now?

3 Dara has 6 blue flowers and 5 pink flowers. She gives Ben some of her flowers. Now Dara has 4 flowers left. How many flowers does Dara give Ben?

Set 3: Add Two-Digit Numbers

Add. Show your work.

1 14 + 29

2 48 + 16

3 13 + 37

4 33 + 29

5 13 + 21

Set 4: Subtract Two-Digit Numbers

Subtract. Show your work.

1 92 − 48 = ?

2 53 − 35 = ?

3 27 − 9 = ?

92 − 48 = ...

53 − 35 = ...

27 − 9 = ...

Set 5: Compare Three-Digit Numbers

Write <, >, or = in each circle to compare the numbers.

1 165 ◯ 212

2 318 ◯ 330

3 611 ◯ 166

4 144 ◯ 79

5 121 ◯ 121

6 429 ◯ 442

7 432 ◯ 423

8 910 ◯ 91

9 725 ◯ 752

Set 6: Read and Write Three-Digit Numbers

Write the numbers in different ways.

1 Write 513 using only words. ....

2 Write 400 + 6 using only words. ....

3 Write 829 using only words. ....

4 Write one hundred fifty using only digits. ....

5 Write 200 + 90 using only digits. ....

6 Write seven hundred two using only digits. ....

7 Write five hundred sixteen in expanded form. .... + ... + ...

8 Write 628 in expanded form. .... + ... + ...

9 Write one hundred four in expanded form. .... + ... + ...

Set 7: Add Three-Digit Numbers

Add. Show your work.

1
$$\begin{array}{r} 452 \\ +\ 154 \\ \hline \end{array}$$

2
$$\begin{array}{r} 347 \\ +\ 138 \\ \hline \end{array}$$

3
$$\begin{array}{r} 716 \\ +\ 262 \\ \hline \end{array}$$

4
$$\begin{array}{r} 458 \\ +\ 275 \\ \hline \end{array}$$

5
$$\begin{array}{r} 648 \\ +\ 130 \\ \hline \end{array}$$

6
$$\begin{array}{r} 302 \\ +\ 324 \\ \hline \end{array}$$

Set 8: Subtract Three-Digit Numbers

Subtract. Show your work.

1 243 − 116

2 468 − 272

Set 9: Add Several Two-Digit Numbers

Add. Show your work.

1 15 + 22 + 19 + 27

2 28 + 25 + 22 + 15

3 12 + 32 + 18

Set 10: Add and Subtract Lengths

Solve the problems. Show your work.

1 Dalton has a ribbon that is 72 inches long. He cuts off 32 inches. How long is the ribbon now?

2 Jess has two scarves. The red scarf is 42 inches long. The yellow scarf is 36 inches long. How much longer is the red scarf than the yellow scarf?

3 Jenna is on a path that is 60 meters long. She walks the first 20 meters. Then she starts skipping. She walks again for the last 15 meters. How far does Jenna skip?

Cumulative Practice

Name: _____

Set 1: Round Numbers

Round each number to the nearest ten for problems 1–6.

1 87 ....

2 438 ....

3 562 ....

4 13 ....

5 724 ....

6 296 ....

Round each number to the nearest hundred for problems 7–12.

7 329 ....

8 849 ....

9 251 ....

10 68 ....

11 595 ....

12 650 ....

Set 2: Add Three-Digit Numbers

Add. Show your work.

1
$$\begin{array}{r} 246 \\ + 382 \\ \hline \end{array}$$

2
$$\begin{array}{r} 408 \\ + 329 \\ \hline \end{array}$$

3
$$\begin{array}{r} 737 \\ + 186 \\ \hline \end{array}$$

Set 3: Subtract Three-Digit Numbers

Subtract. Show your work.

1
$$\begin{array}{r} 835 \\ - 474 \\ \hline \end{array}$$

2
$$\begin{array}{r} 756 \\ - 234 \\ \hline \end{array}$$

3
$$\begin{array}{r} 520 \\ - 398 \\ \hline \end{array}$$

Set 4: Compare Three-Digit Numbers

Write >, <, or = to compare each pair of numbers.

1 576 ◯ 528

2 425 ◯ 426

3 724 ◯ 724

4 389 ◯ 623

5 639 ◯ 639

6 836 ◯ 834

Set 5: Add and Subtract on the Number Line

Use the number line to solve each problem. Show your work.

1 21 + 24 = ?

21 + 24 = ...

2 35 − 17 = ?

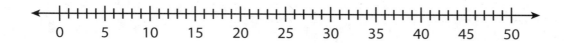

35 − 17 = ...

3 46 − 18 = ?

46 − 18 = ...

Set 6: Two-Step Word Problems

Solve the word problems. Show your work.

1 There are 18 students in a classroom. Then 7 more students enter the classroom. The teacher splits them into two teams. There are 13 students on one team. How many are on the other team?

2 Kemi has 22 pencils in her pencil case. She gives 14 pencils away. Then she gets more pencils from a friend. Now Kemi has 24 pencils. How many pencils does Kemi get from her friend?

3 Cliff has some berries in his basket. He picks 15 more berries. Then he gives away 28 berries to his friends. Cliff now has 12 berries. How many berries did Cliff have in his basket to start?

Set 7: Add and Subtract Three-Digit Numbers

Use any strategy to solve the problems. Show your work.

1 Show how to find 475 + 385.

2 Show how to find 298 + 674.

3 Show how to find 662 − 320.

4 Show how to find 725 − 452.

Set 8: Measure in Inches and Centimeters

Use a ruler to measure the length of each object in inches.

1

.... inches

2

.... inches

3

.... inches

Use a ruler to measure the length of each object in centimeters.

4

.... centimeters

5

.... centimeters

6

.... centimeters

Cumulative Practice

Name: _____

Set 1: Multiplication

Show what each expression means by drawing equal groups. Then write the product.

1 3×6

2 5×3

$3 \times 6 =$ ....

$5 \times 3 =$ ....

Set 2: Multiplying in Word Problems

Solve the word problems. Show your work.

1 Solange has 5 packs of batteries. Each pack has 6 batteries. How many batteries does Solange have?

2 Max is painting cats on 10 windows. In each window, he also paints a ball of yarn. How many balls of yarn does Max paint?

3 Lili has 2 cartons of eggs. Each carton has 8 eggs. How many eggs does Lili have?

Set 3: Break Apart to Multiply

Draw lines on the array and fill in the blanks to show your work.

1 Break apart the array to find 7 × 4.

$7 \times 4 = (7 \times$ ....$) + (7 \times$ ....$)$

$= $ .... $+$ .... $= $ ....

$7 \times 4 = $ ....

2 Break apart the array to find 8 × 6.

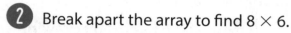

$8 \times 6 = (8 \times$ ....$) + (8 \times$ ....$)$

$= $ .... $+$ .... $= $ ....

$8 \times 6 = $ ....

Set 4: Use Order and Grouping to Multiply

Choose an order and use parentheses to show one way to multiply the factors. Then show the steps to find the product.

1 Multiply the factors 2, 3 and 4.

2 Multiply the factors 7, 2 and 5.

3 Multiply the factors 6, 3 and 2.

4 Multiply the factors 5, 4 and 2.

Set 5: Division

Use any model to show the division expression. Then write the quotient.

1 $35 \div 5$

2 $21 \div 7$

$35 \div 5 =$ ....

$21 \div 7 =$ ....

Set 6: Connect Multiplication and Division

The array shows that $8 \times 7 = 56$. Use this fact to complete the equations.

1 $8 \times 7 =$ .... $7 \times 8 =$ ....

2 $8 \times$ .... $= 56$ $56 =$ .... $\times 8$

3 $56 \div 8 =$ .... $56 \div$ .... $= 8$

4 .... $= 56 \div 7$ $7 = 56 \div$ ....

5 .... $\times 7 = 56$ $7 \times$ .... $= 56$

6 $8 =$ .... $\div 7$ .... $\div 8 = 7$

Set 7: Multiplication and Division Fact Families

Complete the fact families.

1 $6 \times$ .... $= 24$

.... $\times 4 = 24$

$24 \div$ .... $= 6$

.... $\div 6 = 4$

2 .... $\times 8 = 40$

$5 \times$ .... $= 40$

.... $\div 5 = 8$

$40 \div$ .... $= 5$

3 $4 \times$ .... $= 32$

$8 \times$ .... $= 32$

$32 \div$ .... $= 8$

.... $\div 8 = 4$

Set 8: Multiply and Divide Within 100

Solve the problems.

1 $8 \times 8 =$ ....

2 $9 \times 4 =$ ....

3 $6 \times 9 =$ ....

4 $10 \times 6 =$ ....

5 $0 \times 8 =$ ....

6 $1 \times 9 =$ ....

7 $42 \div 7 =$ ....

8 $36 \div 9 =$ ....

9 $24 \div 3 =$ ....

10 $63 \div 9 =$ ....

11 $81 \div 9 =$ ....

12 $72 \div 8 =$ ....

Set 9: Patterns in Numbers

Use the multiplication chart for problems 1–5.

1 Fill in the missing products in the multiplication chart.

2 Which factor, other than 2, has all the numbers you wrote in problem 1 in its row?

....

3 The product of two even numbers is always ....

4 The product of two odd numbers is always ....

5 The product of an odd number and an even number is always ....

×	1	2	3	4	5	6
1	1	2	3	4	5	6
2	2		6		10	
3	3	6	9	12	15	18
4	4		12	16	20	24
5	5	10	15	20	25	30
6	6		18	24	30	36

Glossary/Glosario

English	Español	Example/Ejemplo
Aa		
add to combine or find the total of two or more quantities.	**sumar** combinar o hallar el total de dos o más cantidades.	$$\begin{array}{r} 147 \\ + 212 \\ \hline 359 \end{array}$$
addend a number being added.	**sumando** número que se suma.	$4 + 7 = 11$ addends
algorithm a set of routine steps used to solve problems.	**algoritmo** conjunto de pasos que se siguen rutinariamente para resolver problemas.	$$\begin{array}{r} 1\ 1 \\ 4\ 5\ 6 \\ + 1\ 6\ 7 \\ \hline 6\ 2\ 3 \end{array}$$
AM the time from midnight until before noon.	**a. m.** el tiempo que transcurre desde la medianoche hasta el mediodía.	AM 7:20
analog clock a clock that uses hour and minute hand positions to show time.	**reloj analógico** reloj que muestra la hora con una manecilla de la hora y un minutero.	hour hand / minute hand
angle one of the corners of a shape where two sides meet.	**ángulo** una de las esquinas de una figura en la que se unen dos lados.	angle
area the amount of space inside a closed two-dimensional figure. Area is measured in square units such as square centimeters.	**área** cantidad de espacio dentro de una figura bidimensional cerrada. El área se mide en unidades cuadradas, como los centímetros cuadrados.	Area = 4 square units
array a set of objects arranged in equal rows and equal columns.	**matriz** conjunto de objetos agrupados en filas y columnas iguales.	☆ ☆ ☆ ☆ ☆ ☆ ☆ ☆ ☆ ☆ ☆ ☆ ☆ ☆ ☆

English	Español	Example/Ejemplo
associative property of addition when the grouping of three or more addends is changed, the total does not change.	**propiedad asociativa de la suma** cambiar la agrupación de tres o más sumandos no cambia el total.	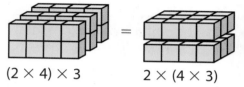 $(2 + 3) + 4 = 2 + (3 + 4)$
associative property of multiplication changing the grouping of three or more factors does not change the product.	**propiedad asociativa de la multiplicación** cambiar la agrupación de tres o más factores no cambia el producto.	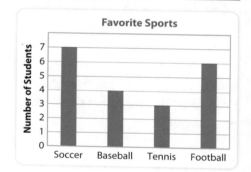 $(2 \times 4) \times 3 \qquad 2 \times (4 \times 3)$
attribute any characteristic of an object or shape, such as number of sides or angles, lengths of sides, or angle measures.	**atributo** característica de un objeto o una figura, como el número de lados o ángulos, la longitud de los lados, o la medida de los ángulos.	attributes of a square: • 4 square corners • 4 sides of equal length

Bb

English	Español	Example/Ejemplo
bar graph a data display in which bars are used to show the number of items in each category.	**gráfica de barras** representación de datos en la cual se usan barras para mostrar el número de elementos de cada categoría.	**Favorite Sports** — bar graph with y-axis "Number of Students" (0–7) and categories Soccer, Baseball, Tennis, Football

Cc

English	Español	Example/Ejemplo
capacity the amount a container can hold. Capacity can be measured in the same units as liquid volume.	**capacidad** cantidad que cabe en un recipiente. La capacidad se mide en las mismas unidades que el volumen líquido.	 capacity of 2 liters

English	Español	Example/Ejemplo
cent (¢) the smallest unit of money in the U.S. One penny has a value of 1 cent. 100 cents is equal to 1 dollar.	**centavo (¢)** la menor unidad monetaria de Estados Unidos. 100 centavos equivalen a 1 dólar.	 1 cent 1¢
centimeter (cm) a unit of length. There are 100 centimeters in 1 meter.	**centímetro (cm)** unidad de longitud. 100 centímetros equivalen a 1 metro.	Your little finger is about 1 **centimeter** (cm) across. 
column a vertical line of objects or numbers, such as in an array or table.	**columna** línea vertical de objetos o números, como las de una matriz o una tabla.	
commutative property of addition changing the order of addends does not change the total.	**propiedad conmutativa de la suma** cambiar el orden de los sumandos no cambia el total.	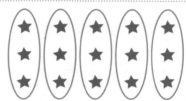 3 + 4 = 4 + 3
commutative property of multiplication changing the order of the factors does not change the product.	**propiedad conmutativa de la multiplicación** cambiar el orden de los factores no cambia el producto.	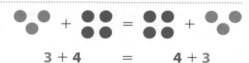 3 × 2 = 2 × 3
compare to decide if numbers, amounts, or sizes are greater than, less than, or equal to each other.	**comparar** determinar si un número, una cantidad, o un tamaño es mayor que, menor que o igual a otro número, otra cantidad u otro tamaño.	$\dfrac{4}{6} < \dfrac{5}{6}$

English	Español	Example/Ejemplo
customary system the measurement system commonly used in the United States that measures length in inches, feet, yards, and miles; liquid volume in cups, pints, quarts, and gallons; and weight in ounces and pounds.	**sistema usual** sistema de medición comúnmente usado en Estados Unidos. La longitud se mide en pulgadas, pies, yardas, y millas; el volumen líquido en tazas, pintas, cuartos, y galones; y el peso, en onzas y libras.	**Length** 1 foot = 12 inches 1 yard = 3 feet 1 mile = 5,280 feet **Weight** 1 pound = 16 ounces **Liquid Volume** 1 quart = 2 pints 1 quart = 4 cups 1 gallon = 4 quarts

Dd

English	Español	Example/Ejemplo
data a set of collected information. Often numerical information such as a list of measurements.	**datos** conjunto de información reunida. A menudo es información numérica, tal como una lista de mediciones.	Number of points scored Alan: 2, Cate: 6, Gary: 10, Mae: 8
denominator the number below the line in a fraction that tells the number of equal parts in the whole.	**denominador** número que está debajo de la línea de una fracción. Dice cuántas partes iguales hay en el entero.	$\frac{2}{3}$
difference the result of subtraction.	**diferencia** el resultado de la resta.	$\begin{array}{r} 475 \\ -296 \\ \hline 179 \end{array}$
digit a symbol used to write numbers.	**dígito** símbolo que se usa para escribir números.	The digits are 0, 1, 2, 3, 4, 5, 6, 7, 8, and 9.
digital clock a clock that uses digits to show the time.	**reloj digital** reloj que usa dígitos para mostrar la hora.	AM 7:20

English	Español	Example/Ejemplo
dime a coin with a value of 10 cents (10¢).	**moneda de 10¢** moneda con un valor de 10 centavos (10¢).	10 cents 10¢
dimension length in one direction. A figure may have one, two, or three dimensions.	**dimensión** longitud en una dirección. Una figura puede tener una, dos, o tres dimensiones.	5 in. 2 in. 3 in.
distributive property when one of the factors of a product is written as a sum, multiplying each addend by the other factor before adding does not change the product.	**propiedad distributiva** cuando uno de los factores de un producto se escribe como suma, multiplicar cada sumando por el otro factor antes de sumar no cambia el producto.	$2 \times (3 + 6) = (2 \times 3) + (2 \times 6)$
divide to separate into equal groups and find the number in each group or the number of groups.	**dividir** separar en grupos iguales y hallar cuántos hay en cada grupo o el número de grupos.	15 balloons 5 groups of 3 balloons
dividend the number that is divided by another number.	**dividendo** el número que se divide por otro número.	$15 \div 3 = 5$
division an operation used to separate a number of items into equal-sized groups.	**división** operación que se usa para separar una cantidad de elementos en grupos iguales.	**Division** $12 \div 3 = 4$ total number of groups number in each group
division equation an equation with a divison symbol and an equal sign.	**ecuación de división** ecuación que contiene un signo de división y un signo de igual.	$15 \div 3 = 5$

English	Español	Example/Ejemplo
divisor the number by which another number is divided.	**divisor** el número por el que se divide otro número.	$15 \div 3 = 5$
dollar ($) a unit of money in the U.S. There are 100 cents in 1 dollar ($1).	**dólar ($)** unidad monetaria de Estados Unidos. Un dólar ($1) equivale a 100 centavos.	

Ee

English	Español	Example/Ejemplo
edge a line segment where two faces meet in a three-dimensional shape.	**arista** segmento de recta donde se encuentran dos caras de una figura tridimensional.	Edge
elapsed time the amount of time that has passed between a start time and an end time.	**tiempo transcurrido** tiempo que ha pasado entre el momento de inicio y el fin.	The elapsed time from 2:00 PM to 3:00 PM is 1 hour.
equal having the same value, same size, or same amount.	**igual** que tiene el mismo valor, el mismo tamaño, o la misma cantidad.	$25 + 15 = 40$ $25 + 15$ **is equal to** 40.
equal sign (=) a symbol that means *is the same value as.*	**signo de igual (=)** símbolo que significa *tiene el mismo valor que.*	$12 + 4 = 16$
equation a mathematical statement that uses an equal sign (=) to show that two expressions have the same value.	**ecuación** enunciado matemático en el que se usa un signo de igual (=) para mostrar que dos expresiones tienen el mismo valor.	$25 - 15 = 10$

English	Español	Example/Ejemplo
equivalent fractions two or more different fractions that name the same part of a whole or the same point on a number line.	**fracciones equivalentes** dos o más fracciones diferentes que nombran la misma parte de un entero y el mismo punto de una recta numérica.	$\frac{2}{4} = \frac{1}{2}$ $\frac{5}{10} = \frac{1}{2}$
estimate (noun) a close guess made using mathematical thinking.	**estimación** suposición aproximada que se hace usando el razonamiento matemático.	$28 + 21 = ?$ $30 + 20 = 50$ 50 is an estimate of the sum.
estimate (verb) to make a close guess based on mathematical thinking.	**estimar / hacer una estimación** hacer una suposición aproximada usando el razonamiento matemático.	$28 + 21$ is about 50.
even number a whole number that always has 0, 2, 4, 6, or 8 in the ones place. An even number of objects can be put into pairs or into two equal groups without any leftovers.	**número par** número entero que siempre tiene 0, 2, 4, 6, o 8 en la posición de las unidades. Un número par de objetos puede agruparse en pares o en dos grupos iguales sin que queden sobrantes.	20, 22, 24, 26, and 28 are even numbers.
expanded form the way a number is written to show the place value of each digit.	**forma desarrollada** manera de escribir un número para mostrar el valor posicional de cada dígito.	$249 = 200 + 40 + 9$
expression one or more numbers, unknown numbers, and/or operation symbols that represents a quantity.	**expresión** uno o más números, números desconocidos o símbolos de operaciones que representan una cantidad.	3×4 or $5 + b$

English	Español	Example/Ejemplo

Ff

English	Español	Example/Ejemplo
face a flat surface of a solid shape.	**cara** superficie plana de una figura sólida.	face
fact family a group of related equations that use the same numbers, but in a different order, and two different operation symbols. A fact family can show the relationship between addition and subtraction or between multiplication and division.	**familia de datos** grupo de ecuaciones relacionadas que tienen los mismos números, ordenados de distinta manera, y dos símbolos de operaciones diferentes. Una familia de datos puede mostrar la relación que existe entre la suma y la resta.	$5 \times 4 = 20$ $4 \times 5 = 20$ $20 \div 4 = 5$ $20 \div 5 = 4$
factor a number that is multiplied.	**factor** número que se multiplica.	$4 \times 5 = 20$ factors
foot (ft) a unit of length in the customary system. There are 12 inches in 1 foot.	**pie (ft)** unidad de longitud del sistema usual. 1 pie equivale a 12 pulgadas.	12 inches = 1 foot
fourths the parts formed when a whole is divided into four equal parts.	**cuartos** partes que se forman cuando se divide un entero de cuatro partes iguales.	fourths 4 equal parts
fraction a number that names equal parts of a whole. A fraction names a point on the number line.	**fracción** número que nombra partes iguales de un entero. Una fracción nombra un punto en una recta numérica.	$\frac{3}{4}$

English	Español	Example/Ejemplo

Gg

gram (g) a unit of mass in the metric system. A paper clip has a mass of about 1 gram. There are 1,000 grams in 1 kilogram.	**gramo (g)** unidad de masa del sistema métrico. Un clip tiene una masa de aproximadamente 1 gramo. 1,000 gramos equivalen a 1 kilogramo.	1,000 grams = 1 kilogram
greater than symbol (>) a symbol used to compare two numbers when the first is greater than the second.	**símbolo de mayor que (>)** símbolo que se usa para comparar dos números cuando el primero es mayor que el segundo.	$\frac{1}{2} > \frac{1}{4}$

Hh

halves the parts formed when a whole is divided into two equal parts.	**medios** partes que se obtienen cuando se divide un entero en dos partes iguales.	halves 2 equal parts
hexagon a two-dimensional closed shape with 6 straight sides and 6 corners.	**hexágono** figura bidimensional cerrada que tiene 6 lados y 6 ángulos.	
hour (h) a unit of time. There are 60 minutes in 1 hour.	**hora (h)** unidad de tiempo. 1 hora equivale a 60 minutos.	60 minutes = 1 hour
hour hand the shorter hand on a clock. It shows the hours.	**manecilla de la hora** la manecilla más corta de un reloj. Muestra las horas.	hour hand

English	Español	Example/Ejemplo

Ii

inch (in.) a unit of length in the customary system. There are 12 inches in 1 foot.

pulgada (pulg.) unidad de longitud del sistema usual. 12 pulgadas equivalen a 1 pie.

The length of a quarter is about 1 **inch** (in.).

Kk

key tells what each symbol in a picture graph represents.

clave dice qué representa cada símbolo de una pictografía.

Points Scored During the Game	
Alan	🏀
Cate	🏀🏀🏀
Gary	🏀🏀🏀🏀🏀
Mae	🏀🏀🏀🏀

Key: Each 🏀 stands for 2 points.

↑
Key

kilogram (kg) a unit of mass in the metric system. There are 1,000 grams in 1 kilogram.

kilogramo (kg) unidad de masa del sistema métrico. Un kilogramo equivale a 1,000 gramos.

1,000 grams = 1 kilogram

Ll

length measurement that tells the distance from one point to another, or how long something is.

longitud medida que indica la distancia de un punto a otro, o cuán largo es un objeto.

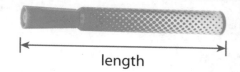

length

English	Español	Example/Ejemplo
less than symbol (<) a symbol used to compare two numbers when the first is less than the second.	**símbolo de menor que** (<) símbolo que se usa para comparar dos números cuando el primero es menor que el segundo.	$\frac{1}{4} < \frac{1}{2}$
line plot a data display that shows data as marks above a number line.	**diagrama de puntos** representación de datos en la cual se muestran los datos como marcas sobre una recta numérica.	**Sea Lion Lengths** X X X X X X X X X X X X 48 49 50 51 52 **Inches**
liquid volume the amount of space a liquid takes up.	**volumen líquido** cantidad de espacio que ocupa un líquido.	When you measure how much water is in a bucket, you measure liquid volume.
liter (L) a unit of liquid volume in the metric system. There are 1,000 milliliters in 1 liter.	**litro (l)** unidad de volumen líquido del sistema métrico. Un litro equivale a 1,000 mililitros.	1,000 milliliters = 1 liter

Mm

English	Español	Example/Ejemplo
mass the amount of matter in an object. Measuring the mass of an object is one way to measure how heavy it is. Units of mass include the gram and kilogram.	**masa** la cantidad de materia que hay en un objeto. Medir la masa de un objeto es una manera de medir qué tan pesado es. Las unidades de masa incluyen el gramo y el kilogramo.	The mass of a paper clip is about 1 gram.
measure to find length, height, or weight by comparing it to a known unit.	**medir** determinar la longitud, la altura o el peso de un objeto comparándolo con una unidad conocida.	0 inches 1 2 0 1 2 3 4 5 centimeters

English	Español	Example/Ejemplo
meter (m) a unit of length in the metric system. There are 100 centimeters in 1 meter.	**metro (m)** unidad de longitud del sistema métrico. 1 metro es igual a 100 centímetros.	100 centimeters = 1 meter
metric system the measurement system that measures length based on meters, liquid volume based on liters, and mass based on grams.	**sistema métrico** sistema de medición. La longitud se mide en metros; el volumen líquido, en litros; y la masa, en gramos.	**Length** 1 kilometer = 1,000 meters 1 meter = 100 centimeters 1 meter = 1,000 millimeters **Mass** 1 kilogram = 1,000 grams **Volume** 1 Liter = 1,000 milliliters
minute (min) a unit of time. There are 60 minutes in 1 hour.	**minuto (min)** unidad de tiempo. 60 minutos equivalen a 1 hora.	60 minutes = 1 hour
minute hand the longer hand on a clock. It shows minutes.	**minutero** la manecilla más larga de un reloj. Muestra los minutos.	minute hand
mixed number a number with a whole-number part and a fractional part.	**número mixto** número con una parte entera y una parte fraccionaria.	$2\frac{3}{8}$
multiplication an operation used to find the total number of items in a given number of equal-sized groups.	**multiplicación** operación que se usa para hallar el número total de objetos en un número dado de grupos de igual tamaño.	**3 groups** of **2 balls** is **6.** $3 \times 2 = 6$
multiplication equation an equation with a multiplication symbol and an equal sign.	**ecuación de multiplicación** ecuación que contiene un signo de multiplicación y un signo de igual.	$3 \times 5 = 15$

English	Español	Example/Ejemplo
multiplication table a table showing multiplication facts.	**tabla de multiplicación** tabla que muestra multiplicaciones y sus resultados.	<table><tr><td></td><td>0</td><td>1</td><td>2</td><td>3</td><td>4</td><td>5</td></tr><tr><td>0</td><td>0</td><td>0</td><td>0</td><td>0</td><td>0</td><td>0</td></tr><tr><td>1</td><td>0</td><td>1</td><td>2</td><td>3</td><td>4</td><td>5</td></tr><tr><td>2</td><td>0</td><td>2</td><td>4</td><td>6</td><td>8</td><td>10</td></tr><tr><td>3</td><td>0</td><td>3</td><td>6</td><td>9</td><td>12</td><td>15</td></tr><tr><td>4</td><td>0</td><td>4</td><td>8</td><td>12</td><td>16</td><td>20</td></tr><tr><td>5</td><td>0</td><td>5</td><td>10</td><td>15</td><td>20</td><td>25</td></tr></table>
multiply to repeatedly add the same number a certain number of times. Used to find the total number of items in equal-sized groups.	**multiplicar** sumar el mismo número una y otra vez una cierta cantidad de veces. Se multiplica para hallar el número total de objetos que hay en grupos de igual tamaño.	42 36 30 24 18 12 6 $7 \times 6 = 42$

Nn

English	Español	Example/Ejemplo
nickel a coin with a value of 5 cents (5¢).	**moneda de 5¢** moneda con un valor de 5 centavos (5¢).	5 cents 5¢
number line a straight line marked at equal spaces to show numbers.	**recta numérica** recta que tiene marcas separadas por espacios iguales; las marcas muestran números.	0 1 2 3 4
numerator the number above the line in a fraction that tells the number of equal parts that are being described.	**numerador** número que está encima de la línea de una fracción. Dice cuántas partes iguales se describen.	$\frac{2}{3}$

Oo

English	Español	Example/Ejemplo
odd number a whole number that always has 1, 3, 5, 7, or 9 in the ones place. An odd number of objects cannot be put into pairs or into two equal groups without a leftover.	**número impar** número entero que siempre tiene el dígito 1, 3, 5, 7, o 9 en la posición de las unidades. Los números impares no pueden ordenarse en pares o en dos grupos iguales sin que queden sobrantes.	21, 23, 25, 27, and 29 are odd numbers.

English	Español	Example/Ejemplo
operation a mathematical action such as addition, subtraction, multiplication, or division.	**operación** acción matemática como la suma, la resta, la multiplicación, y la división.	$15 + 5 = 20$ $20 - 5 = 15$ $4 \times 6 = 24$ $24 \div 6 = 4$

Pp

English	Español	Example/Ejemplo
parallel always the same distance apart.	**paralelos** que siempre están a la misma distancia.	
parallelogram a quadrilateral with opposite sides parallel and equal in length.	**paralelogramo** cuadrilátero con lados opuestos paralelos e iguales en longitud.	
partial sums the sums you get in each step of the partial-sums strategy. You use place value to find partial sums.	**sumas parciales** las sumas que se obtienen en cada paso de la estrategia de sumas parciales. Se usa el valor posicional para hallar sumas parciales.	The partial sums for $124 + 234$ are $100 + 200$ or 300, $20 + 30$ or 50, and $4 + 4$ or 8.
partial-sums strategy a strategy used to add multi-digit numbers.	**estrategia de sumas parciales** estrategia que se usa para sumar números de varios dígitos.	312 + 235 Add the hundreds. 500 Add the tens. 40 Add the ones. + 7 547
pattern a series of numbers or shapes that follow a rule to repeat or change.	**patrón** serie de números o figuras que siguen una regla para repetirse o cambiar.	
penny a coin with a value of 1 cent (1¢).	**moneda de un 1¢** moneda con un valor de 1 centavo (1¢).	1 cent 1¢
pentagon a two-dimensional closed shape with exactly 5 sides and 5 angles.	**pentágono** figura bidimensional cerrada que tiene exactamente 5 lados y 5 ángulos.	

English	Español	Example/Ejemplo

perimeter the distance around a two-dimensional shape. The perimeter is equal to the sum of the lengths of the sides.

perímetro longitud del contorno de una figura bidimensional. El perímetro es igual al total de las longitudes de los lados.

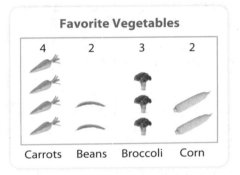

60 yards
40 yards   40 yards
60 yards

The perimeter of the soccer field is 200 yards.
(60 yd + 40 yd + 60 yd + 40 yd)

---

picture graph a data display in which pictures are used to show data.

pictografía representación de datos en la cual se usan dibujos para mostrar datos.

Favorite Vegetables

4	2	3	2
Carrots	Beans	Broccoli	Corn

---

place value the value assigned to a digit based on its position in a number.

valor posicional valor de un dígito según su posición en un número.

Hundreds	Tens	Ones
4	4	4
↓	↓	↓
400	40	4

PM the time from noon until before midnight.

p. m. tiempo desde el mediodía hasta la medianoche.

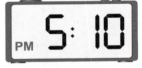

PM 5:10

---

product the result of multiplication.

producto el resultado de la multiplicación.

$5 \times 3 = \mathbf{15}$

Qq

quadrilateral a two-dimensional closed shape with exactly 4 sides and 4 angles.

cuadrilátero figura bidimensional cerrada que tiene exactamente 4 lados y 4 ángulos.

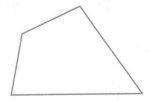

English	Español	Example/Ejemplo
quarter a coin with a value of 25 cents (25¢).	**moneda de 25¢** moneda con un valor de 25 centavos (25¢).	25 cents 25¢
quotient the result of division.	**cociente** el resultado de la división.	$15 \div 3 = 5$

Rr

English	Español	Example/Ejemplo
rectangle a quadrilateral with 4 right angles. Opposite sides of a rectangle are the same length.	**rectángulo** paralelogramo que tiene 4 ángulos rectos. Los lados opuestos de un rectángulo tienen la misma longitud.	
regroup to put together or break apart ones, tens, or hundreds.	**reagrupar** unir o separar unidades, decenas, o centenas.	10 ones can be regrouped as 1 ten, or 1 hundred can be regrouped as 10 tens.
rhombus a quadrilateral with all sides the same length.	**rombo** cuadrilátero cuyos lados tienen todos la misma longitud.	
right angle an angle that looks like the corner of a square.	**ángulo recto** ángulo que parece la esquina de un cuadrado.	90°
round to find a number that is close in value to a given number by finding the nearest ten, hundred, or other place value.	**redondear** hallar un número que es cercano en valor al número dado hallando la decena, la centena, o otro valor posicional más cercano.	48 rounded to the nearest ten is 50.
row a horizontal line of objects or numbers, such as in an array or table.	**fila** línea horizontal de objetos o números, tal como las que aparecen en una matriz o una tabla.	

English	Español	Example/Ejemplo
rule a set way that is followed to go from one number or shape to the next in a pattern.	**regla** procedimiento que se sigue para ir de un número o una figura al número o la figura siguiente de un patrón.	17, 22, 27, 32, 37, 42 rule: add 5

Ss

English	Español	Example/Ejemplo
scale (on a graph) the value represented by the distance between one tickmark and the next on a number line.	**escala (en una gráfica)** el valor que representa la distancia entre una marca y la marca siguiente de una recta numérica.	 **Points Scored During the Game**
second (s) a unit of time. There are 60 seconds in 1 minute.	**segundo (s)** unidad de tiempo. 60 segundos equivalen a 1 minuto.	60 seconds = 1 minute
side a line segment that forms part of a two-dimensional shape.	**lado** segmento de recta que forma parte de una figura bidimensional.	 side
square a quadrilateral with 4 square corners and 4 sides of equal length.	**cuadrado** cuadrilátero que tiene 4 esquinas cuadradas y 4 lados de igual longitud.	
square unit the area of a square with side lengths of 1 unit.	**unidad cuadrada** el área de un cuadrado que tiene lados de 1 unidad de longitud.	1 unit 1 unit 1 unit 1 unit
subtract to take away one quantity from another, or to compare two numbers to find the difference.	**restar** quitar una cantidad a otra, o comparar dos números para hallar la diferencia.	365 − 186 = 179

English	Español	Example/Ejemplo
sum the result of addition.	**suma** el resultado de la suma.	$34 + 25 = 59$

Tt

English	Español	Example/Ejemplo
thirds the parts formed when a whole is divided into three equal parts.	**tercios** partes que se forman cuando se divide un entero en tres partes iguales.	thirds 3 equal parts
three-dimensional solid, or having length, width, and height. For example, a cube is three-dimensional.	**tridimensional** sólido, o que tiene longitud, ancho, y altura. Por ejemplo, los cubos son tridimensionales.	
trapezoid (exclusive) a quadrilateral with exactly one pair of parallel sides.	**trapecio** cuadrilátero que tiene exactamente un par de lados paralelos.	
trapezoid (inclusive) a quadrilateral with at least one pair of parallel sides.	**trapecio** cuadrilátero que tiene al menos un par de lados paralelos.	
triangle a two-dimensional closed shape with exactly 3 sides and 3 angles.	**triángulo** figura bidimensional cerrada que tiene exactamente 3 lados y 3 ángulos.	
two-dimensional flat, or having measurement in two directions, like length and width. For example, a rectangle is two-dimensional.	**bidimensional** plano, o que tiene medidas en dos direcciones, como la longitud y el ancho. Por ejemplo, un rectángulo es bidimensional.	

English	Español	Example/Ejemplo
Uu		
unit fraction a fraction with a numerator of 1. Other fractions are built from unit fractions.	**fracción unitaria** fracción cuyo numerador es 1. Otras fracciones se construyen a partir de fracciones unitarias.	$\frac{1}{4}$
Vv		
vertex the point where two rays, lines, or line segments meet to form an angle.	**vértice** punto donde dos semirrectas, rectas, o segmentos de recta se unen y forman un ángulo.	Vertex
Yy		
yard (yd) a unit of length in the customary system. There are 3 feet, or 36 inches, in 1 yard.	**yarda (yd)** unidad de longitud del sistema usual de Estados Unidos. 1 yarda equivale a 3 pies o a 36 pulgadas.	3 feet = 1 yard 36 inches = 1 yard

Acknowledgments

Common Core State Standards © 2010. National Governors Association Center for Best Practices and Council of Chief State School Officers. All rights reserved.

Photography Credits

United States coin images (unless otherwise indicated) from the United States Mint

Images used under license from **Shutterstock.com**.

iii ArtMari, lendy16; **iv** Dimedrol68; **v** akiyoko, Vadim; **vi** Artismo, Hurst Photo, Rashad Ashurov, trekandshoot; **vii** sumire8, TerryM; **viii** CyrilLutz, Kaiskynet; **1** Kristina Vackova; **3** Erica Truex, Iraidka; **4** En min Shen, Erica Truex; **9** Erica Truex, Seregam; **10** Billion Photos, Erica Truex, EtiAmmos; **13** Erica Truex, Ralko; **14** blue67design, Erica Truex, Jagodka, LHF Graphics, Nina_Susik; **15** Edwin Verin, Erica Truex, palform; **16** Erica Truex, palform, Rich Koele; **19** Bogdan ionescu, Erica Truex; **20** Northallertonman; **23** Erica Truex, GOLFX, Lightspring; **24** Lane V. Erickson; **27** likekightcm; **30** Erica Truex, Javier Brosch, RomanJuve; **31** Erica Truex, Fabio Berti, palform; **34** Dudarev Mikhail, Erica Truex; **40** Erica Truex, S-ts; **41** Erica Truex, Gavrylovaphoto, palform; **42** Erica Truex, Kithanet, palform; **45** Andrey Lobachev, Art'nLera, olllikeballoon; **49** pattara puttiwong; **52** Dima Sobko; **53** IROOM STOCK, palform; **54** palform, studiolovin; **56** PhotoProCorp; **57** Federico Quevedo; **58** Erica Truex, palform, Plumdesign; **59** Erica Truex, Shebeko; **60** Ed Samuel, Erica Truex; **61** Erica Truex, Kzww; **62** Erica Truex, lendy16; **69** AfricaStudio, Erica Truex; **70** Erica Truex, Natu, palform; **74** Stephen Orsillo; **75** Cmnaumann, palform; **76** Dangdumrong, otsphoto; **80** Triff; **81** SeDmi, smilewithjul; **82** David Franklin; **83** Wsantina; **89** Shuter; **91** Kovalchuk Oleksandr, Kyselova Inna; **92** Pete Spiro, Photosync; **93** KK Tan; **96** Petlia Roman; **97** Rose Carson; **99** Fotofermer, Irin-k; **100** freestyle images; **101** Tim UR; **102** Pete Spiro; **105** Pets in frames; **108** Timothy Boomer; **109–110** charles taylor; **112** Coprid, marssanya; **113** M. Unal Ozmen, Maks Narodenko; **114** Mario7, Tim UR; **116** Elnur, Lubava; **119** CrackerClips Stock Media; **120** Studio DMM Photography, Designs & Art; **122** SOMMAI; **125** Lubava, Valentina Razumova; **126** Jiri Hera, showcake, Stockforlife, Vitaly Zorkin; **127–128** Valentina Rozumova; **130** Viacheslav Rubel; **131** Natasha Pankina, SUN-FLOWER; **132** Hannamariah, marssanya; **134** Iriskana, Photo Melon; **136** Le Do, liskus; **137–138** Aopsan, Claudio Divizia; **141** Sashkin; **143** AS Food studio, smilewithjul; **144** AS Food studio; **147** Lukas Gojda, Valentina Proskurina; **148** Yaping; **149** Kyselova Inna, Triff; **150** KMNPhoto; **152** Elena Schweitzer, Iriskana; **153** Lifestyle Graphic; **154** Tropper2000; **159** Dimedrol68; **160** Dimedrol68, liskus, SOMMAI; **163** Danny Smythe; **164** normallens; **165–166** Tadeusz Wejkszo; **169** Andrea Izzotti, Celso Diniz, Chris Bradshaw, Christian Musat, Denton Rumsey, Don Mammoser, f11 photo, FloridaStock, GUDKOV ANDREY, Henryk Sadura, Jason Patrick Ross, Jayne Carney, liquid studios, moosehenderson, Romrodphoto; **171** Rido, smilewithjul; **172** Bajinda, liskus, Maks Narodenko; **174** Elnur, Ksuxa-muxa; **177** Narong Jongsirikul; **179** Alexey D. Vedernikov; **180** Kletr, smilewithjul; **181** ArtMari, Nattika, palform; **182** Claudio Divizia, palform; **183** Africa Studio, palform; **184** Drozhzhina Elena; **186** mayer kleinostheim, palform; **187** palform, Natalia D; **190** Boris Sosnovyy, palform; **192** Africa Studio, palform; **193** palform, Redchocolate, Lenorko; **194** Lenorko, palform, Redchocolate, TerraceStudio; **197** Karkas, Coprid, Olga Popova, palform; **199** stockcreations; **200** Gbuglok, palform; **202** Olga Lyubkin, palform; **207** Erofeeva Natalya, palform; **208** palform, Phase4Studios, Picsfive; **209** ArtnLera, palform, paulaphoto; **211** ajt, palform; **212** ArtnLera, FabrikaSimf, palform; **214** Balabolka, EtiAmmos, monticello, palform; **215** ArtnLera, Cergios, palform; **216** Caimacanul, Design56, Redchocolate; **218** Balabolka, Michelle D. Milliman; **221** Balabolka, Odua Images; **222** palform, Vstock24; **223** Ocram, palform; **224** palform, Vangert; **225** Ivaschenko Roman, palform; **226** Juthamat8899; **227** Andrey_Kuzmin; **228** mr.chanwit wangsuk palform; **230** COLOA Studio, LHF Graphics; **231** Cheers Group, HelgaLin, palform; **233** Anneka, Kschrei, palform, Vesna cvorovic; **234** Denis Pepin, palform; **235** Ivory27; **236** palform, Pao Laroid; **237** nld, Runrun2; **238** HamsterMan, Robyn Mackenzie; **239** Craig Wactor, palform; **240** AlexPic, mohamad firdaus bin ramli; **242** AlexPic, Quang Ho; **243** Natalia7, palform; **245** Bryan Solomon, motorolka, palform; **246** r.classen, palform, Valentina Proskurina; **247** Maria Jeffs; **250** En min Shen; **251** oksana2010; **252** Somboon Bunproy; **254** artnLera, Hong Vo, sevenke, Tiwat K; **255** Shippee; **256** HodagMedia; **259** Kletr; **262** Africa Studio; **264** smilewithjul, Steve Cukrov; **268** Dontree; **272** Jiradet Ponari; **283** palform, Shuter; **286** Vdimage; **289** Alekseykolotvin; **290** Suzanne Tucker; **291** Victor Moussa; **299** JARIRIYAWAT; **303** Kovalenko Dmitriy, Route55; **306** Roman Dick; **314** Gl0ck, Tiwat K; **315** Tom Pavlasek; **318** Undrey; **320** Plufflyman; **322** Irina Fischer; **325** Bragin Alexey; **326** Ksenia Palimski; **329** areeya_ann; **333** Coprid; **334** balabolka, MaxCab; **335** Drozhzhina Elena, palform; **337** Vadim Sadovski; **338** palform; **340** palform, RomanStrela; **341** Fotokostic, Oleg Romanko, VVO; **346** cherezoff, palform; **345–348** akiyoko, palform; **356** artnLera, Dmitry Zimin, En min Shen; **357** artnLera, Olivier Le Queinec; **358** EHStockphoto; **359** Maks Narodenko; Matt Benoit; **360** Pavlo_K; **361** Svetlana Serebryakova, Olga Nikonova; **362** LAURA_VN, Quang Ho; **363** bluehand, Olga Nikonova; **364** Miroslav Halama; **366** LittleMiss, MarGi; **367** lana rinck; **369** Roma Borman; **370** Roma Borman; **372** aquariagirl1970, Tim UR; **373** Africa Studio, Simon Bratt; **374** balabolka, Max Lashcheuski; **375** Madlen; **378** Aopsan, Claudio Divizia, Natasha Pankina; **379** krurapoto; **380** Ultimax; **383** vikky; **384** palform, YUTTASAK SAMPACHANO; **385** anna. q, Iriskana, Quanthem; **386** Iriskana, ES sarawuth, topform; **387** Surrphoto; **390** BW Folsom; **391** balabolka, Leigh Prather; **392** Lotus_studio; **394** Mauro Rodrigues; **395** Alchena; **396** Andrey Eremin, Iriskana; **397–398** abdrahimmahfar; **400** marre; **402** jannoon028; **403** Aluna1, Pandapaw; **404** Aluna1, Tropper2000; **407** Simic Vojislav; **408** Iriskana, Peshkova; **411** photosync, redchocolate; **412** NinaM; **414** Erica Truex, irin-k; **415** Cherdchai charasri, Erica Truex; **418** CrackerClips Stock Media; **419** Aliaksei Tarasau, Flower Studio, LilKar; **420–421** Aliaksei Tarasau; **422** Aliaksei Tarasau, Smit; **423** Erica Truex, Valdis Skudre; **424** Joshua Lewis, Tiwat K; **425** STILLFX; **426** Chones; **428** Erica Truex, Sergiy Kuzmin; **430** Katstudio, Tiwat K; **431** attapoljochosobig, Iriskana; **432** JUN3, Iriskana; **434** Protasov AN; **435–436** Aliaksei Tarasau; **438** Smileus; **439** David Franklin, Iriskana, palform; **440** irin-k, Iurii Osadchi; **441** Oksana2010; **442, 444** Khvost, Ronald Sumners, Surrphoto; **446** Sergey Chayko; **455** Africa Studio; **457** Hurst Photo; **458** Olga Nayashkova; **462** CKP1001;

Front Cover credits

©Teri Lyn Fisher/Offset

468 Africa Studio, blue67design; 469 IB Photography; 471 Grynold; 474 Nata-Lia; 475 Artsimo; 480 SunshineVector, trekandshoot; 481 PhotoMediaGroup; 486 GreenArt; 492 baibaz; 494 balabolk; 495 Scruggelgreen; 498 t50; 499 MaskaRad; 500 Palokha Tetiana; 502 bestv; 505 Exopixel; 506 ANGHI, liskus; 508 Africa Studio, Natasha Pankina; 509 Jessica Torres Photography; 511–512 Tsekhmister; 514 Vladimir Jotov; 515 Mybona, Zeligen; 521 Anyunov, Iriskana; 522 balabolka, Julia-art; 526 images.etc, Iriskana; 529 balabolka, KAWEESTUDIO; 530 Iriskana, Mamuka Gotsiridze; 531 6493866629; 532 Africa Studio, Erica Truex, GraphicsRF; 534 En min Shen, Samathi; 538 Gargantiopa; 539 balabolka, CameraOnHand; 540 Sommai damrongpanich; 542 Iriskana, Maryna korotenko; 546 ImagePixel; 547 balabolka, Iriskana, nechaevkon, Zeligen; 548 Studio KIWI; 549 Hintau Aliaksei; 550 Mega Pixel; 551 Billion Photos; 552 Billion Photos; 553 Yellow Cat; 554 serg_dibrova; 555 Domnitsky; 558 Tetiana Rostopira, Tiwat K; 559 FeellFree; 560 FeellFree; 561 Hsagencia; 564 Africa Studio, Arka38, Tiwat K; 566 Valeri Potapova; 567 Alslusky; 568 Mega Pixel; 569 Anutr Yossundara; 570 vvoe; 571 Tiwat K, Tobik; 572 Arnon Phutthajak, goir; 574 Mark Herreid, smilewithjul; 576 Beautiful landscape, smilewithjul; 578 Krungchingpixs, Kubias; 585 SUN-FLOWER; 588 DenisNata, Natasha Pankina; 589 baibaz; 592 Iriskana, Roxana Bashyrova; 593 Brenda Carson; 594 Sumire8; 599 Africa Studio; 600 Anton Havelaar, Iriskana; 602 Peter Kotoff; 603 Happy monkey, Iriskana; 604 Iriskana, supachai sumrubsuk; 605 Ivan Smuk; 606 Africa Studio, Iriskana; 608 Olena Mykhaylova; 609 Ruth Black; 610 Oleksandr Lysenko, Primiaou; 612 Elnur; 614 Ever; 615 Kellis, Steve Collender, somchaij, Suzanne Tucker; 616 sabza; 617 Mega Pixel, Quang Ho, Kaiskynet Studio; 618 higyou, Kellis, posteriori, photo one somchaij, Suzanne Tucker; 619 chromatos, TerryM; 620 Chones, Kaiskynet Studio, kolopach, Quang Ho; 621 robert_s; 622 Iriskana bioraven; 625 Africa Studio, Keith Homan, somchaij, Timmary; 626 Fleuraya, lacote, somchaij; 627 Hortimages; 628 Steve Collender, Lestertair; 630 Vector things; 631 gowithstock; 632 Steve Collender; 634 Fleuraya; 635 Maksym Bondarchuk; 636 Dorottya Mathe, Natasha Pankina; 637 Alina Cardiae Photography, Iakiv

Pekarskyi, Iasha, M. Unal Ozmen, More Images; 638 Take Photo, design56, Hong Vo; 639 Domnitsky, Vitaly Zorkin; 641 GrigoryL, Roman Samokhin; 642 IB Photography; 643 Khumthong; 644 amero, Mariusz Szczygiel; 646 jiangdi; 647 Alex Mit, Denis Churin; 648 s_oleg; 649 Tim UR, ZoneCreative; 650 More Images; 652 Iriskana, JGade; 653 Jim Vallee; 654 TanyaRozhnovskaya; 657 Maks Narodenko, Zirconicusso; 658 Quang Ho; 659 SUN-FLOWER; 662 PeachLoveU; 664 George3973, Grigor Unkovski, smilewithjul, Timquo; 665 Sia-James; 666 Nito; 667 Africa Studio; 673 Besjunior; 675 Jojoo64; 676 Africa Studio, Creative icon styles, CyrilLutz, ParvinMaharramov, Joe Belanger, UltimaS; 680 artnLera, Kaspri; 681 smilewithjul, Standard Studio; 684 Kaiskynet Studio, liskus; 687 Hank Shiffman, Joe Belanger, jannoon028; 688 Cbenjasuwan, Mtsaride, Mega Pixel, Yanas, rzstudio; 692 goran cakmazovic, marssanya; 700 valkoinen; 707 balabolka, endeavor; 709 KhanunHaHa, Ksuxa-muxa, Natasha Pankina; 710 palform, Sanzhar Murzin; 711 fotoscool, Irin-k, palform; 714 Anucha Tiemsom, Moxumbic; 715 yevgeniy11; 716 Effective stock photos, palform, Tiwat-K; 718 Ksuxa-muxa, Roblan, Tiwat K; 719 STILLFX; 724 Sergey Sizov; 726 Natasha Pankina, M Kunz; 730 donatas1205; 731 boivin nicolas; 732 Natasha Pankina, Evgeny Tomeev; 734 MicroOne; 735 liskus, SHUTTER TOP; 736 Ksuxa-muxa, Palmform; Seregam; 737 YUU-ME; 738 Vladislav Lyutov; 743 GO DESIGN, Suradech Prapairat; 744 Suradech Prapairat; 745 Optimarc; 746 Iriskana; 747 akiyoko; 752 Diana Elfmarkova, runLenarun; 753 artnlera, Redstone; 760 Nortongo; A5 Amfoto, Gts; A10 P Maxwell Photography

Student Handbook, appearing in Student Bookshelf and Teacher Guide only: HBi ArtMari, Rawpixel.com, Pixfiction, Disavorabuth; **HB1** Africa Studio, opicobello; **HB2** iadams; **HB3** Palabra; **HB5** Havepino; **HB6** Tatiana Popova; **HB8** Chiyacat; **HB9** Kyselova Inna, Markus Mainka; **HB10** ArtMari; **HB11** Disavorabuth; **HB12** ArtMari, Disavorabuth; **HB13–HB14** ArtMari; **HB18** Rawpixel.com